Explorations
in
Classroom Observation

Explorations in Classroom Observation

Edited by

MICHAEL STUBBS
Department of English Studies, University of Nottingham

and

SARA DELAMONT
School of Education, University of Leicester

JOHN WILEY & SONS
London · New York · Sydney · Toronto

Library of Congress Cataloguing in Publication Date:

Stubbs, Michael, 1947–
Explorations in classroom observation.

1. Educational research — Addresses, essays, lectures.
2. Observation (Educational method) — Addresses, essays,
lectures. 3. Teacher-student relationships — Addresses,
essays, lectures. I. Delamont, Sara, 1947 –   joint author.

LB1028. S846   1975   375.1'02   74–13166

ISBN   0 471 83481 5

Set by Lightbown & Co., Ryde, Isle of Wight; printed in
Great Britain by The Pitman Press Ltd., Bath

Preface

There is something radically wrong with educational research. Few teachers read it. Planning ignores it. And it has rock-bottom status in the universities. (Who expects to receive intellectual challenge from their Dip. Ed. year?)

The authors of this book believe that one of the major faults in educational research is the almost total neglect of classroom studies—that is, the neglect of direct *observation* of teachers and pupils *inside classrooms*. It is a paradox that research concerned with teaching and learning has often so assiduously avoided looking directly at what happens between teacher and pupil.

A major reason why educational researchers have avoided going into classrooms is that classroom events are so complex. But it is easy to point out the fallacy in this kind of retreat from complexity. The situation in educational research has often been analogous to the old story of the drunk who lost his doorkey somewhere along a particularly dark stretch of the street but insisted on looking for it under the lamp — because the light was better there. Educational research has tried to find the key to understanding educational processes by staying outside the classroom, and administering tests and questionnaires to samples of 'subjects'. Such research is easy to carry out and the data are numerical, tidy and relatively easy to handle. But it is unclear whether there is any relation between such data and what goes on inside classrooms.

Events in classrooms *are* complex. The papers in this book explore precisely that complexity. They are concerned to develop concepts and a descriptive language which do capture some aspects of the behaviour of teachers and pupils. They do this by exploring *different* methods and *different* theories.

There is no single accepted methodology for observational studies of social settings. The papers use a variety of different methods of collecting data: audio-recording, film, observation and note-taking, prepared observation schedules, and formal and informal interviews with both pupils and teachers.

Much less is there a single widely accepted theory of social behaviour. Again, this book deliberately brings together papers which draw on a variety of *different* theoretical backgrounds: psychology, social psychology, social anthropology, different schools of sociology, and sociolinguistics. This explicitly multi-theoretical approach is put forward in opposition to the narrow focus of much previous educational research, which has typically been artificially restricted to a single method (questionnaires/tests) and a single theory ('psychometry'). In a developing field, it is necessary to have a variety of research strategies.

These introductory remarks are somewhere along the way to being a manifesto. The whole book argues for genuinely *exploratory* studies, in an area where any new orthodoxy would be premature, and for approaches which address complexity, rather than playing safe with topics which are manageable because they are trivial.

The papers are different, then, when compared amongst themselves. But they present a concentrated alternative to the vast amount of educational research which never looks inside the classroom. All these points are argued in detail in the introductory chapter by Delamont and Hamilton.

We hope that the collection may also be of interest to a wider audience of sociologists, social psychologists and sociolinguists. If the classroom is regarded simply as one setting for social interaction, then much of the exploratory methodology and descriptive theory proposed and used in these papers will be seen to be equally applicable to other social settings.

MICHAEL STUBBS

Birmingham,
April 1974

Acknowledgements

In 1970, at the University of Lancaster, John Garner organized a conference on classroom research which, despite itself, provided one stimulus for this book. A group of researchers from Edinburgh came away from the Lancaster conference dissatisfied with the prevailing orthodoxy in educational research and determined to write a series of papers presenting alternatives. Since 1970, the original group members have discovered other researchers with similar views and the present volume has gradually taken shape. Whilst each of the papers remains the responsibility of its individual author, the arguments are all interrelated. All attack the orthodoxy of classroom research as it was spelled out in Lancaster and as it has continued to develop since.

The editors wish to acknowledge in particular the advice and support of Liam Hudson, Malcolm Parlett and Peter Sheldrake of the Centre for Research in the Educational Sciences, University of Edinburgh. Paul Atkinson, Margaret Reid and other members of CRES have often helped us clarify our ideas; and John Garner, Ted Wragg and Arnold Morrison have encouraged the project. The Social Science Research Council has provided financial support for much of the research presented. Our thanks go also to Christine Avern-Carr for her conscientious help in the preparation of the manuscript.

It goes without saying that we all owe a debt to the teachers and pupils on whose classroom lives this book is based.

Contents

PART 1

Introduction:
The Research Context

1. Classroom research:
A critique and a new approach

By Sara Delamont and David Hamilton

Editorial introduction

This paper contains a brief section explaining why there should be discussion of classroom research in Britain *now;* a detailed critique of the restricted techniques of much previous observational classroom research; and an argument for genuine *exploration of different* types of research based on direct *observation* and recording of classroom events. The paper opens up the theoretical and methodological area for the range of research presented in all the papers which follow.

Delamont and Hamilton's main critique is levelled at the exclusive and unthinking adoption of the type of classroom research, known as 'interaction analysis', which has become a dominant tradition in the U.S.A. (This is a reasearch technique whereby an observer uses a set of pre-specified categories to 'code' or classify the behaviour of teachers and pupils). They argue that interaction analysis contains a number of severe biases and limitations when it is used as a research tool. (They distinguish sharply its use in teacher-training).

In a positive vein, Delamont and Hamilton then argue that interaction analysis should be supplemented—not necessarily always replaced—by a range of 'anthropological' techniques such as participant observation, taking field-notes, recording and in-depth interviewing. Note particularly that they are not arguing for the supremacy of any single 'method' — no single technique or theory can capture the complexity of classroom life.They are arguing that the nature of the research problem should determine the choice of the method and that a wide range of methods requires to be explored.

Delamont and Hamilton have characterized their paper as 'contextual, not descriptive'. It does not describe or summarize the other papers in the book, but places them in the context of recent research traditions in Britain and the U.S.A.

Note finally that the 'we' of this chapter should be taken to imply, amongst the authors of the book, broad agreement on broad issues. It should not be taken to imply that the papers which follow will all look the same.

M.S.

This collection of papers is intended to show a selection of new approaches to the study of the classroom. All the authors believe that, for educational research, the classroom is a very important arena which has been too long neglected. In addition, we all believe that the researchers who have attempted to study classroom phenomena have concentrated their attentions upon a restricted range of techniques, which obscure the real problems. The papers in this volume are designed to suggest alternative perspectives for studying the classroom, and hence for educational research of all kinds, which we hope will stimulate the growth of a new research tradition for education — one which is both intellectually exciting and also relevant to people working in the field.

Because the papers are putting forward slightly different perspectives on the classroom, each speaks for itself. This chapter therefore has two purposes — it shows the underlying themes which unify the various approaches put forward, and it offers a critique of the prevailing type of classroom research, which we all feel to be inadequate in several important respects.

The form of this chapter is as follows. First, there is a brief section which explains why we feel that there should be discussion about classroom research in Britain at the present time — there are clear signs that research effort is about to be concentrated on the classroom, but that this will be only one restricted kind of research. Second, we deal with the position in America, where classroom studies have been funded for over ten years — the present position in America is a cautionary tale for Britain. Third, we contrast the two major types of classroom observation which do exist, to show how they are in fact designed to do very different things and how they carry implicit assumptions that are not usually appreciated by their practitioners. Finally, we make a plea for a more eclectic approach to the study of the classroom and for tolerance of different perspectives, as exemplified by the papers which follow. Throughout this introductory chapter, the unifying philosophy of the papers which follow is stressed and used to illustrate the arguments.

THE CLASSROOM — A NEW RESEARCH AREA

Educational research in Britain is currently entering a new phase. As its preoccupations with mental testing, the results of streaming and curriculum development gradually diminish, a variety of other research interests seek to achieve pre-eminence. One area in which all the funding agencies are becoming increasingly active is classroom research.[1]

To anyone outside education it may seem paradoxical that such a central area of educational life has previously been a peripheral area for research. But it remains the case, overall, that the classroom has been a 'black box' for researchers, providing merely a vehicle for 'input-output' research designs or a captive audience for psychometric testing programmes. Even research on *teaching* has been carried on outside the classroom settings where the teaching occurs! While reviewing this field ten years ago, Medley and Mitzel (1963, p. 247) commented that

> The research worker limits himself to the manipulation or studying of antecedents and consequents . . . but never once looks into the classroom to see how the teacher actually teaches or the pupil actually learns.

Even today this comment could be applied with justice to most educational research in Britain.

Morrison and McIntyre highlight the doubtful origins of this disregard for the classroom in their remark that 'it is *almost a cliché* of modern educational thinking that pupils' behaviour in the classroom derives largely from their lives outside it' (1969, p. 119, emphasis added).

One consequence of this neglect of classroom life is that teachers have remained largely indifferent, or even antagonistic, to the claims made for educational research. For insight into their daily lives they turned elsewhere, to 'travellers' tales' (e.g. Holt, 1969), to 'non-fiction novels' (e.g. Blishen, 1955), or to the compounded folk-tales, myths and mores of the staffroom.

Unquestionably, however, there is now a shift in research interests, with the classroom as the new focus. It is not difficult to find reasons for this shift. From various quarters more and more recognition is being paid to the fact that an appreciation and understanding of classroom events is essential to any analysis of educational processes. Thus, for example, problems found with certain new curricula at the classroom stage (see MacDonald and Rudduck, 1971), the 'ineffectiveness' of much teacher training (see Stones and Morris, 1972) and the survival of 'streaming attitudes' among teachers in unstreamed primary schools (see Barker Lunn, 1970) all point towards the classroom as a relevant, indeed essential, field of research.

Basically, classroom research aims to study the processes that take place within the classroom black box. Hitherto such research in Britain has been small-scale, pursued largely by isolated individuals using *ad hoc* methods and theory. In the U.S.A., however, classroom research has been extensively funded and vigorously promoted for over a decade. Like the better known curriculum reform movement, it grew from a concern with the quality of educational practice.

Despite such widespread attention, classroom research in the U.S.A. has not been without its problems. While results have grown to voluminous proportions, their contribution to *understanding* has been disproportionately small. Gaze, summarizing several decades of research on teacher effectiveness, could only damn with faint praise:

> . . . here and there, in research on teaching methods, on teacher personality and characteristics, *and on social interaction in the classroom* it might be possible to come up with more sanguine judgements about the meaning of research findings! (1971, p. 31, emphasis ours)

In America, therefore, a decade of classroom research has not produced the revolution in educational understanding which its proponents expected. In this chapter we argue that this 'failure' is due to an over-emphasis on one type of observation, 'interaction analysis', at the expense of other kinds, which we will call 'anthropological'. In the following section we contrast the main American traditions — interaction analysis and anthropological classroom research — in the American context. By contrasting interaction analysis (the dominant tradition) with anthropological classroom research, we hope to demonstrate the reasons for our argument that a wholesale and uncritical adoption of the former in Britain is premature if not misguided.

THE AMERICAN TRADITIONS

Interaction analysis

In this section, the American experience with interaction analysis is discussed and certain issues are raised that we feel are relevant to the successful development of classroom research in Britain.

Interaction analysis[2] is a research tradition true to the behavioural core-assumptions of American psychology. Characteristically, research of this type involves using an observational system to reduce the stream of classroom behaviour to small-scale units suitable for tabulation and computation. *Mirrors for Behavior* (Simon and Boyer, 1968 and 1970), the interaction analyst's 'pharmacopoeia', details seventy-nine different systems. These various systems cover slightly different kinds of small-scale units — some provide lists of pre-specified categories (e.g. 'teacher asks question' or 'student replies'), others give the observer a checklist of events to watch for (e.g. 'teacher leaves room' or 'pupil talks with visitor'). The best known system, that of Flanders (1970), is described by Delamont (in this volume). Figure 1 shows the categories which make up the system.

Figure 1. Flanders's interaction analysis categories* (FIAC)

	Response	1. *Accepts feeling.* Accepts and clarifies an attitude or the feeling tone of a pupil in a nonthreatening manner. Feelings may be positive or negative. Predicting and recalling feelings are included.
		2. *Praises or encourages.* Praises or encourages pupil action or behavior. Jokes that release tension, but not at the expense of another individual; nodding head, or saying "Um hm?" or "go on" are included.
		3. *Accepts or uses ideas of pupils.* Clarifying, building, or developing ideas suggested by a pupil. Teacher extensions of pupil ideas are included but as the teacher brings more of his own ideas into play, shift to category five.
Teacher Talk		4. *Asks questions.* Asking a question about content or procedure, based on teacher ideas, with the intent that a pupil will answer.
		5. *Lecturing.* Giving facts or opinions about content or procedures; expressing *his own* ideas, giving *his own* explanation, or citing an authority other than a pupil.

	Initiation	6. *Giving directions.* Directions, commands, or orders to which a pupil is expected to comply. 7. *Criticizing or justifying authority.* Statements intended to change pupil behavior from nonacceptable to acceptable pattern; bawling someone out, stating why the teacher is doing what he is doing; extreme self-reference.
Pupil Talk	Response	8. *Pupil-talk—response.* Talk by pupils in response to teacher. Teacher initiates the contact or solicits pupil statement or structures the situation. Freedom to express own ideas is limited.
	Initiation	9. *Pupil-talk—initiation.* Talk by pupils which they initiate; expressing own ideas; initiating a new topic; freedom to develop opinions and a line of thought, like asking thoughtful questions; going beyond the existing structure.
Silence		10. *Silence or confusion.* Pauses, short periods of silence and periods of confusion in which communication cannot be understood by the observer.

*There is *no* scale implied by these numbers. Each number is classificatory; it designates a particular kind of communication event. To write these numbers down during observation is to enumerate, not to judge a position on a scale.

(From N. Flanders, *Analyzing Teaching Behavior,* 1970, Addison-Wesley, Reading, Mass. Reproduced by permission).

The categories of Figure 1 appear in slightly different versions in Flanders's various publications. For convenience, the version reproduced here is from Flanders's main book (1970). In this version the terms 'response' and 'initiation' replace the terms 'indirect' and 'direct' influence with respect to teacher-talk. See Flanders (1970, p. 102) for discussion of this slight alteration. Flanders (1970) still uses the concept of I/D ratio (indirect to direct) in his discussion of teaching styles.

Some try to tackle more complex phenomena — in one scheme, ideas expressed verbally as 'thought units' are coded according to their 'thought level' and their 'function'. The majority (sixty-seven) of the seventy-nine systems in *Mirrors for Behavior* are described as suitable for use in classrooms; fifty-nine as suitable for any school subject; and fifty-two as suitable for coding 'live'. (Some kind of audio-visual device for recording the events is essential for the remainder.) Although all the systems in *Mirrors for Behavior* were developed for research purposes, perhaps their most successful application has been as teacher-training tools. In fact, according to Simon and Boyer (1970, p. 27), 'forty-seven of the seventy-nine systems have been transferred from research to training instruments'.

The interaction analysis tradition has, of course, both strengths and weaknesses. On the credit side can be placed the simplicity of most of the observation systems. They are well-tried, reliable and easy to learn. In addition, they can be used to study large numbers of classrooms and readily generate a wealth of numerical data suitable for statistical analysis.[3] The data produced with such systems tell one something about life in an average classroom and allow one to 'place' a teacher in relation to his or her colleagues — the data are therefore numerical and normative. Like the results of a survey or of a psychological test, they refer to samples and populations.

In the debit column, however, must be placed factors which impose certain restrictions upon the use of these systems:

(1) All but ten of the interaction analysis systems ignore the temporal and spatial context in which the data are collected. Thus although this is not made explicit in the description of the schedules, most systems use data gathered during very short periods of observation (i.e. measured in minutes and single lessons rather than hours or days); and the observer is not expected to record information about the physical setting like that discussed in the papers by Hamilton and Delamont (in this volume). Divorced from their social and temporal (or historical) context in this way, the data collected may gloss over aspects relevant to their interpretation.

(2) Interaction analysis systems are usually concerned only with overt, observable behaviour. They do not take directly into account the differing intentions that may lie behind such behaviour. Where intention is relevant to the observational category (as in Flanders's Category 2, 'Teacher praises or encourages') the observer has himself to impute the intention, making no attempt to discover the actor's actual or self-perceived intention. In such cases only the observer's interpretation is considered relevant. Thus by concentrating on surface features, interaction analysis runs the risk of neglecting underlying but possibly more meaningful features. A comprehensive understanding of classroom life may, for example, depend upon the translation of 'silent languages' (Smith and Geoffrey, 1968) or the uncovering of 'hidden curricula' (Snyder, 1971). The papers by Walker and Adelman, Stubbs and Torode (in this volume) are examples of the kinds of analysis which may be necessary to understand the underlying features of verbal interaction in the classroom.

(3) Interaction analysis systems are expressly concerned with 'what can be categorized or measured' (Simon and Boyer, 1968, p. 1). They may, however, obscure, distort or ignore the qualitative features which they claim to investigate, by using crude measurement techniques or having ill-defined boundaries between the categories. (The distinction between 'accepting student's feeling' and 'using student's idea' to take an example from Flanders's system, cannot, by its nature, be clearly defined, yet is important if the system is to 'work' properly.)

(4) Interaction analysis systems focus on 'small bits of action or behaviour rather than global concepts' (Simon and Boyer, 1968, p. 1). Thus, inevitably, they have a tendency to generate a superabundance of data which, for the purposes of analysis, must be linked either to a complex set of descriptive concepts — customarily the original categories — or to a small number of

global concepts built up from these categories (e.g. Flanders's 'direct/ indirect ratio' built up from combinations of Categories 1, 2, 3, 6 and 7). But since the categories may have been devised in the first place to reduce the global concepts to small bits of action or behaviour, the exercise may well be circular. The potential of interaction analysis to go beyond the categories is limited. (The paper by Delamont, in this volume, in fact goes 'behind' rather than beyond them.) This circularity and lack of potential necessarily impede theoretical development.

(5) The systems utilize pre-specified categories. If the category systems are intended to assist explanation, then the pre-specification may render the explanations tautological. That is, category systems may assume the truth of what they claim to be explaining. For example, if a set of categories is based on the assumption that the teacher is in the same position as the leader of a T-group, any explanation of 'teaching' in other terms is not possible.

(6) Finally, we feel that, by placing arbitrary (and little understood) boundaries on continuous phenomena, category systems may create an initial bias from which it is extremely difficult to escape. Reality frozen in this way is not always easy to liberate from its static representation.

All these limitations inherent in interaction analysis systems are implicitly or explicitly acknowledged by their originators (e.g. Flanders, 1970, Chapter 2). However, they are not usually acknowledged by other researchers and soon slip from view even in the writings of the originators themselves. We believe that if such systems are to be used, these limitations must not be allowed to become implicit, but must be openly acknowledged all the time. The methods must not be seen as something they are not. To be valid as methods for studying the classroom, the techniques must be constantly scrutinized, not once accepted and then taken for granted.

In spite of the 'credits' which we accept for interaction analysis, its proponents make other claims which we dispute. First, interaction analysis claims to be objective. Its proponents argue that, compared to other forms of observation, interaction analysis systems provide unambiguous data uncontaminated by observer 'bias'. However, the price paid for such 'objectivity' can be high. We believe that by rejecting, as invalid, non-scientific, or 'metaphysical', data such as the actor's ('subjective') accounts, or descriptive ('impressionistic') reports of classroom events, the interaction analysis approach risks furnishing only a partial description. Furthermore, in justifying the rejection of such data on operational rather than theoretical or even educational grounds, the interaction analysis approach may divert attention from the initial problem towards more 'technocratic' concerns such as the search for 'objectivity' and 'reliability'. (In the instructional handbook of the Flanders system, ten pages deal with observer reliability, but only two with how to understand classroom phenomena (see Flanders, 1966). All of us would question the exclusion of so-called subjective data in favour of a striving for superficial objectivity.

Another preoccupation which can be seen in all the papers in the present collection is a consideration of the role of the observer. With one exception, all the systems in *Mirrors for Behavior* make a rigid distinction between the observer and the observed. The former is considered a 'fly on the wall', detached from the classroom events. For example, in an observational study of English infant classrooms, Garner (1972) devotes no discussion to the impact of the observer. More particularly, his checklist makes no reference to infant behaviour directed towards the observer, though it is reasonable to assume that it did (or could) occur.

By maintaining a strict 'distance' from those being observed, interaction analysis may again promote an incomplete appraisal. As Louis Smith has pointed out, teaching must be viewed as an intellectual, cognitive process:

> The way [the teacher] poses his problems, the kinds of goals and sub-goals he is trying to reach, the alternatives he weighs . . . are aspects of teaching which are frequently lost to the behavioural oriented empiricist who focuses on what the teacher does, to the exclusion of how he thinks about teaching. (Smith and Geoffrey, 1968, p. 96)

In much of interaction analysis these aspects are rarely considered. They too are labelled 'subjective' and placed beyond the bounds of the empirical world. In contrast, all the authors in the present volume believe that rigid distances between the observer and the teacher and pupils can be maintained only in certain circumstances, and so have generally opted for participant observation.

Finally, in the interests of objectivity, many interaction analysis research studies feel compelled to survey large numbers of classrooms. It is argued (correctly) that small samples may fail to provide statements relevant to the population at large. Such an approach (even if it can achieve true randomness) may however fail to treat as significant local perturbations or unusual effects. Indeed, despite their potential significance for the classroom or classrooms to which they apply, atypical results are seldom studied in detail. They are ironed out as 'blurred averages' and lost to discussion. All the papers in this volume comprise in-depth studies of small numbers of classrooms and do not assume that the particular examples studied are 'typical' of any wider sample.

In addition to our reservations about the use of interaction analysis, we have doubts about the historical tradition from which the research is derived. We feel that interaction analysis is plagued by a number of deep-rooted theoretical and ideological constraints. Most of the American classroom research is ethnocentric — based on a model of the classroom and a conception of education that is not always relevant in Britain. Many of the systems assume the 'chalk and talk' paradigm and focus predominantly upon the teacher. (Flanders's interaction analysis system has ten categories, seven devoted to 'teacher-talk' and two devoted to 'pupil-talk'. The tenth is a 'junk' category, 'silence or confusion'.)[4] They imply a classroom setting where the teacher stands out front and engages the students in some kind of pedagogical or linguistic ping-pong (teacher asks question/pupil replies/ teacher asks question/ . . .).

Interaction analysis systems frequently have built in to them outdated assumptions about teaching and learning. Flanders's system concentrates upon the 'affective' domain and *Mirrors for Behavior* classifies techniques according to their 'affective' or 'cognitive' focus. This split between affective and cognitive domains, dating at least from Bloom (1956),[5] is no longer accepted without question by educationalists in general. Certainly none of us would want to use such a simplistic dichotomy when talking about the complexities of classrooms in Britain.

Interaction analysis may also involve ideological assumptions in more subtle ways. Like much of the social-psychological and educational research conducted in the U.S.A. since the Second World War, it has developed from certain premises concerning 'democracy', 'authoritarianism', 'leadership' and 'mental hygiene'. Ned Flanders is expressly concerned to encourage 'indirect' teaching and, as a result, there is a latent evaluative residue in his observational system. It can be seen, for example, in Flanders's operational statement:

> Direct influence consists in those verbal statements of the teacher that restrict *freedom* of action, by focusing attention on a problem, interjecting teacher *authority* or both. (Flanders, 1965, p. 9, emphasis added).

This fact may not always be appreciated when the system is used in other, less experienced, hands.

These then are some of the major objections which all the authors of this volume have to interaction analysis, the classroom research method which has dominated the American research scene for ten years and now threatens to be adopted wholesale, and without critical thought, in Britain. The next section deals with another American tradition of classroom research which is little known in this country but which all of us feel has greater potential for Britain.

'Anthropological' observation

Outside the interaction analysis tradition in the U.S.A. there have been certain other important but widely neglected programmes of classroom research. Often described as 'anthropological', this work has developed beyond the margins of mainstream educational psychology and relates instead to social anthropology, psychiatry and participant observation research in sociology. No satisfactory name exists for this tradition. It has been described as 'microethnographical' (Smith and Geoffrey, 1968), 'naturalistic' (MacDonald, 1970) and 'ecological' (Parlett, 1969). Unlike the interaction analysis tradition, whose origins are clearly rooted in behavioural psychology, the anthropological tradition has no established roots. Some of its members are 'straight' anthropologists (e.g. Jules Henry), some are sociologists (e.g. Howard Becker), some are psychiatrists (e.g. Zachary

Gussow) and some are 'converts' from behavioural psychology (e.g. Philip Jackson, Malcolm Parlett and Louis Smith).

In the U.S.A. this tradition is perhaps better known for its work in higher education (see, for example, Becker *et al.* (1968), Kahne (1969) and Parlett (1969)). It contrasts strongly with interaction analysis and can be thought of as representing an alternative tradition: one that goes back to Malinowski, Thomas and Waller, rather than Watson, Skinner and Bales.

While both interaction analysis and anthropological classroom research are concerned with developing 'metalanguages' (Simon and Boyer, 1968, p. 1) adequate to the complexity of the behaviour they countenance, the latter uses an approach based on ethnography rather than 'psychometry'; and a conceptual framework which considers education in broad socio-cultural terms, rather than, say, in 'cognitive' or 'affective' terms. In each case, 'knowledge', the 'curriculum', and even 'learning' are regarded differently. Methodologically, 'anthropological' classroom studies are based on participant observation, during which the observer immerses himself in the 'new culture'. That is, they involve the presence of an observer (or observers) for prolonged periods in a single or a small number of classrooms. During that time the observer not only observes, but also talks with participants; significantly, the ethnographer calls them informants, rather than subjects. Also, the anthropologist does not make such a strong category distinction between observer and observed as the interaction analyst does. Gussow and Vidich put the anthropological case most clearly:

When the observers are physically present and physically approachable the concept of the observer as non-participant though sociologically correct is psychologically misleading. (Gussow, 1964, p. 240)

Whether the field-worker is totally, partially or not at all disguised, the respondent forms an image of him and uses that image as a basis of response. Without such an image, the relationship between the field-worker and the respondent by definition does not exist. (Vidich, 1935, p. 35)

In addition to observing classroom life, the researcher may conduct formal interviews with the participants and ask them to complete questionnaires. Usually, to record his observations, the observer compiles field-notes or, more recently, field-recordings. Compared with the results of the interaction analyst, the data of the 'anthropological' researcher are relatively unsystematic and open-ended.[6]

The 'anthropologist' uses a holistic framework. He accepts as given the complex scene he encounters and takes this totality as his data base. He makes no attempt to manipulate, control or eliminate variables. Of course, the 'anthropologist' does not claim to account for every aspect of this totality in his analysis. He reduces the breadth of enquiry systematically to give more concentrated attention to the emerging issues. Starting with a wide angle of vision, he 'zooms' in and progressively focuses on those classroom features he considers to be most salient. Thus, ethnographic reasearch clearly dissociates itself from the a priori reductionism inherent in interaction analysts.

'Anthropological' classroom research, like interaction analysis, begins with description. But, whereas the former is governed by pre-ordained descriptive categories (e.g. 'verbal', 'non-verbal', 'teacher', 'pupil') the latter allows and encourages the development of *new* categories. Anthropological research can freely go beyond the *status quo* and develop new and potentially fertile descriptive languages. The papers in this volume show some of these descriptive languages and reveal their empirical basis.

Unlike ethnographic classroom research, interaction analysis is, as stated above, often concerned with generating normative data, that is, in extrapolating from sample to population. It should be remembered, however, that statistical norms (e.g. 'teacher-talk percentages' (Flanders, 1970) apply to the population *taken as a whole,* not to its individual members. They apply to individual settings only in probabilistic terms. And since settings are never equivalent, such statistical generalizations may not always be relevant or useful. The papers which follow are primarily intended to *be* relevant and useful; not to be normative, but to illuminate.

It is often argued against anthropological studies that their results cannot be generalized to other settings. This criticism refers only to statistical generalizations. To an anthropological researcher, the development of generally or universally applicable statements is quite a different task, one that is never achieved merely by carrying out a survey. Despite their diversity, individual classrooms share many characteristics. Through the detailed study of one particular context it is still possible to clarify relationships, pinpoint critical processes and identify common phenomena. Later, abstracted summaries and general concepts can be formulated, which may, upon further investigation, be found to be germane to a wider variety of settings. Case studies, therefore, are not necessarily restricted in scope. Indeed, unlike interaction analysis, they can acknowledge both the particulars and the universals of classroom life. In this respect, interaction analysis is akin to demography or census-taking, whereas anthropological studies are equivalent to the small-scale studies commonly reported in medical journals.[7]

Thus, interaction analysis and anthropological traditions can be seen to differ in a number of respects. In the U.S.A. they are sharply insulated from one another. Interaction analysis has largely ignored classroom research conducted outside its own territorial preserve. For example, the A.E.R.A. curriculum evaluation monograph on *Classroom Observation* (Gallagher *et al.,* 1970) contains no discussion or even acknowledgement of any of the anthropological literature related to curriculum evaluation (e.g. Russell (1969), Smith and Keith (1967), or Hanley *et al.* (1969)). Also, *Mirrors for Behavior* fails to acknowledge that there are (or even can be) ' "metalanguages" for describing communication of various kinds' (p. 1) that are based on anything other than measurement or a *priori* categorization.

Anthropological research has developed outside the prestige universities of the American east coast and is concentrated in the mid- and far west. By comparison with interaction analysis, it is poorly funded, its findings are difficult to obtain and its formal outlets (journals and conferences) are minimal. In Britain, this unenviable state has yet to come about. Dialogue still takes place: recent classroom observation conferences have included papers reflecting both interests and British literature reviews (e.g. Delamont (1973) and Walker (1972)) have considered the merits of both traditions. This volume is intended as a contribution to this continuing dialogue. We hope that proponents of interaction analysis will admit the value of other types of study, such as those reported here, and vice versa.

THE FUTURE DEVELOPMENT OF CLASSROOM RESEARCH IN BRITAIN

In concluding this introductory chapter, we should like to raise a number of issues which we feel are essential to what is an important, yet largely unargued, debate in Britain. Although the issues relate in general to the practice of classroom research, they are particularly concerned with the theoretical and methodological substrata upon which it is founded.

(1) In its rush to the classroom, there is a danger that research will cease to consider the wider educational and social context of the classroom. It contrast 'classroom' with 'society' is to construct a false opposition. While it is possible, for research purposes, to regard the classroom as a social unit in its own right, it is only with considerable difficulty that it can be regarded as self-contained. An adequate classroom study must acknowledge and account for both the internal and external aspects of classroom life. In particular, classroom research should not be treated as a substitute for studies which look at the broader societal aspects of education. As Walker (1970, p. 143) has warned,

> any descripttion of classroom activities that cannot be related to the social structure and culture of the society is a conservative description.

(2) Development of audio-visual techniques has meant that much classroom research can work from recorded rather than 'live' data, that is, at one remove from the classroom. While this allows for *post hoc* analysis, it has the disadvantage that much of the (usually implicit) contextual data normally made available to the on-site observer may be lost. It is significant, we suggest, that at least some studies which have used visual and/or audio recordings still consciously supplement them with the physical presence of an independent observer (see Walker and Adelham, and Stubbs, in this volume, and Smith and Brock forthcoming). We believe that, while an

elaborate technology can facilitate *description* of behaviour, it cannot furnish *explanations* for that behaviour. The methods themselves do not provide such a link, nor do they supplant the conceptual processes needed to generate explanations. In the past, classroom research — particularly the interaction analysis tradition — has poured forth an endless stream of comparative studies, hoping presumably that some conceptual clarity would mysteriously emerge; and technological sophistication threatens to increase the flow of data without adding to our understanding. The use made of recordings in two studies reported here (Walker and Adelman, and Stubbs) does not fall into this trap. Both studies concentrate on illuminating aspects classroom phenomena by means of recording, not recording for its own sake.

(3) We also feel that much classroom description has been simply behavioural. It has tended to disregard the meaning(s) that behaviour entails. As already suggested, such an approach may miss important differences that underlie the behaviour. To the extent that classroom research claims to illuminate the processes associated with classroom life, it cannot afford to divorce what people do from their intentions. If it treats teachers and students merely as objects, it can only obtain a partial analysis, one that falls short of explanation in terms of the subjective processes that inform a teacher's or student's actions.

To inquire into subjectivity or relative truth is not, as is sometimes imagined, to accept solipsism or relativism. It can still be a central theme for empirical research, as Harré and Secord (1972, p. 101) point out,

> to treat people as if they were human beings it must still be possible to accept their commentaries upon their actions as authentic, though revisable, reports of phenomena, subject to empirical criticism.

This is related to the successful use of interaction analysis systems as training rather than research tools. As training instruments, they are used to give information back directly to the people being observed. Indeed, when audio-visual systems are employed, the observer and the observed can be one and the same person. Clearly, when interaction analysis is used in this way, the observer is more aware of the intentions and subjective processes involved and, at the same time, is sensitized to their temporal and social context. Thus, he or she has the necessary data to reach a more powerful understanding of the interaction. In this respect, interaction analysis as 'research' is fundamentally different from interaction analysis as 'training'. In that it necessarily incorporates a phenomenological understanding as well as a behavioural description of the situation, its use in training is much closer to the 'anthropological' research model.

(4) We all recognize that, like all other research, every classroom study develops from certain premises, suppositions and interests held by the researcher. Typically, these reflect the ethos, especially the intellectual ethos, of his time. As we have noted, there is an insidious danger of an

uncritical acceptance of techniques developed from different (and often forgotten) standpoints — the 'mental hygiene' overtones, research methods and statistical techniques, just as much as the theoretical constructs with which they are sustained, may bear the hallmarks, if not the scars, of an earlier and possibly outdated regime. (Perhaps the clearest examples of this can be drawn from the chequered history of mental testing — see, for example, papers by Rex, and Daniels and Houghton, in Richardson and Spears (1972)).

The reader is not expected to accept, uncritically, the arguments put forward in the papers in the present volume. Rather we hope to show that, starting from unusual assumptions, new understandings of the classroom can arise, relating to aspects of problems which interaction analysis ignores or takes for granted.

(5) There is one final issue on which we wish to dissociate ourselves from the prevailing pattern of educational research. This is the congenital and manic optimism with which much educational research is suffused. Absolute truth is heralded as lying just beyond the horizon. For example:

> A revolution in teaching is being fomented. If successful it will over-throw the hegemony of the centuries-old pattern whereby one teacher and 20–40 pupils engage for most kinds of instruction in a teacher-dominated discourse . . . If the revolution succeeds the teacher will spend much less time each day with groups of students in time-honoured ways . . . In short, a spectre is haunting research on teaching—the spectre of programmed instruction. (Gage and Unruh, 1967)

This optimism and its associated, essentially nineteenth-century, belief in rational man and the power of science (with its implicit denial of the historicity of truth) has been of considerable consequence, not least for classroom research. In a field where instant solutions are at a premium, this belief, surely, is unlikely to bear much fruit. Rather, it can often lead to premature closure (when an exploratory or heuristic stance would be more useful), to the presentation of cautionary notes dressed up as 'conclusions', and to the pursuit of short-term reliability at the expense of long-term validity. In summary, this belief can produce 'tunnel vision', a mental state where a clear view ahead is achieved at the expense of a fading appreciation of the past and an ignorance of what is taking place close by.

The purpose of this volume is not to put forward yet another utopian solution to all the ills of educational research. Indeed, given the differing views of the various authors, this would hardly be practicable. We are pleading, rather, for a new attitude towards research, in which eclectic combinations of research methods can be used and in which different problems can be tackled by different, and mutually appropriate, methods. Instead of looking for one solution to all problems, we suggest that more consideration be given to the nature of the specific problems being faced and, hence, to choosing a particular research strategy.

CONCLUSION

Although for the purposes of this discussion we have divided classroom research in two fields, we do not regard them as necessarily mutually exclusive. Indeed, in our own work we are concerned to go beyond this distinction. The task is not easy, as the differences are clear and deep-rooted, and the respective positions entrenched. For this reason we suggest that significant advances will ultimately depend, not on increased techno-logical sophistication nor upon some kind of methodological convergence, but instead upon a reconceptualization and transformation of the dimensions which divide the two traditions.

While research awaits this advance, it is still incumbent upon researchers to treat interaction analysis and anthropological classroom research for what they are. Confusion still exists as to their aims and objectives. Too often, questions such as 'What are they for? What can (or cannot) they do?' are not considered. As different tools, they are better suited to different tasks. A knowledge of their deficiencies is as important for their successful use, as an appreciation of their potential. Neither is, or can be, a universal panacea.

Thus, for example, to criticize anthropological studies for not providing demographic information is as misplaced as it is narrow-minded. Likewise, to complain that interaction systems are not as sensitive as, say, in-depth interviews, is to forget that they were never intended as clinical devices — their focus is the *average* rather than the *individual* classroom.

At the beginning of this paper we noted that the classroom was likely to become an important 'new' field in British educational research. All of us are afraid that the American experiences in the area will be repeated here. We do not want to see large sums of money spent, and valuable time and good-will expended, making the same mistakes. Some work should be done with systematic classroom techniques of various kinds; but we feel that other perspectives, like those which follow, are equally fruitful lines of enquiry.

Acknowledgements

A slightly different version of our argument has appeared in *Research in Education*, 11, May 1974. The authors wish to thank the editor for permission to reproduce it here. In addition we wish to thank all those who commented on earlier drafts of this paper, particularly those at the Centre for Research in the Educational Sciences, University of Edinburgh, and to thank the Social Science Research Council, the Scottish Council for Research in Education, and the Scottish Education Department for financial support during our research and the preparation of this paper.

Notes

1. During 1972 programmes were announced by N.F.E.R. (The 'Secondary School Day' project and the 'Evaluation of the Primary School'); by the O.E.C.D. (The International Microteaching Unit, University of Lancaster); and by the Scottish Education Department (The Interaction Analysis Project, Callender Park College). These projects together represent a funding commitment approaching £¼ million.

2. For the sake of our discussion, 'interaction analysis' refers to any research technique which fulfils the criteria for inclusion in *Mirrors for Behavior* (Simon and Boyer, 1970). Strictly speaking, interaction analysis is the name given to the system developed by Ned Flanders. However, as 30% of the classroom systems in *Mirrors for Behavior* are expressly related to interaction analysis (referring to Flanders or his forbears Bales and Withall in their abstracts) we feel the designation to be valid.

3. It is more correct, though perhaps tautological, to say that all the *widely used* systems are simple. Of the remainder, five require four observers, one requires an extensive knowledge of psychoanalysis, and one requires a knowledge of the foreign language being taught in the classroom. A few systems are also restricted in the situations in which they can be used (e.g. a 'correctional institution for delinquents').

4. For critiques of Flanders's system see Silberman (1970, p. 455 ff.) and Mitchell (1969, pp. 704–710).

5. This affective-cognitive category distinction dates back to Wolff (1679–1754) when it formed the foundation of faculty psychology — now largely disregarded (see O'Neil, 1968, pp. 24–5).

6. This is not, however, to imply that all anthropological research is open-ended 'pure' research. Like interaction analysis it has been used in curriculum evaluation (e.g. Smith and Pohland, forthcoming, Parlett and Hamilton, 1972) and in teacher-training (e.g. Goldhammer, 1969).

7. See Glaser and Strauss (1967) and Strodtbeck (1969) for separate discussions of theory building and case-study research.

References

Barker Lunn, J. C., 1970, *Streaming in the Primary School,* National Foundation for Educational Research, Slough.

Becker, H. S. *et al.,* 1968, *Making the Grade,* Wiley, New York.

Blishen, E., 1955, *Roaring Boys,* Thames and Hudson, London.

Bloom, B. S. *et al.,* 1950, *Taxonomy of Educational Objectives Handbook 1: Cognitive Domain,* McKay, New York.

Delamont, S., 1973, *Academic conformity Observed: Studies in the Classroom,* unpublished Ph.D. thesis, University of Edinburgh.

Flanders, N. A., 1965, *Teacher Influence, Pupil Attitudes and Achievement,* Cooperative Research Monograph, University of Michigan.

Flanders, N. A., 1966, *Interaction Analysis in the Classroom: A Manual for Observers,* revised edition, School of Education, University of Michigan.

Flanders, N. A., 1970, *Analyzing Teaching Behavior,* Addison-Wesley, Reading, Mass.

Gage, N. L., 1971, *Teacher Effectiveness and Teacher Education: the Search for Scientific Basis,* Pacific Books, California.

Gage, N. L. and W. H. Unruh, 1967, 'Theoretical formulations for research on teaching', *Review of Educational Research,* 37, 358–370.

Gallagher, J. J. *et al.,* 1970, *Classroom Observation,* A.E.R.A. Monograph Series on Curriculum Evaluation No. 6, Rand McNally, Chicago.

Garner, J., 1972, 'Some aspects of behaviour in infant school classrooms', *Research in Education,* 7, 28–47.

Glaser, B. G. and A. Strauss, 1967, *The Discovery of Grounded Theory,* Weidenfeld and Nicholson, London.

Goldhammer, R., 1969, *Clinical Supervision: Special Methods for the Supervision of Teachers,* Holt, Rinehart and Winston, New York.

Gussow, Z., 1964, 'The observer-observed relationship as information about structures in small group research', *Psychiatry,* 27, 236–247.

Hanley, J. P. *et al.*, 1969, *Curiosity, Competence, Community,* Education Development Centre, Cambridge, Mass.

Harré, R. and P. F. Secord, 1972, *The Explanation of Social Behaviour,* Blackwell, Oxford.

Holt, J., 1969, *How Children Fail,* Penguin, Harmondsworth.

Kahne, M. J., 1969, 'Psychiatrist observer in the classroom', *Medical Trial Technique Quarterly,* **23,** 81–98.

MacDonald, B., 1970, 'The evaluation of the humanities curriculum project', unpublished paper.

MacDonald, B. and J. Rudduck, 1971, 'Curriculum research and development: barriers to success', *British Journal of Educational Psychology,* **41,** 148–154.

Medley, D. M. and H. E. and H. E. Mitzel, 1963, 'Measuring classroom behaviour by systematic observation', in N. L. Gage (ed.), *Handbook of Research on Teaching,* Rand McNally, Chicago.

Mitchell, J. V., 1969, 'Education's challenge to psychology: the prediction of behaviour from person–environment interaction', *Review of Educational Research,* **39,** 695–721.

Morrison, A. and D. McIntyre, 1969, *Teachers and Teaching,* Penguin, Harmondsworth.

O'Neil, W. M., 1968, *The Beginnings of Modern Psychology,* Penguin, Harmondsworth.

Parlett, M. R., 1969, 'Undergraduate teaching observed', *Nature,* **223,** 1102–1104.

Parlett, M. R. and D. Hamilton, 1972, *Evaluation as Illumination: A New Approach to the Study of Innovatory Programs,* Occasional Paper 9, Centre for Research in the Educational Sciences, University of Edinburgh.

Richardson, K. and D. Spears, 1972, *Race, Culture and Intelligence,* Penguin, Harmondsworth.

Russell, H., 1969, *Evaluation of Computer-Assisted Instruction Program,* C.E.M.R.E.L., St. Ann, Mo.

Silberman, C. E., 1970, *Crisis in the Classroom,* Vintage Books, New York.

Simon, A. and G. E. Boyer (eds.), 1968, *Mirrors for Behavior,* Research for Better Schools, Philadelphia.

Simon, A. and G. E. Boyer (eds.), 1970, *Mirrors for Behavior II,* Research for Better Schools, Philadelphia.

Smith, L. M., 1971, 'Dilemma in educational innovation: a problem for anthropology as clinical method', paper presented to A.E.R.A. symposium 'Anthropological approaches to the study of education', New York.

Smith, L. M. and P. M. Keith, 1967, *Social Psychological Aspects of School Building Design,* U.S.O.E. Cooperative Research Report No. S–223, Washington D.C.

Smith, L. M. and W. Geoffrey, 1968, *The Complexities of an Urban Classroom,* Holt, Rinehart and Winston, New York.

Smith, L. M. and J. A. M. Brock, 1970, *'Go Bug', Go!: Methodical Issues in Classroom Observation Research,* C.E.M.R.E.L., St. Ann, Mo.

Smith, L. M. and P. A. Pohland, forthcoming, 'Educational technology and the rural highlands', in A.E.R.A. Monograph Series on Curriculum Evaluation No. 7, Rand McNally, Chicago.

Smith, L. M. and J. A. M. Brock, forthcoming, *Teacher Plans and Classroom Interaction,* C.E.M.R.E.L., St. Ann, Mo.

Snyder, B. R., 1971, *The Hidden Curriculum,* Knopf, New York.

Stones, E. and S. Morris, 1972, *Teaching Practice: Problems and Perspectives,* Methuen, London.

Strodtbeck, F., 1969, 'Considerations of meta–method in cross–cultural studies', in D. R. Price–Williams (ed.), *Cross–cultural Studies,* Penguin, Harmondsworth.

Vidich, A. J., 1955, 'Participant observation and collection and interpretation of data, *American Journal of Sociology,* **60,** 354–360.

Walker, R., 1971, *'The Social Setting of the Classroom—a Review of Observational Studies and Research,* unpublished M.Phil. thesis, University of London.

Walker, R., 1972, 'The sociology of education and life in school classrooms', *International Review of Education,* **18,** 32–43.

PART 2

Pupils'-Eye Views

Education research often disregards how pupils see school. The three papers in this section propose three ways of exploring pupils' perceptions of teachers and teaching.

2. Interaction sets in the classroom: Towards a study of pupil knowledge

By Viv Furlong

Editorial introduction

This paper presents a preliminary demonstration that classroom behaviour must be directly observed in order to reveal its complexity. Furlong argues that some researchers have tried to explain classroom life by supposing that it is determined by *external* constraints and pressures, referred to, for example, as 'norms', 'values', and 'group cultures'. But such a model over-simplifies pupils' behaviour in the classroom, by making it appear more stable and rigid than it is. Furlong views 'culture' rather as what you have to 'know' to be able to behave appropriately from minute to minute in changing circumstances.

He argues that observation of individual pupils with different teachers shows that their behaviour *changes* across different situations within short periods of time. If pupils' interaction is observed as it happens, and if the researcher attempts to discover how pupils themselves see their behaviour, then their behaviour is seen as a continual adjustment to the changing social scene — not simply as 'determined' by whichever 'group' they spend time with. In commonsense terms, different teachers see 'different sides' of their pupils. The paper proposes a concept of 'interaction set' to describe a group of pupils who perceive what is happening in a similar way and who communicate this to each other to communally define appropriate behaviour. This paper, and also the following two papers by Gannaway and Nash, thus tackle directly the question of how pupils 'make sense' of school.

This paper is, then, a preliminary demonstration, based on many quoted classroom incidents, that direct observation of teachers and pupils can reveal what no indirect questionnaire or 'testing' methods can. All the other papers in the collection, taking this argument for granted, are concerned to further develop methods and descriptive concepts which can capture aspects of this complexity and thus specify more closely the nature of the 'complexity'.

M.S.

Not all pupils 'know' the same things about their school lives. They do not all form the same commonsense judgements about their teachers or the curriculum; they do not all see other pupils in the same way. Because of this, a study of pupil experience or 'knowledge' of school life must begin by looking at the way some pupils come to share common perspectives and how pupils influence each other in what they 'know'. In other words, we need a more detailed understanding of pupil interaction. Only when this process is fully understood will it be possible to go on to document what individuals or groups actually 'know'. This paper is therefore intended to provide the groundwork for a more detailed study of pupil knowledge.

The ways in which pupils influence each other, both in their behaviour and in their interpretation of their school experience, is of great interest to both teachers and parents. That interest is often expressed in phrases such as, 'He's getting into bad company', or, 'She's a good influence on her class'. Despite this interest, there has been relatively little research which examines pupils' informal school life. Most classroom observation, whether 'systematic' or 'anthropological', seems to be directed at throwing light only on the teacher-pupil relationship; this study is an attempt to redress that imbalance.

The field work was carried out in a secondary modern school, in a large English city, for two terms during 1972 and 1973. I had taught in the school since 1970. The data presented relate to one class of sixteen fourth-year girls whose average age was 15 years.[1] The material has come from two main sources. First, notes made during my extensive observations of lessons with each of their ten teachers: I simply sat at the back of the class and wrote down what the girls did and said, concentrating in particular on situations where they communicated with each other. The second source of data was tape-recorded interviews with groups and individual girls.

Many of the quotations selected for this paper relate to one particular girl, whom I call Carol. (All names of pupils and teachers in this paper are of course pseudonyms.) In this way the reader can build up a consistent picture of interaction as it takes place in the classroom. For this purpose, any of the sixteen girls could have been chosen, for Carol is not seen to be in any way unusual.

Of the sixteen girls, thirteen, including Carol, were of West Indian origin, although most of them had spent the major part of their school career in England.[2] This class was considered below average intelligence and they occupied a 'one from bottom' position in the streaming system. The general assessment of the staff was that they were 'difficult' but not the 'worst' class in the school.

The paper is divided into two main sections. The first part is devoted to building up an understanding of what interaction is and how it takes place in the classroom. Patterns of interaction are seen to be related to how individuals or groups define classroom situations, what they 'know' about them. The second section develops this model, illustrating Carol's typical pattern of interaction and typical ways of looking at classroom situations.

I begin by comparing my approach with some of the existing work on pupil interaction, most of which has been based on a key theory of social psychology, that of groups. I argue the results are less than adequate.

The social psychological approach

Various authors[3] have applied a social psychological model to the study of schools. The process of pupil interaction in the classroom is assumed to take place within the context of peer groups or friendship groups. It is suggested that these groups have a 'culture' of norms and values which colour the pupils' whole school experience.

This approach does not, however, examine how the pupils *themselves* see their social relationships. Researchers have not asked how pupils actually interact with each other in the classroom, or examined the different action they see as appropriate in different circumstances.

The studies by David Hargreaves (1967) and Colin Lacey (1970) are probably the best known in this field. Their analysis is simple. They both believe that social interaction can best be understood by using the concept of the informal group. They assume that friends will 'interact' more frequently than pupils who are not friends and that, in so doing, they will develop their own norms and values. Interaction is therefore understood only in terms of groups membership and it is a simple task, using a sociometric question-naire, to discover exactly who is in the group. (A sociometric questionnaire is a means of obtaining quantitative data on the preferences of individuals for associating with each other. For example, Hargreaves asked pupils to write down the names of the friends they went around with at school. Pupils who chose each other were assumed to form a peer group).

Once Hargreaves and Lacey have plotted their different groups, they proceed to 'measure' the norms and values associated with each. They assume that these groups form 'cultures' which will be consistent in their approach to the school, and Hargreaves goes so far as to identify the 'central norms' of each of the classes he studied. For example, the main value of his 4B is seen as 'having fun' while the values of his 4C are characterized in terms of delinquency (Hargreaves, 1967, p. 27).

Conformity to these central norms is explained in terms of 'social pressure' or 'power'. Conforming to the demands of the group culture is something the individual must do if he is not going to sacrifice his social status. Those who do not conform are called 'deviants'.

There are three major difficulties with this model. First, interaction does not just 'happen' in friendship groups but is 'constructed' by individuals. When classes are observed, it becomes obvious that who interacts with whom can change from minute to minute depending on a great many circumstances. Pupil interaction in a classroom will not necessarily include all friends at the same time, and it will often involve pupils who are not friends at all.

The second difficulty with this model relates to the idea that norms and values will be consistent. It would be obvious, even to the most casual observer of classroom behaviour, that there is no *consistent* culture for a group of friends. Even the most delinquent pupils will be well behaved in certain circumstances.[4] Teachers do not always invite the same amount of conformity or hostility; some lessons allow for greater feelings of personal achievement than others. Classroom situations change in the meaning they have for pupils and, as they change, so will the pupils' assessment of how to behave.

Finally, the model suggests that there is a pressure on group members to conform to the group's demands. The culture is presented as an external reality and social behaviour is shown not so much as an interaction between two or more individuals but rather as one person responding to some reified group. The implication is that the individual has little choice in his action, as he is controlled by something outside him: the group.

The 'external analysis of interaction is inadequate, because it misses the main point, that participants have to build up their own respective lines of conduct as they go along. They must continually interpret each others' actions and, therefore, continually 'redefine' the situation for themselves. Norms and values are significant only in so far as they are interpreted by the participants during the interaction process.

I am therefore arguing for an alternative understanding of classroom interaction, where the pupils are seen to be continually adjusting their behaviour to each other, where those actually interacting are always changing and where norms of behaviour are not consistent. In these circumstances it is impossible to use the necessarily static methods implied by the social psychological model. Questionnaires and paper-and-pencil tests become inadequate and it is necessary to observe pupils' interaction as it actually happens in the classroom. It is also important to record what the pupils say about their classroom situations and try and understand how they form rules for interpreting these situations. Anthropological observation must therefore become the major tool of analysis and cannot simply be used to resolve ambiguities, as Lacey, for example, has suggested (1970, p. 98).

1. INTERACTION

The object of this study, then, is to develop a more sensitive analysis of the way in which pupils influence each other, both in their undersanding of their school experience and in the types of behaviour they consider appropriate. The assumption that this somehow 'happens' in groups is inadequate and it is necessary to study interaction as it takes place and as the pupils themselves see it.

By interaction, I mean situations where individuals come to a common 'definition of the situation', by drawing on similar commonsense knowledge, and make common assessments of appropriate action. That is, they 'see' what is happening in the same way and agree on what are appropriate ways to behave in the circumstances. This does not mean that those interacting will behave in the *same* way, simply that they behave in a way that can be interpreted by others as showing similar 'definitions of the situation'. Nor do pupils have to 'tell' each other how they see things, for their actions will symbolically tell this to the whole class.

In this way, running out of a class or shouting an answer to a teacher can be examples of interaction, when the individual takes into account that he is being given support by smiles or laughter from others present. He knows by their support that they 'see' the classroom situation in the same way; they share the same commonsense knowledge about it. Here it is not enough to look at the individual on his own, for he is aware that his behaviour is a 'joint action', that others are taking part, that he is interacting.[5]

The following example of interaction comes from my observational notes. The incident occurred after Carol had been told to leave the room because she had been rude to the teacher. My notes show her interacting with Valerie and Diane and taking into account what they are doing in choosing her own action:

> She (Carol) wanders out slowly, laughing and looking round at Valerie and Diane, who laugh as well. She stands outside the door, looking though its window for a few minutes . . . trying to catch the eyes of the people inside the room.

While she is walking out of the room, Carol is aware of Valerie and Diane and is making continual non-verbal contact with them. Even when she is outside the door, she maintains this contact for a few minutes but, after a while, she gives up and wanders off out of sight.

In this example, Carol is communicating with two other girls in the room, each of whom 'see' what is happening in the same way. They symbolically communicate this to her by the way they act (laughing and looking at her) and therefore support her action. These three girls, who are choosing their behaviour together, form a group or a set. To distinguish those taking part in this sort of grouping from any other, I am going to call it an 'interaction set'. That is to say, the interaction set at any one time will be those pupils who perceive what is happening in a similar way, communicate this to each other and define appropriate action together.

Now consider this example of Carol interacting with a much larger group of girls; she is aware of them and directs what she says to them all. They are all part of an interaction set.

> Eight of the girls are sitting round the same bench in the Science Lab. Carol and Diane run in thirty minutes late and sit down with them all.

CAROL: (to the whole table) *I went home to get some tangerines.*

MRS. NEWMAN: *Where have you been?*

DIANE: (aggressively) *Dentist . . . .*

MRS. NEWMAN: *Where have you been?*

CAROL: (aggressively) *None of your business.*

MRS. NEWMAN ignores or does not hear this remark.

The interaction set in the second example is much larger than in the first: nine girls are involved, as opposed to three.

The descriptions above show that the girls are aware of each other in choosing their behaviour. This awareness of others is implied in the way they describe classroom situations. For example, in an interview, Carol uses the term 'we' rather than 'I': *

> *We sneak out of class, or ask to go for a drink of water . . . and we don't come back, we don't come back in again at all.*[6]

This is a generalized classroom description and Carol thinks in terms of herself and her friends; she does the same when describing specific situations:

> *We had R.E....We had that stupid teacher, and he just sits there and gives us these stupid books to read, so I just sit there reading them . . . so Anne says 'Let's go out', so me, Jill, Linda and Diane just follow her out.*

A lot of Carol's classroom behaviour takes place in the context of an interaction set. She takes others into account in deciding how to behave and is aware that they share a common definition of the situation. Similar observations were made for all the other pupils in the class. Each spends a great deal of her classroom time interacting rather than behaving individually.

Who is in the interaction set?

Consider the following descriptions of classroom situations, which show different interaction sets in operation. In the first, the set comprises Carol and Diane alone; they are late for the lesson and are talking to each other in the corridor. Angela tries to distinguish herself from them in the teacher's eyes by 'telling on them'.

> When Mrs. Alan comes in, Carol and Diane are missing: she asks where they are. Angela says they were in the last lesson.

> ANGELA: *Them lot are outside, Miss.*

> Mrs. Alan goes out and sends in Carol and Diane who enter, laughing loudly, and start to sit down. They are followed in by Mrs. Alan who shouts, *Stand at the front.* They continue to laugh and look round the room, though less confidently than before. Other class members are no longer laughing with them and Carol's and Diane's eyes rove round the room, but come into contact with no-one in particular.

*Compare the paper by Torode, in this volume, for a detailed analysis of the importance of such small shifts in language for implying alignment or distance between speakers. Ed., *M.S.*

In this second example, the interaction set includes Carol and five other girls.

> Carol, Valerie, Diane, Anne, Angela and Monica sit round one of the benches in the Science Lab. There is continual talking throughout the lesson from these girls even though they carry on copying down the notes that Mrs. Newman has written down on the board. At times the noise from these girls is so great that Mrs. Newman can't be heard. The rest of the class, sitting round the other bench, are comparatively quiet.

It is obvious from these examples that quite different interactions sets are in operation. In the first situation Carol and Diane form a distinct unit. They are defined as an interaction set both by themselves and by others' assessment of their action, as shown by Angela's behaviour. In the second example, a much larger interaction set is in operation. Again, Carol, Valerie and Diane take part, but this time, Anne, Angela and Monica participate as well, each legitimating the action of the others.

There are other situations which illustrate different patterns of classroom interaction. In the following example, which describes a test, the pattern of interaction continually changes.

> When the test begins, they slowly move to different seats without being told to . . . Linda does not know the answer to the first question and does not write anything. Diane whispers across the room to Carol. *You doing it?* Carol holds up a blank piece of paper and giggles, she hasn't been able to do the first two questions either. Miss Lane asks the next question: *Name a common cooking cheese* . . . Linda smiles, looks round the class and does not write anything. Next question: *Name one use the body puts calcium to.* Linda behaves differently. She writes, then looks up to the ceiling for a moment, and then writes again. *Name common egg drink.* Linda and Jill's eyes meet; they both seem to know the answer and quickly look away, covering their papers from each other with their arms.

Here the girls are moving in and out of interaction depending on whether or not they know the answers. When they know the answer, they act alone: when they do not, they interact.

The changing pattern of interaction is reflected in the way the girls describe each other. For example, in an interview, Carol, Valerie and Diane discuss who they are 'friends with' in the class:

CAROL: *Yes, we're all friends together, really . . . not Monica though, she's not really with us.*

VALERIE: *No she works too hard, she's too good.*

DIANE: *Well, she used to be last year.*

CAROL: *Well I suppose she is most of the time.*

They seem confused about whether Monica is or is not a 'friend';

observations show that Monica only interacts with these three girls at certain times, but at others she has nothing to do with them, often sitting on the other side of the room.

Patterns of interaction can vary a great deal. Sometimes, these girls act quite alone without obvious communication between them, apparently defining situations for themselves. At different times interaction sets form, involving varying numbers of girls and occasionally the whole class. Each interaction set relates to a specific definition; all of the girls interacting share the same commonsense knowledge of the situation.

Norms and values

A great many researchers have tried to study the 'culture' of different adolescent groups, by trying to identify both norms of behaviour and the underlying values to which members subscribe.[7]

I have already argued that action cannot be understood in terms of friendship groups, for these are not the same as interaction sets where membership can vary from minute to minute. Consistent groups do not exist in reality; and observation has also shown that there is no consistent culture for a group of pupils. Norms and values relate to specific definitions of the situation and to typical interaction sets, rather than to a particular group of friends. We have already seen that there is a great variety of behaviour in the class — a variety too great to be described in terms of a consistent 'culture' as the word has traditionally been used. This diversity is even more strongly brought out by the following description of some girls going to two different lessons on the same afternoon.

> The girls are standing in the corridor talking to me before the beginning of a Commerce lesson.
>
> MARY: *Quick — Mrs. Alan!*
>
> She runs violently into the class, smiling. The other girls all enter quickly and find their places and sit talking.
>
> MRS. ALAN: (through the noise) *Good afternoon 4G.*
>
> GIRLS: (in unison) *Good afternoon.*
>
> There is silence as they wait for the register to be taken, each girl answering her name as it is called. They then wait quietly for the lesson to begin.

Contrast this with the beginning of the Science lesson that followed immediately afterwards:

> . . . the girls all enter the lab. Carol, Valerie, Diane, Debbie, Monica, Anne and Angela are talking, shouting and laughing. They find their places, and continue talking, all completely ignoring the teacher, Mrs. Newman. She takes the register, but is not able to call out the names as there is too much noise, and she spends a considerable time looking to see who is there.

The way the girls behave in these two situations is quite different: different norms are being used and different interaction sets are in operation. In the first example the whole class shares a common definition of the lesson whereas, in the second example, seven girls form one specific interaction set.

The following examples related to History, but with two different teachers. They bring out just how varied behaviour can be:

> Carol, Valerie, Diane and Mary are sitting close together, though there is no visible interaction between them, verbal or non-verbal . . . Mr. Marks moves to the back of the class and talks to me in whispers for the last ten minutes of the lesson. None of the girls show any signs of hearing us, they all seem too involved in their work to notice us.

As Mary says, in an interview:

> *We all love it, it's our favourite subject . . . we all like History.*

During my period of observation, the History teacher, Mr. Marks, left. Carol describes an incident with the new teacher who replaced him.

> *I just started to laugh and he hold my collar until I get out of the chair so I hit him . . .then I push him and he fall down.*

Extreme behaviour like this is very rare, but the girls are quite frequently rude and hostile to their teachers, and sometimes do not bother to turn up to lessons at all.

The idea that different norms and values are appropriate at different times is borne out by what the teachers wrote on a questionnaire about the pupils. Take for example the comments made about Carol by two teachers, Mr. Marks, the History teacher, and Mrs. Newman, who taught Science.

MRS. NEWMAN: *Carol is restless, awkward and often very noisy . . . I can get a lot more done when Carol isn't there.*

MR. MARKS: (writing after he had left) . . . *amenable to discipline and not at all unintelligent . . .*

Obviously these teachers saw very different 'sides' of Carol in their lessons and for this reason the girls' behaviour cannot be described as a 'culture' in the normal use of the word. The range is too great and, at first glance at least, their actions often look contradictory: Carol can arrive one day at a lesson and work quietly and well, and the next day not bother to turn up at all for the same lesson.

I am not suggesting that the action of these girls is random; there are patterns and common ways of behaving, as will be shown below. Yet these patterns are much more complex than has been implied by other researchers. Norms of behaviour relate to specific definitions of classroom situations.

People who interact regularly function with a limited number of typical definitions; and there will be typical patterns of action related to each. Before discussing norms and values for any one girl, therefore, it is necessary to examine how she sees situations, what she 'knows' about them, and who else shares that knowledge. Only in this light can her specific actions be interpreted.

The individual and the set

A large proportion of the classroom behaviour of the girls observed took place in the context of interaction sets; there was a great deal of joint rather than individual action. In these circumstances it is important to examine the relationship between the individual and the other interaction set members. Are pupils 'forced' to act in a certain way simply by being a member of an interaction set, or do they choose their action for themselves?

There are two ways of examining the relationship between the individual and the set. The first is to look at the behaviour of pupils when they are not in interaction, when they define situations in a different way from those around them. The second method is to look at the variety of action that takes place in any one interaction set.

(a) *Individual action* Most of Carol's classroom behaviour is interactive, but sometimes she acts alone. On these 'individual' occasions she shows the same types of behaviour as when part of a set. What is different is not the behavioural content but the times when Carol considers that behaviour appropriate. Carol can be seen as having the same 'repertoire'[8] of classroom behaviour in individual or interactive situations. For example she can be just as hostile to a teacher when acting alone as when part of an interaction set. When she 'greeted' her new History teacher, by pushing him over, she was acting alone. Other girls describing the same incident seemed slightly shocked by the extremity of Carol's action; they were not participating or supporting.

A quite different example of very individual action comes in a cooking lesson:

> Carol . . . works alone, all lesson; she talks to no-one, not even Dorothy who is working at the same table.

In an interview, she explains how she sometimes acts alone:

> *Valerie . . . and them lot sometimes start to muck about you know, and I says to them all, "Why can't you lot behave? — you know, start to tell them off. Sometimes I just sit down in the corner, you know — just sit down by myself.*

Carol can therefore be extremely hostile and disruptive in some lessons, but at other times is very work-oriented. In the examples above she was acting alone, defining situations for herself. Yet, as is well documented below, she frequently shows exactly the same type of behaviour in interactive situations.

Particular 'pieces' of behaviour can, then, be displayed in both social and individual settings. Action should therefore be considered not so much a product of a social situation, in some way 'manufactured' by it, but much more 'facilitated' by that situation. The choice of action remains with the individual and belongs to her. Only the general situation is interactively defined.

(b) *Variety of action* Girls who assess situations in a similar way and define appropriate action together do not necessarily act in the *same* way. When Carol and Diane run in late to a Science lesson, it is Carol who makes most of the comments to the teacher, saying, 'None of your business', when asked where they have been. Diane, on the other hand, is much quieter and begins getting out books and finding out what they have missed. Despite the fact that they are in full communication with each other, each legitimating the action of the other, they negotiate different 'social identities', Carol being outspoken and Diane being supportive. Similar examples occur in less hostile situations. For example, Carol often shouts out answers to questions, or wanders round the room while Diane and Valerie support her by watching and laughing. They seldom, if ever, take over this sort of action themselves.

Thus joint action does not always imply the same action. It simply demands behaviour that can symbolically communicate to another a particular definition of the situation; it must show that interactions have the same commonsense knowledge. Thus the range of any one individual's joint action can, theoretically at least, be quite varied, as long as it symbolically implies a common definition. It is the willingness to take others into account and share interpretations and definitions of situations that is important. Carol chooses her own action, but is dependent for support on others. She does not act in the same way as she would if she were alone, but decides how to behave in the light of commonly negotiated definitions of the situation.

2. DEFINITIONS OF CLASSROOM SITUATIONS

Goffman (1959) has suggested that definitions of the situation tend to be 'idealized'. That is, a group's or interaction set's definition of the situation is likely to differ to some extent from the individual's own. Establishing a common point of contact demands compromise from all. Action itself may be drawn away from what the individual wants towards what is appropriate to the idealized definition. Goffman has also pointed out that most groups function with a limited number of 'typical' definitions: people 'see' situations in certain set ways. Of course, individuals can extract themselves from interaction and groups as a whole can establish new definitions. Goffman is simply suggesting that this will not be the usual experience.

In this section, I illustrate some of the 'idealized' and 'typical' definitions of classroom situations that Carol often subscribes to. That is, I will examine some of the criteria she uses in making assessments of situations and show some of the more common interaction sets related to these.

Before proceeding, a number of points should be made. First, my objective will be to provide a series of simplified 'ideal/typical' definitions, so that the interaction sets associated with them can be specified. These definitions are not intended to be rigid categories for analysing behaviour, since real life situations would be unlikely to correspond to any of them exactly. Second, the picture to be presented will necessarily be static. The more abstract knowledge Carol uses to move from one definition to the next is beyond the scope of this paper. Finally, it must be remembered that these definitions relate only to Carol and her interaction sets. It is not suggested that they have wider validity.

For Carol, and those she interacts with, the most significant factor involved in making definitions of classroom situations is the teacher. Many of her criteria of assessment related to teachers, both in the way they taught and in the methods they used for controlling the class. The following example comes from a group interview:

> QUESTION: *When you work in class, is it because you like the subject, or is it the way the teacher teaches?*
>
> DIANE: *It's the subject.*
>
> CAROL: *Mmmmmmmmm. It's the teacher as well, isn't it?*

In another interview:

> QUESTION: *Why do you think you all muck about so much?*
>
> CAROL: *The teachers look for it if you ask me.*
>
> QUESTION: *Why?*
>
> CAROL: *I don't like no subjects, they're boring, they make me feel like going to sleep.*

Obviously, then, the teacher was very important. How was he assessed?

(a) *'Strict' and 'soft' teachers* One of the major distinctions between teachers, was between those who are seen as 'soft' and those who were 'strict' or 'tough'. Valerie often interacts with Carol; in an interview:

> VALERIE: *Some of the teachers are soft, you could stand up and they don't teach you nothing, they don't teach anything that way.*
>
> QUESTION: *What would you do if you were a teacher and you came in and everyone was mucking about?*
>
> VALERIE: *Well it would depend on what sort of teacher I was. If I was a tough teacher, I'd go 'Sit down'. You know, once you hit one of them, the rest are frightened, and everybody just do the same thing just sit down.*

As criteria of definition, though, 'soft' and 'strict' are not adequate. Take, for example, two teachers, Mrs. Alan, who taught Commerce, and Mrs. Newman, who taught Science. Both of them were characterized as 'soft' by Carol. But she and her friends responded quite differently when these two teachers told them off for something. In a lesson with Mrs. Alan, Carol, Valerie and Diane had arrived late and were instructed to stand at the front of the class. They were then severely told off. The three girls became extremely hostile and made abusive comments to the teacher. Mrs. Alan ignored these for a while but, when Carol called her an 'ignorant pig', she asked her to leave the room.

This example can be contrasted with Carol's interactive behaviour when being told off by Mrs. Newman for coming in late. When asked where she had been, she simply said 'None of your business!' and continued discussing what she had been doing with seven or eight of her friends.

Carol, Valerie and Diane seem to take the 'telling off' from Mrs. Alan far more seriously than from Mrs. Newman. Even though both teachers were thought as as 'soft', one seemed to pose a more serious threat to the girls than the other, and their response was different. Other girls in the class also defined these situations differently. In the first instance, the rest of the class was quiet and avoided contact with Carol, Valerie and Diane. In the second case they eagerly participated and were keen to listen to Carol's latest exploits. Obviously, some teachers were 'softer' than others!

(b) *'Learning a lot'* Carol made further distinctions between teachers. She readily admitted that while taught by Mr. Marks, History was her best subject.

> *You can't talk in Mr. Marks' lesson, you just have to work . . . so after a while you work, and you enjoy it because you're learning a lot.*

This may be compared with her comments on her new History teacher who came after Mr. Marks had left. He was also 'strict', but

> *. . . he don't make sense, I don't understand nothing.*

There is obviously an additional criterion being applied, for Carol seemed to be concerned about how much different teachers actually managed to teach her. For example,

> QUESTION: *What do you think about teachers who aren't strict, but who are really soft?*
>
> CAROL: *Some of them are all right. I learn a lot from some of them . . . Mrs. Alan's soft, but I learn a lot from her, because it's kind of funny the way she gives jokes.*

Obviously, 'learning a lot' was important to Carol, but we must ask what she actually means by this. It seemed to be important that teachers 'explain'.

> *Mr. Marks would talk to us as well. Not talk them big words you know; talk words we understood.*

But the new History teacher

> . . . *talks and writes things on the board, like diagrams, names and you're supposed to keep them in your head, and then after he talks, it don't even make sense.*

Also important was whether she was actually involved in doing something rather than just listening.

CAROL: *I can't stand people talking when I'm not doing anything!*

DIANE: *Yes, like Mr. Stacks, in Art. He puts you to sleep. We have on Wednesday, and he just talks and talks for two lessons.*

Actually giving these girls a feeling of 'learning a lot' was extremely difficult for any teacher, whether they were defined as 'soft' or 'strict'. Linda probably best sums up the difficulty:

> *I don't like doing Maths. I can't do it, it's too hard. I don't know how to add. Well, I know how to add, but I don't know how to do the other sums. They're too hard anyway. I don't do nothing in Maths lessons, I've always got a headache . . . I enjoy doing things I know, I can sit all morning doing that, but when something's hard and I don't really know how to do it, I don't want to do it. I don't even want to try. I get bored.*

Linda expresses her difficulty in trying to learn when she does not really understand. She must learn immediately or not at all. The whole class seemed to have little interest in their subjects *per se* and were strongly dependent on the learning context provided by the teacher.

Members of staff who did not live up to Carol's particular criteria of assessment, that is, those who 'can't teach you nothing', were 'written off'. Carol approached their lessons 'knowing' that she was not going to learn anything.

Naturally, this is simplified assessment of what classroom situations meant to Carol. Nevertheless, if particular lessons are looked at in terms of a combination of the simple criteria of definition (that is: 'strict/soft', 'effective/ineffective'), then typical interaction sets and patterns of behaviour emerge.

Typical patterns of interaction

Teachers who were assessed as potentially 'effective' and able to provide some lessons where it was possible to 'learn a lot' were approached in a very different style from those who were considered 'ineffective'. Naturally, 'effective' teachers were not always successful in providing the right learning context for the girls, but when they were, a fairly standard pattern of interaction emerged.

(a) 'Successful' lessons

In lessons where the context enabled the girls to 'learn a lot', they would act as a unified group and the whole class was included in the same interaction set. Although they were not always in verbal contact, each girl was aware that the others defined the lesson as one where they could 'learn'. In these circumstances it was irrelevant whether the teacher was 'strict' or 'soft'. Mr. Marks was considered 'strict' and the whole class worked quietly and well. Miss Keene, on the other hand, was 'soft', yet in 'successful' lessons no-one took advantage of this fact. Consider this example of a typing lesson with Miss Keene.

Miss Keene is teaching the girls how to file alphabetically. It is a revision lesson, though evidently the girls do not understand the principles fully.

MISS KEENE: *Carol, how would you file 'The Borough of East Hamilton'?*

CAROL: *Under H.* (She obviously does not realize that the name is East Hamilton) . . .

GENERAL QUESTION: *How would you file Miss Mary Brown-Curtis*

SOMEONE: *'C'* (not realizing it is a double-barrelled name).

CAROL: *M* (she is going by the other rule they have just learnt which says that if it does not go under the surname as a person, it must be the name of a company and therefore goes under the first name. She seems to be trying to apply the rules as she understands them, but is still confused) . . .

Miss Keene goes round the room asking questions . . .

CAROL: *My turn now!*

MISS KEENE: *20th Century Films Limited.*

Carol says *'C'* then *'F'* applying the rules she knows. But this is a new one. As 20th is short for twentieth it should go under 'T'.

Here the girls are willing to take risks, struggle to understand and consistently keep applying rules to make sense of what they are being told, even though they make a lot of mistakes. They take into account that others are behaving similarly in choosing to act in this way.

When the girls assess a lesson this way, they will often ignore attempts to 'redefine' it. In the example below, everyone in the class but Debbie is working and her attempts to communicate with the other girls are ignored.

Debbie is eating an ice lolly. Mrs. Alan tells her to put it in the bin, but Debbie refuses and turns round in her seat to face the rest of the class. Mrs. Alan grabs the hat Debbie is wearing, and says: *Right, you are in school to do as you are told. When you have put your sweet in the bin as I asked you can have your hat back.*

> DEBBIE: *You give me that hat back. I paid for it. Give it back to me!*

As she says this she looks towards Diane and Carol, but they continue with their work. Debbie sulks for the rest of the lesson, making no attempt to do any work whatsoever. She is totally ignored by the rest of the class, who carry on working enthusiastically.

Here, it is only Debbie who sees her action as appropriate. The rest of the class are too interested in their work. They form an interaction set, but Debbie is left outside it.

(b) *Judgement of 'effective' teachers*

Lessons as 'successful' as those shown above were very rare, but the ability of teachers to provide such a context, even occasionally, was extremely important in the girls' eyes. When a teacher was considered 'potentially effective', the girls seemed more likely to approach the lesson with an open mind and reserve judgement until they had seen the content of the lesson. Of course, with 'strict, effective' teachers, this was not so important, for as Carol says of History, 'you just have to work'. With 'soft, effective' teachers, specific lesson content becomes much more significant. An extreme example of the sort of assessment that took place was shown in Domestic Science. These lessons were often 'successful', particularly when the girls were actually cooking, rather than learning theory:

> Valerie, Jill, Diane, Carol and Linda are all missing at the beginning of the lesson. Carol rushes in and says to Monica: *What have we got to do, write notes?*
>
> MONICA: *Yes.*
>
> CAROL: *I'm going out then.*
>
> She runs out . . .

Writing notes in Domestic Science was considered a 'non-learning' situation.

(c) *'Non-learning' situations*

Two factors seemed to lead to a lesson being defined as a 'non-learning' situation. The first was when teachers who were judged 'potentially effective' did not provide an adequate learning context. The second was when teachers were considered 'ineffective'. In thse latter circumstances the specific content of the lesson was irrelevant. The judgement had already been made and the girls would arrive 'knowing' they would not learn anything.

This was Carol's most frequent definition of the situation. Most lessons were not able to provide her with the sort of learning context she wanted. Her interactive behaviour at these times could be called mildly anti-authoritarian. It involved joking, laughing, talking on topics such as boys and clothes, while at the same time, at least nominally, carrying on with the classwork. The interaction set usually included nine or ten girls. They were: Carol, Valerie, Diane, Debbie, Anne, Angela, June and Monica, with Linda and Jill taking part when present.[9]

An example of this sort of interaction with a 'potentially effective' teacher comes in a typing lesson. Carol is interacting with a large group of girls who all sit close to each other. Although they are working they still manage to make jokes among themselves.

> Miss Keene has asked the class how to go about 'tabulating'.
> She says: *How many spaces do you go in?* Various people shout out answers, all of which are wrong; eventually Debbie gives the right answer. After it has been said, Carol jumps up and shouts out the right answer again, looks round the room, and giggles.

> ANNE: (out loud to the class) *Oh, God, she waits till someone else has said it.*

> All of the girls sitting nearby laugh.

It is to this type of interaction that Carol is referring when she says of her class 'We're all friends together really', and Valerie says 'You get a lot of fun, a lot of jokes in the classroom'. Valerie points out that Carol is best at making jokes, but also says that others are involved:

> *She's good at making jokes* (pointing at Carol) *and she* (Diane)... *and Anne and June... and this other girl, Debbie, she's good at laughing...*

The next example comes from an R.E. lesson which Carol considers a 'waste of time' and 'boring'. It is an example of how they behave when they consider the teacher 'ineffective'.

> Carol, Valerie, Diane, Jill, Debbie, Anne, Angela and Monica are sitting close together. Debbie is playing with one of Carol's shoes; Valerie and Diane are reading comics and Carol is combing her hair and occasionally making jokes quietly to those around her. By and large no-one in the class seems very interested in the content of the lesson ... eventually the teacher 'notices' that Valerie and Diane are reading comics and demands to have them. Diane quietly gives hers up but Valerie says, *Oh no, sir, please don't take it.* The teacher insists and takes it away until lunchtime. Carol immediately gets out another magazine from her bag, turns round to Valerie and Diane, and they all start looking at it.

When a particular teacher's lessons were defined in this way, it was fairly irrelevant what specific material they presented. They always met the same style of interaction. By Easter of her fourth year, with the Typing and History teachers leaving, Carol had 'written off' six out of her ten teachers in this way. Most of these assessments were shared by several of the other girls in the class.

(d) 'Bunking it'

Another response when it was not possible to 'learn' was to run out of the lesson or not bother to turn up at all — in their terms, they would 'bunk it'.

This involved a different interaction set, as only Carol, Valerie, Diane, Jill and Linda would 'bunk' lessons.

In an interview, Carol explained how 'bunking' was related to specific definitions.

> With Mr. Marks in History, them lot sometimes say 'let's muck about', or 'let's bunk it', and I say 'yeah', and then I goes in the lesson and them lot comes in and calls me 'snide'. If I don't feel like bunking it, I don't. But now (i.e. with the new History teacher) if they tell me 'don't go to History', I don't go.

She describes how they make the decision to miss a lesson:

QUESTION: *When you and your friends say 'let's bunk a lesson', who actually suggests it?*

CAROL: *When we don't want to go nowhere, like if we say we don't want to go to this lesson . . . Valerie comes up and says 'let's bunk it', sometimes Diane do, sometimes I do. I say, 'let's bunk it' and they all agree.*

This interaction set is far more specific than the others described. Carol, Valerie, Diane, Linda and Jill were the only girls in the class who would 'bunk' lessons. They also formed a separate interaction set when teachers who were regarded as 'soft' tried to become 'strict'.

(e) Teachers who become 'strict'

When a 'soft' teacher tried to become 'strict', for example if he threatened to discipline the girls in some way, a specific pattern of interaction emerged. This situation occurred regardless of whether teachers were considered 'effective' or not.

In the following example, Valerie and Jill had arrived late for Science.

MRS. NEWMAN: (to Valerie and Jill) *Where have you been?*

CAROL: (aggressively) *Shut your mouth.*

This is said loud enough for Mrs. Newman to hear, but she ignores it.

Another time, Carol, Valerie, Diane, Jill and Linda arrived late for Domestic Science and became aggressive.

MISS LANE: *I think one of you ought to go and tell Mr. Kraft (Deputy Head) where you've been.*

VALERIE: (aggressively) *I ain't going nowhere.* She turns to talk to Carol.

CAROL: (to those round her) *Where's Monica?*

LINDA: *Oh! She's at the front* (of the class).

CAROL: *Oh! Look at that lot. She's too brainy for me.*
They all laugh.

In this example the girls who arrived late sat physically separated from the rest of the class and at each successive 'joke' they laughed heartily. Even though the rest of the pupils and probably the teacher could hear what they said, none of them laughed or made any comment.

Again, it was only Carol, Diane, Valerie, Jill and Linda who would interact in this manner. On these occasions the rest of the class sat very quietly, seldom interacting with anyone but the teacher. Carol and her friends were defined as an interaction set by themselves and by the rest of the class.

I have shown that interaction sets represent shared knowledge amongst a group of pupils and are associated with regular patterns of behaviour. But the definitions presented above are necessarily incomplete as is shown by the way Carol will sometimes, for no apparent reason, extract herself from a common definition and act alone. A very good example of this sort of 're-definition' came in a Science lesson. The rest of the class were chattering and laughing in their usual way and not taking much notice of what the teacher was saying.

Carol and Diane sit at the top of the bench, farthest from the board. They are correcting or finishing a diagram of a skeleton, and seem very engrossed in it. Carol says, *and this is the arm, the femur . . .* Eventually they put their folders away and then begin writing the notes written on the board.

Here for some reason the girls were willing to extract themselves from their typical definition of Science and establish new appropriate behaviour. Obviously, additional criteria of assessment are being applied and a new pattern of interaction emerges.

Why is it that Carol will come to one Science lesson and work very hard, while the next day she will take part in a common definition and 'bunk it' completely? Why is it that even with teachers who are assessed as 'able to teach', some lessons are more 'successful' than others? Obviously more detailed analysis of pupil knowledge is necessary before these questions can be answered with any certainty.

What can be said, however, is that how to define the situation is a constant problem for these girls and one that demands continual negotiation. Unlike the successful Grammar School pupil who knows how to look at his school experience, these girls constantly have to make sense of frustrating and often confusing situations. This, together with the fact that all interaction sets tend to function with a limited number of definitions makes it progressively difficult for individuals to extract themselves from their usual way of seeing things. Attempts by teachers to reach these girls were only effective when they conformed to the girls' own standards of assessment. They no longer blindly accepted all teachers as the Grammar School pupil might do.

Presumably because of their own unsuccessful learning experiences they had established their own criteria of judgement. They seemed to want to learn quickly, effectively and, at least to begin with, with the minimum of effort. Teaching these girls in the way they wished to be taught was something which many members of staff (myself included) found almost impossible.

CONCLUSION

Pupil knowledge about school life is differentially distributed. An interaction set presents a static picture of a group of pupils making the same commonsense judgements about classroom situations. Their behaviour is chosen in the light of what they agree to 'know' about that situation. The fact that different pupils take part in interaction sets at different times simply illustrates the point that they do not always agree about what they know. Teachers, subjects and methods of teaching mean different things to different pupils. A study of pupil knowledge must take this fact into account and begin by specifying situations where pupils do agree. Only then would it be possible to ask what they agree about — what they know.

In describing some of Carol's definition, I have already illustrated some of the things she knows about school life and pointed out which girls agree with her and when. Unfortunately, the whole concept of 'definition of the situation' is a static one.[10] What is now needed is an understanding of Carol's abstract knowledge so that we can tell how she goes about classifying situations in the typical ways I have shown.

Both teachers and researchers seem extremely ignorant of what school life means to pupils. The present study already brings into question some of the more popular beliefs amongst teachers about 'non-academic' adolescents. There is a common assumption that such pupils will only be interested in subjects that will be immediately relevant to their life when they leave school. It is for this reason that many timetables are heavily laden with 'practical' subjects such as Typing, Domestic Science, Woodwork, Metalwork and (if all else fails) Games. Yet the girls described in this paper were much more concerned with 'learning' no matter what the subject. History or Typing could be of equal interest to them if they provided the sort of learning situation that they looked for. Further case studies of pupil knowledge will not only be of interest to sociologists, but may even be some practical use to teachers, both in preparing their material, and in understanding their pupils.

Perhaps the last words should be left with Carol herself:

QUESTION: *What do you think the teachers think of you as an individual?*

CAROL: *I don't think they like me much . . . I'm not a good girl anyway . . . I don't blame them, if you've got a child and she's rude, you can't like her very much . . . I mean, if I was in their place, I wouldn't like me 'cos the way I act — you know, I won't learn, keep making jokes and muck about. I don't blame them, but I'm not worried at all, you know!*

Acknowledgements

I would like to begin by thanking the pupils of 4G for allowing me to observe their lessons and for their open and frank discussions with me; without them there would have been no paper. I am grateful to the Local Education Authority for allowing me to carry out the research, and to the staff of the school where I have worked for four years. The continued cooperation and interest of many teachers, particularly those who allowed me to observe their lessons, was a great help. I would also like to thank Dr. Ed Sherwood and Dr. Diana Leat for their encouragement and support throughout my research. For financial support, I am indebted both to the Social Science Research Council and to the Lawrence Atwell Charity, administered by the Skinners' Company. For comments on the first draft of this paper, I am grateful to Dr. Diana Leat and to my wife Ruth.

Notes

1. Because of the high proportion of 'immigrant' pupils, the staff/pupil ratio was considerably better than in many neighbouring schools. Most of the 'lower ability' classes comprised twenty pupils or less.

2. About 50% of the school population were classed as 'immigrants' by the Local Education Authority, i.e. they had not been born in Great Britain or Ireland. The majority of these 'immigrants' were West Indian. The remainder of the school were mainly working-class English or Irish.

3. See for example Hollinshed (1949), Coleman (1960), Hargreaves (1967), Sugarman (1966, 1967, 1968) and Lacey (1970).

4. See for example Lacey's discussion of a pupil called Short (1970, p. 98), or some of the comments made to Hargreaves about Maths (1967, p. 100).

5. For a fuller discussion of 'joint action' see Blumer (1965).

6. One of components of Bernstein's (1971) 'restricted code' is a strong sense of loyalty to the group, as is implied here.

7. See, in particular, Cohen (1955).

8. The notion of 'repertoire' in behaviour is developed in Goffman (1959).

9. As part of the 'remedial group', Linda and Jill did not take all of their lessons with the other girls.

10. This limitation on the usefulness of the concept of 'definition of the situation' characterizes the distinction between ethnomethodology and symbolic interactionism. For a useful comparison of these two approaches on these lines, see Zimmerman and Wieder (1970).

References

Bernstein, B., 1971, *Class, Codes and Control*, Routledge and Kegan Paul, London.

Blumer, H., 1965, 'Sociological implications of the thought of George Herbert Mead', *American Journal of Sociology*, **71**, 535–544.

Cohen, A., 1955, *Delinquent Boys; the Culture of the Gang*, Free Press, Illinois.

Coleman, J. S., 1960, *The Adolescent Society; the Social Life of the Teenager, and its Impact on Education*, Free Press, New York.

Dale, R., 1973, 'Phenomenological perspectives and the sociology of the school', *Educational Review*, **125**, 3, 175–189.

Filmer, P., M. Phillipson, D. Silverman and D. Walsh, 1972, *New Directions in Sociological Theory*, Collier Macmillan, London.

Goffman, E., 1959, *The Presentation of Self in Everyday Life*, Doubleday Anchor, Garden City, New York; Penguin, Harmondsworth, 1971.

44

Hargreaves, D., 1967, *Social Relations in a Secondary School,* Routledge and Kegan Paul, London.

Hollinshed, A. B., 1949, *Elmstown's Youth; the Impact of Social Class on Adolescents,* Wiley, New York.

Keddie, N., 1971, 'Classroom knowledge' in M. F. D. Young (ed.), *Knowledge and Control: New Directions for the Sociology of Education,* Collier Macmillan, London.

Lacey, C., 1970, *Hightown Grammar; the School as a Social System,* Manchester University Press, Manchester.

Sugarman, B. N., 1966, 'Social class and values as related to achievement in school', *Sociological Review,* **14,** 287–302.

Sugarman, B. N., 1967, 'Involvement in youth culture, Academic achievement and conformity in school', *British Journal of Sociology,* **18,** 151–164.

Sugarman, B. N., 1968, 'Social norms in teenage boys peer groups — a study of their implications for achievement and conduct in four London schools', *Human Relations,* **21,** 41–58.

Werthman, C., 1963, 'Delinquents in schools; a test for the legitimacy of authority', *Berkeley Journal of Sociology,* **8 (I),** 39–60.

Werthman, C., 1970, 'The functions of social definitions in the development of delinquent careers', in P. E. Garbedian and D. C. Gibons (eds.), *Becoming Delinquent,* Aldine, Chicago, 1971.

Young, M. F. D. and N. Keddie, 1973, 'New directions: is there anything happening in Sociology?', *Hard Cheese,* no. 2, May 1973, 29–36.

Zimmerman, D. H. and D. L. Wieder, 1970, 'Ethnomethodology and the problem of order: comment on Denzin', in J. D. Douglas (ed.), *Understanding Everyday Life; Towards the Reconstruction of Sociological Knowledge,* Routledge and Kegan Paul, London.

3. Making sense of school

By Howard Gannaway

Editorial introduction

Gannaway's paper continues the theme that Furlong discussed in the last paper: what do pupils 'know' about school? how do they 'make sense' of it? and how do they talk about it? But this paper tackles the question from a different angle, with different methods.

All the papers in this book explore methods of direct observation of real classrooms and often derive from close collaboration between teachers, pupils and researcher. And most of the authors have teaching experience themselves. But the papers have nevertheless been written from the point of view of 'researchers', not 'teachers'. (This is true even of the paper by Furlong, who taught in the school while he was doing his fieldwork). Gannaway, however, gives a fuller meaning to the term 'participant observation': by using data gathered in the school in which he was teaching and by discussing these data explicitly from the perspective of a teacher's reflections on pupils' views of school.

Note, then, the nature of the data. The paper comprises not only a teacher-observer's reflections on classroom events and conversations but also a teacher-observer's reflection on *children's* classroom observations: an adult talking to pupils about what they have experienced in the classroom and talking to them as part of a classroom lesson.

Hymes, in his introduction to a recent book on the ethnography of the classroom has argued that teachers must be their own ethnographers: 'The ethnography of a situation is not for a non-participant to say'. Ultimately, only the participants in the situation can provide an adequate understanding of 'what was really going on'. Most of the papers in this book try to develop new techniques for understanding real classrooms. Perhaps this paper will encourage not only researchers, but teachers themselves, to try out some of the ideas. Why stop at the teachers? The paper mentions some pupils carrying out a survey of pupils' attitude to school as part of an 'A' level Sociology course . . .

On the one hand, Gannaway is less concerned with theory and methodology than the other contributors. On the other hand, he points to areas which the other papers tend to neglect. And he raises problems of the status of the observer which the other papers do not tackle.

M.S.

Reference

Hymes, Dell, 1972, 'Introduction', in C. Cazden, V. John and D. Hymes (eds.), *Functions of Language in the Classroom*, Teachers College, Columbia University, New York.

This paper was written while I was a student teacher at Goldsmiths' College. It was submitted as my main Education essay for a Postgraduate Teaching Certificate. The observation and recording of data took place while I was on a term's teaching practice at a large mixed comprehensive school in the Greater London area.

The observations were made in several situations. I was operating as a teacher and 'took' lessons in Social Sciences. In addition, I sat in on lessons taken by other teachers, in particular by another Social Science teacher. In some of the lessons which I 'took', I talked to the pupils about the school and their impressions of it. Sometimes the pupils offered such statements without my asking. The tape-recordings, some ten hours in all, were mostly made in the lessons taken by the Social Science teacher whose class appears in the transcripts in Appendixes 1 and 2 at the end of this chapter. The pupils knew that the discussions were being recorded, and indeed the teacher had asked them at the beginning if they minded the recordings being made. I explained to the class my purpose in making them.

As well as the observations made in the classroom during lessons, I was, of course, aware of some of the other social interactions in the school: informal conversations in the corridor or the staffroom, staff meetings and assemblies, to name but a few. I have selected extracts from the tape-recordings and from the few longhand notes I took when the tape-recorder was not to hand. Some extracts of these are used in the text of the paper, as well as the fairly long transcripts of two of the lessons in Appendixes 1 and 2. I chose these two lessons, not because I thought them typical, but because they contained many things which helped to clarify my own ideas. In addition, Appendix 1 should give the reader a fairly clear idea of the nature of my own involvement in the discussions. The term 'participant observer' partly describes it but with a heavy emphasis on the participation.

1. WHY AM I WRITING ABOUT THIS?

The initial stimulus for this piece of writing was something which happened during a seminar at Goldsmiths'. We had been discussing organizational models of schools and education, when someone asked the teacher taking the seminar if any work had been done on children's models of school, and the teacher said, as far as he knew, no. This seemed to me incredible. I thought it was an important area for a number of reasons.

First, schools bring together people of different ages, experiences and backgrounds. The teachers all have a certain number of years and certain types of educational experience beyond those of the pupils. Given these differences, then, it is reasonable to expect that teachers and pupils may well view the school quite differently. Providing for the possibility of 'school' may be different for teachers and pupils.

Second, if we view pupils as consumers of a welfare service (admittedly an unfashionable opinion today but nevertheless . . .) then some idea of how the clients make sense of the service seems a reasonable feedback to expect.

Third, many people involved in education, teachers and administrators, include in their frameworks of reference notions about the needs, perceptions and activities of the pupils: such views as 'children like to work in a secure framework where they know what's what'. Frequently, these ideas are supported by causal references which extend beyond the teacher's immediate experience of the pupil to embrace the pupil's home background and social life outside the school. I am referring to views which I have often heard expressed in words such as: 'How can you expect him to pass his Maths/Physics/Geography when he comes from a home like *that*'. Ideas such as these, by which the teacher orientates himself in relation to the official aims of the formal education process, are presumably derived partly from professional training, partly from the teacher's own observations and work within the school, and partly from prevailing school doctrines, not to mention all the influences outside the school that may contribute to the formation of a person's views about young people. These views form a basis for the practice of education in the classroom. One doubts instinctively whether the pupils share the same theories of causation as the teachers, but to what extent *do* they share aims, or definitions of everyday reality. How far do pupils understand 'official' aims of education and how does their understanding reflect upon the processes and interaction in the school?

Lastly, from my own experience it seems that few teachers actually communicate their 'professional'[1] view of education to the pupils. Indeed it is an integral part of the 'professional' code of teaching that many of these theories and processes should *not* be communicated to pupils and, in many cases, not even to parents. Nevertheless, teachers do represent the school and education to pupils in ways thought to be appropriate to the needs of the pupil, the aims of the school and so on. If one had to enumerate the different contexts in which teachers represent and communicate about the school and education, one might add to Nell Keddie's (1971) 'teacher' and 'educationalist' contexts (which are both situations where teachers talk to other teachers) further contexts in which teachers meet pupils, parents, administrators, inspectors, governors and other social welfare agencies. In each of these cases it is reasonable to expect a different part of the teacher's total stock of experience and knowledge of school to be communicated. We may also look for parallel differences between pupils and other people with whom they have communications about their existence as school pupils.

By and large the comment of the teacher has proved true. I have read and searched, looking for some learned assistance, some way into the subject, but I have found none. I have found some encouragement in the writings of John Holt (1965) and Herbert Kohl (1969), but even they are still writing from the perspective of 'teacher', albeit a new, reformed teacher. Their writings offer much food for thought to the teacher, but not much for my line of enquiry. But why should it matter that they write from this perspective? The main reason is that, no matter how child-centred they may be, they have certain assumptions about school and about the value of education which their pupils *may* not share with them.

One book which does start with the children's own expressions is *The School I'd Like,* edited by Edward Blishen (1969), which is a collection of extracts from children's essays on the topic in the title. It is a fascinating book but not very helpful to me for the following reasons. First, it is in writing, a medium which is very difficult for some pupils, and for others, as the editor himself says,[2] is at best a process removed from their everyday expression. Second, the published extracts have been subjected to at least one selection and editing process by an adult. Third, most of the essays show a mode of generalization which differs from the everyday verbal expression I am used to hearing in schools. Now, it may be that these children were, in fact, committing to paper their everyday thoughts, but it may also be that this type of generalization was motivated either by the title, or by teachers, or in general by what the pupils saw as appropriate writing for a competition, which is, after all, what prompted the essays.

2. WHAT AM I TRYING TO DO?

I find the whole subject of children's understandings of school problematic because of my own experience. During my teaching I had always been aware that much of what teachers present is not understood by pupils as it is *meant* to be. When a pupil says, 'I've done a bit of writing, Sir. Can I do another drawing now?', the aims of that pupil are almost certainly at odds with the aims of the teacher. One could write at length about the points of difference, but perhaps the main ones would be the relative value that the teacher and the pupil each attach to writing and drawing and, second, the teacher would probably consider that the content of the writing is at least as important as the mode of expression and presentation: a view which the pupil ignores.

This paper arose out of an opportunity I had, in a school which was new to me, to stand back from the teaching situation a little and consider the issues which had only been felt previously as frustrations. So I set out from the standpoint of the teacher crying, 'Why don't they understand?', and tried to work my way towards the standpoint of the pupil, I could not become a pupil.[3] And, without observing a great deal more of pupil's life outside the school, I could not hope to be clear about the part that school plays in the whole life of a young person. In focusing on the pupil *in the school* I have probably made certain assumptions which are not shared by my subjects. For instance, the use of the word 'pupil' denotes a category which may not be meaningful to the 'pupils'. It is certainly a word that one seldom hears used by young people in schools. Perhaps the majority of young people are not interested in stressing their membership of the school as a group and along with this their particular status in that group. Perhaps they would rather stress friendship groups, which frequently cut across school boundaries. This paper might be a point of departure for such an enquiry. Indeed, had circumstances not forced me to restrict the focus of my observations to the school, I might have looked to see whether these categories have any life outside it, whether they play any part in the ways in which young people represent their school experiences outside the school.

My subjects

They are young people who spend part of each weekday in a secondary school undergoing full-time education. My aim is to observe how they talk about school. I am aware that, in concerning myself only with verbal statements, I have only the statements of those pupils who were prepared to make them public in the school situation. In the class discussions which I recorded, the number of pupils who spoke was rarely above half the class, and sometimes much lower.[4] Throughout the paper a few names will reappear, those people who talk publicly in this way. It could be said that this represents a bias as strong as the written form of Blishen's essays. I am not claiming that the pupils on whom I concentrated were in any way *typical*. I am suggesting that for the pupils whose words I have recorded, speaking represents a more natural form of expression than writing. I am interested in making sense of how this limited number of pupils makes sense of school. I am aware that I have no observations of those who did not speak in class. It might be called non-participation, but this residual category may itself obscure important facts about the phenomenon. Now that I reflect upon the matter, perhaps I should have addressed myself to the silence of the many, rather than to the words of a few.

What they say

I assume that the statements the pupils make represent to some extent the way in which they make sense of the experience of school. At the same time it should not be thought that the child's understanding of the school is contained in a static set of conceptions. His awareness may be changed from minute to minute by what happens to him, what he does, what people say to him, how he thinks about his actions and the actions of others, how he communicates his thoughts and the responses these thoughts arouse in others. In addition, all the talk is produced in a physical setting within the school: in a classroom before or during a lesson, or in a corridor during a break. These things will all affect what the pupil says.

One area where I felt this was an important consideration was that of *generalization*. Here I draw a fairly simple distinction between *anecdote* and *general statements*. By anecdote I refer to statements about actual events which are essentially narrative; and by general statement I refer to statements containing notions about regular patterns in the nature of things but which do not refer specifically to actual events. Now one only has to look at the transcripts to see that the children did make general statements about school, but at the same time many children declared a dislike of generalization. I can illustrate this by recounting an incident in a fourth year class I was taking. I was explaining some ideas about the nature of learning processes and, when I came to explain the concept of generalization, the whole class groaned and said that when a teacher turned from talking about specific cases to make generalizations, then the lesson invariably became boring. Generalization in class frequently involves writing 'notes' in exercise books, an activity not usually rated highly by pupils. Or else, it nearly always takes the form of the teacher attempting to 'draw together' thoughts and statements which have been made previously *in the lesson*: it is essentially a repetitive activity. In contrast to this, pupils' generalizations rarely take the form of statements referring to actions or statements made *just prior* to the generalizing activity itself. In this I think that the teacher must appear unnatural to pupils. After all, why repeat something that has just been said?

Another factor about generalization is that the school context may play a direct part in pupils' mode of expression in the classroom. When a teacher (or an observer) asks a question in the form, 'Do you . . . ', it may evoke a response which, had the question not been asked, might never have become part of the pupil's consciousness. It may also be the case that, since the pupils know that some teachers place a high value upon generalization compared with anecdote, pupils consciously adopt a generalizing mode in certain circumstances if they wish to have a statement accepted in, for instance, a classroom discussion.

The observer

Clearly, the observer has a personality or role thrust on him by his subjects and it is better to try to be aware of it than to wish it back in the bottle. In the school where I did this study I was a student teacher, a curiously anomalous status. It was not apparent to all the pupils that I was a student teacher: some pupils claimed they could distinguish between a student and a regular teacher (see Appendix 1) and some classes assumed that I was their 'new teacher' for some time after I started to take them for lessons. I unwittingly added to the confusion by assuming that they would have been told that I was a student. But I could not perceive any differences in behaviour between a class when they thought I was 'our teacher' and when they were told I was a student teacher. But, whether or not I was seen as a student, I was still acting in the role of teacher as far as the pupils were concerned, in that I was distinct from them, in that I conducted lessons and so on. I assume therefore, that the statements made to me were of the same order as would be made to a similar teacher. My own participation as observer in the talk will be apparent on reading the transcripts where 'Obs' indicates my statements.

So I have my data but what am I to make of them? What does it mean for me to make sense of the pupils' understandings. I have my *own* understandings of school which I have acquired and which change with new experiences. The interaction of the pupils' understandings and my own is complex. Faced with their statements about school, many of which conflict with 'official' aims and definitions of schooling, I have tried to see they *can* make sense. For me the question is: How can a pupil come to say such things? What does a pupil need to know and understand in order to be able to make such statements? For some of my explanations I have looked inside the school and for others I have looked at the way pupils make sense of school in the light of experience and knowledge derived from their lives outside school — an area of speculation we teachers find so hard to give up!

I have divided my analysis into three sections which I introduce briefly below. Some draw upon ideas which I am sure are shared with many pupils, while some are based on ideas which are mainly my own.

Order and authority One of the topics most mentioned by pupils was how they related to teachers in the area of order and discipline. In other situations I came to see that this had connections within the wider area of choice and decision making in the school.

The ideal teacher and his subject Central to Nell Keddie's (1971) paper 'Classroom knowledge' is Becker's notion of the ideal pupil as conceived of by teachers. This made me wonder whether the evaluation of teachers by pupils might be similar, i.e. do pupils rate teachers according to the degree to which the teacher acts in harmony with the pupil's own notions of what is 'expected' or even 'good' teacher behaviour?*

Work and boredom 'Boring' is certainly one of the most common words in pupil vocabulary. (Blishen (1969, p. 10) says of his school pupil writers: '(boring) is the word that unites all the essays that allow themselves to be freely critical'.) But, as a teacher, I have in the past been aware that pupils' use of this word differs from my use of it. What do they mean? How do pupils rate 'good' activities in school and how do these evaluations compare with 'official' ones?

3. ORDER AND AUTHORITY: 'WILL THE REAL MR. TEACHER PLEASE MAKE US SIT DOWN?

It became clear to me that, for some pupils, the most important parameters for evaluating not only the performance of teachers in school, but also their own enjoyment as pupils, were order and discipline. John frequently made comments of this sort when asked about teachers. Once, when I asked 4X how they would describe an ideal teacher, the following conversation took place:

> JOHN: *One who has a laugh with you.*
>
> ANN: *And one that understands you.*
>
> JOHN: *And one that won't let you get too stroppy . . . and stops the lessons getting boring . . . he doesn't let the class get all stroppy and do what they want . . . and, wait a minute, whether he's human. Right, didn't sort of sit here on a desk, right? He didn't sort of, you know, sort of being mucked about . . . sort of doing what we wanted him to do.*
>
> ANN: *. . . took advantage of him.*

*The paper by Nash, in this volume, explores one way of investigating this question. Ed., *M.S.*

JOHN: *Yeh, yeh, we didn't take advantage of her . . . swearing at her and things like that.*

OBS: *You prefer someone who doesn't let you do that?*

ANN: *Yeh.*

Similar statements were made at other times by other pupils. Altogether they led me to the view that there is a widely held picture of two extreme types of teacher: the soft and the hard, if you like. In operation, the difference consists in whether he can keep order or not. This order relates to various preventative measures: not allowing rudeness, maintaining control over the physical layout of the room (e.g. movement of desks), controlling noise and preventing unauthorized movement about the room (or outside the room) by pupils. In another lesson where the class had been discussing the possibility of making a film about the school it was said (this conversation is reconstructed from written notes):

TEACHER: *What sort of lessons are you going to show?*

PUPIL: *Ones with soft teachers. Before the teacher comes in, pellets flying about and all that.*

JULIE: *No, you want to show different teachers: ones you play up and ones where you sit down.*

This type of 'playing up' is not always accidental or motiveless. On one occasion John explained how a class will 'push' a teacher to 'see how far he will go'. The tactics for this activity are unauthorized talking, walking about and contravening all the other norms of an ordered class. This is not done in the form of an all-out attack but rather a steady process which seems to be a very important part of meeting a teacher for the first time and establishing a relationship. What is required is that the teacher shows some signs of what he considers to be acceptable behaviour and what is not. The teacher's performance can have fairly important results for the class and for the teacher. Tony recounts a failure:

TONY: *. . . last year 3M (laughter) there was one teacher, a Mrs. G. and she was coming in the first week and everyone was chatting as she said, 'Be quiet' and no-one took any notice of her at first until she ran out of the room.* (Talk by class). *We swapped over for a Mr. M. and he isn't very tough like . . . but he kept us quiet. You know: 'I'm the teacher. I'm taking the lesson. You can either get out or listen'. So you kind of kept quiet while he was in there.*

KEITH: *We had a laugh in that class last year* (laughter).

Stories of teachers who had at the first attempt failed to keep order and either left the school or ceased to teach the class (which in a large school can amount to the same thing from the pupils' point of view), recurred in several discussions. I attempted to find out what attitude the pupils had, on reflection, to these teachers. (It is interesting that these stories always referred to teachers who no longer took the class and never to someone *teaching them at present*.) When I asked whether they would want to include in the film (which, as I have already mentioned, they were planning to make about the school) a scene of the female teacher crying, there was general agreement that it was all right to show pranks, but showing *that* was going *too* far. One way of shedding light on the stories of the 'non-starter' and the pupils' apparent embarrassment about it, is to see the 'non-starter' as part of a mythical structure in the Lévi-Straussian sense of a story or stories which represent conflicting extremes of accepted behaviour or social structure and by which the 'middle way', as represented by the hero, is to be ascertained. (I will deal with the other extreme — woodwork teachers — below.) The hero, or embodiment of the 'middle way', I have referred to as The Ideal Teacher (see Section 4) who is a very difficult person to describe, both for pupils and teachers, as he represents a fine balance between conflicting opposites, namely, freedom and control. The nature of this conflict is very complicated and sometimes leads to apparent contradictions. In a myth, the extremes are a way of indicating the conflicting values that the hero finally manages to encompass. The extremes are all, in some sense, desirable, but individually inadequate. The 'middle way' shows how they can find valid expression.

I suggest that the 'non-starter' represents, for the pupil, freedom carried to absurd extremes. The teacher (who, in the accounts, is invariably a young woman) fails even to establish a presence in the class. The game cannot really begin. In a 'normal' situation the teacher establishes his presence, his personality and his codes of behaviour, by means of his responses to the disruption techniques and to the other happenings in the classroom. In a normal situation the process is seen by the pupils as 'natural' and quite straightforward. It is worth noting that there are few teachers who, in the course of initiation into the profession, have not encountered a similar definition of the situation presented to them by one of their superiors, in words such as: 'You've got to let them know who's in charge right from the start'. This may even be formalized into an official instruction or piece of advice.[5] Here it would seem that both 'sides' have compatible definitions of the situation. Both see the first meeting as an occasion when rules are laid down. It is not difficult to see why, from the point of view of the pupils, the 'non-starter' comes as a great shock and may even raise feelings of guilt. In a successful situation, the question of guilt never arises; the structure of the process is unproblematic although the actual outcome may be uncertain in terms of what sort of relationship emerges.

Perhaps pupils who adopt disruption tactics see it as a necessary ordeal for the new teacher. The primary test of a real teacher is: can he keep order? I find it difficult to make any other sense of the following statements from John:

OBS: *Supposing in a class the teacher picked on one of the class, all right? I know that people . . . kids in a class do get upset*

54

> *when that sort of thing happens and they resent the teacher*
> *doing that and yet you all seem to think it's a really great*
> *laugh when this happens to a teacher.* (Laughter).

JOHN: *Well, that's the way it is, isn't it?*

OBS: *Is it? Do you mean it's O.K. for a teacher to do it to kids as*
well? (Calls of NO.)

JOHN: *Yeh, but it doesn't work that way, does it?*

OBS: *Tell me what you mean.*

JOHN: *It's all right for us to muck a teacher about and make her cry*
(laughter from class) and that . . . but as soon as she starts on
us it's not all right, you know? (Laughter and noise.) *That's*
the way it is, isn't it?

OBS: *Perhaps this is not quite the thing to say, but does that not*
seem to you a little unfair?

JOHN: *Of course it's unfair!!*

On another occasion John said: 'Some teachers are weak and some teachers shout all the time'. Teachers' shouting was frequently mentioned by pupils, referring to House Heads and others mainly in posts of responsibility. Whenever this topic was raised, there was nearly always a body of opinion to contradict such statements and to counter them with a comment like: 'Oh, but he's nice when you get to know him'. After a time I realized that there were some teachers who frequently had stories told about them shouting or losing their tempers which no-one ever contradicted: they were all woodwork teachers. Some of these stories are remembered from four years previously and concerned teachers who had now left the school. Here is an example (and a fairly mild one!) from James:

JAMES: *We was in the craft room with Mr. C. and he was telling*
us to shut up but we kept going so he got hold of this saw
and he whammed it down on the bench and it went
flying and hit him on the head (laughter from class) *and he*
was swearing!

The structure of these stories is fairly consistent and concerns the woodwork teacher's unsuccessful attempts to keep order or to discipline someone. The teacher loses his temper and takes some wild action which rebounds upon himself, making him appear ridiculous and adding to the lack of order. Other examples of these stories concerned a woodwork teacher who, in a fit of temper, had thrown a chisel at his bench and pierced right through his attendance register; and another about a teacher who had, in an enraged attempt to discipline a boy, lifted him by the shoulders to sit him on a bench and in the process was (accidentally?) kicked in the groin by the boy.

Whenever these tales were recounted they too, like the 'non-starter' stories, evoked laughter which I would describe as partly embarrassed and guilty. Mike's reaction to James' story about the woodwork teacher (above;

Mike had been present when the incident had occurred) was very untypical; but, even though it bordered on the sympathetic, it too was greeted with further laughter:

> MIKE : *I never thought a teacher was human until I heard him swear . . . because he didn't seem sort of . . . right* (laughter) *. . . I couldn't imagine him going home and sort of . . . having a house . . . a car and everything like that until I heard him swear and then I felt sorry for him. He was standing all on his own talking to a goldfish.* (Laughter).

I suggest that the reason stories such as these were greeted with laughter from a class which at other times showed that they were very sensitive to human feelings, is because the 'mad woodwork teacher', like the 'non-starter', gives rise to grave doubts among the pupils. Neither is capable of providing a secure relationship for the pupils, or of assembling meaningful order for the class. Despite the apparent levity accorded to these tales, they are really very moral in the sense that they are concerned with the basic quality necessary to establish a relationship with a teacher. As mythical opposites, the 'non-starter' and the 'mad woodwork teacher' are essentially caricatures and express only one feature of a personality. The former is female, passive and cries; the latter is male, over-active and aggressively temperamental. It is tempting to see these as extreme sex-role stereotypes. Both of these failures were contrasted unfavourably with the good teacher who can keep order.

Our 'hero' then is someone between these two poles, a complex character capable of generating freedom within an ordered framework. Although being able to keep order is a necessary quality, it is only the start. For instance, a teacher who is able to keep order but is too strict is also frowned on:

> PHIL : (replying to the question : what makes a teacher human?) *If a teacher treats you like a human being and jokes with you . . .* (inaudible). *But if he's strict with you and goes by the book we think 'we don't like you' so we'll give him trouble.*

The idea of 'having a laugh' is a very important one; the phrase was used very often by many pupils. Formality is definitely frowned on. John's first response to the question about the ideal teacher was 'one who has a laugh with you' (see the extract at the beginning of Section 3 above). This idea of having a laugh is a complex one; it is an interaction between class and teacher which preserves a finely balanced tension, allowing the class to push the pace while the teacher holds invisible reins.

4. THE IDEAL TEACHER AND HIS SUBJECT: 'OH, TO BE IN ENGLISH . . . '

I wish now to look at some of the other ways in which pupils rate or evaluate their teachers. This is a complex subject, as the evidence which I have shows a high degree of interconnection between the ratings. It was fairly easy to isolate the idea of 'order' in the last section, as I feel that *most* pupils see this as a necessary preliminary evaluation: if a teacher does not pass the order-test then he does not go forward to be assessed on any other criteria. I have said that humour and flexibility seem to be the key to the order-test but how do these relate to other evaluations? Who are the *good* teachers?

I will start from the end and refer to Appendix 1 where Ann says her Geography teacher was 'a good teacher but she does drag on a bit'. The class teacher translated 'drag on a bit' into 'a hell of a bore' and this new expression was accepted by Ann. They threw this problem about a bit and finally Ann withdrew from the debate with 'she teaches you things but it's boring . . . '. These statements from Ann were clearly taken to be problematic by the class teacher, whose comments imply that he feels that the terms 'good teacher' and 'boring' are mutually contradictory. Ann, however, see no difficulty: the teacher does teach you things but they are boring things. I think that this evaluation is closely related to the 'have a laugh' versus 'sticking to the book' criteria. The Geography teacher seems to have been one who stuck to the book and who could be seen by Ann to be doing a good job *per se* but nevertheless she was boring. That a teacher could be a good practitioner of his art and yet bore his pupils is probably an idea which would appal most teachers, but then Ann is not a teacher. Why should the pupil want to address the *teacher's* philosophy of teaching? When the class teacher asked the pupils how they would recognize a teacher if one came into the room (Appendix 1), the first reply he received was 'because he'd start teaching you things'. In the context of the analysis which the teacher seems to have been trying to develop, this statement may sound tautological, which may be why it was not followed up by the teacher. But subsequently none of the pupils actually came up with any deeper analysis of the word 'teach'. So, a teacher is someone who teaches you. The identification of teachers and strategies of teaching are not susceptible of consideration in the abstract.

I want now to move on to another aspect of the evaluation of teachers: the subject that they teach. Some weeks after Ann had made her statement about the Geography teacher I raised the matter again with her and in the course of her reply she said:

> ANN: *With a subject like Geography . . . it's boring itself. She's teaching it to you . . . she's a good teacher but the subject's boring.*

However, she went on to talk about Geography lessons she had had at a previous secondary school which *had* been interesting. The teacher, a woman, was described as 'terrific' — Ann had come top in Geography 'because she was such a good teacher'. When I put it to her that this contradicted her previous statement that Geography was always boring she explained that in her previous school she had become involved in what they were learning about the products of various countries. She prefaced these remarks with the words: 'I know it sounds funny but . . . ', as though anticipating that the class would not believe this tale of interesting Geography lessons. John then remarked that it was the teacher that made all the difference to a lesson and the rest of the class seemed to agree with this. It was said that a good teacher is one who understands the pupils.

As I listened to accounts of various teachers and their personalities I began to realize that for many of the pupils there is one subject where the sort of problems which Ann outlined for Geography did not apply. That subject is English. In English the situation is almost exactly the reverse; both the subject matter and the teachers are interesting. It is almost as if one has to be a really *bad* teacher of English in order not to be rated highly by the pupils, and a number of reasons were given for liking English teachers. It would appear that English lessons and teachers represent a happy coincidence of agreeable features, so that many pupils find something good about the lessons. And this fact also, that many pupils come to the lessons in pleasant anticipation, may contribute to their success.

For Mike, as for some others, English was contrasted with Maths, a contrast which Mike sees in terms of the freedom of expression and variability allowed in English:

> MIKE: *English is sort of about what you think. But in Maths you can't. There's just sort of one answer and that answer's right. But in English you could have about four or five answers which are correct.*
>
> OBS: *So you prefer English on account of that, do you?*
>
> MIKE: *Oh yeh, because English is sort of more free . . . because in Maths if you get the answer right then your answer's the same as everyone else's but if they ask you in English what do you think of . . . uh . . . that Warhol bloke . . .*
>
> TEACHER: *Oh yes, Andy Warhol.*
>
> MIKE: *. . . someone might say, 'he's great' and someone might 'he's stupid' but to you that answer's right.* (Appendix 2)

Success in Maths means conformity, whereas success in English can mean that you establish the uniqueness of your personality by expressing your individual opinions on a topic.

As it happens, the English teachers in the school are nearly all under thirty and the majority of women. They nearly all dress fashionably and very informally. Pupils often made general statements about the age of teachers and attributed different characteristics to young and old teachers.

> JOHN: *Young teachers are more adaptable, old teachers go by the book.*

This is a context in which pupils made far more detailed analyses of lessons than we saw previously. Mike, talking about two of his past English teachers, said:

> MIKE: *If a teacher's not too remote . . . like we had this Miss L. last year and she was sort of like an overgrown one of us — dressed*

*like us and everything and you could really sort of talk to
her. But, was it the year before, we had another English
teacher and it was all English composition, English speaking
and things like that.*

OBS: *Oh, so you would like someone to be as much like you as
possible?*

MIKE: *Yeh, yeh but* . . . (class laughter) *well, not too aloof. Not too
far departed, sort of thing.*

Later on he added:

MIKE: *She was like us but if she wanted to be firm she could be.*

Not only was Miss L. seen as having more pleasing personal characteristics
and as being close to the pupils in age, or at least manner, but also, this
was all related to her work in the classroom. I note that Mike contrasts
Miss L.'s dress and her easy manner of speaking with the English composition and speaking lessons of the other teacher. Who can fail to picture
the difference between 'really talking to her' and 'English speaking'? Miss
L. *is a part* of the content of her lesson in a way that the other teacher
is not.

Another aspect of teacher evaluation which relates especially to English
teachers is the use of the teacher's christian name by the pupils. In the
problem of how close the pupils wanted their teachers to be to them.
Most of the examples cited by the teacher and the pupils were English
teachers and both Keith and Phil said that they would incline towards
calling an English teacher rather than another subject teacher by his first
name, according to Phil, 'because they've got the right ideas'. It is almost
as if English represents an outpost for some pupils; and the English teacher
is a man or woman apart. At no time did I ever hear of English teachers
having discipline problems. In addition, I heard more accounts of the actual
content of English lessons (books read, subjects discussed, etc.) than for
all other subjects put together. In fact I rarely heard mentioned the
content of any other subject lesson.

One exception to this was Mike's sustained critique of Environmental
Studies (Appendix 1) which I think throws some light upon his liking for
English. I quote part of it below:

MIKE: *When we first come to this school and they told us what
subjects we were going to do and I was really baffled because I
didn't know what Classics was. I had no idea, and at one stage
I thought it was classical music* . . . *They didn't tell you what
you were going to do. It was just put on a plate. I went into
Environmental Studies with my eyes shut and didn't know what
that was going to be. I thought it was going to be almost
identical to this* (i.e. Social Science) . . . *Environmental Studies:
I thought: well it's environment so it's going to be about where
you live but it isn't really. It's all sorts of things* . . . (And on
the question of whether it makes sense 'doing' Eskimos): . . .
but it doesn't (make sense) *in a practical way because no-one
here has ever lived in an igloo, I don't think, so they can't
really compare it with us, can they?* . . . *We're doing Aborigines*

next week (class laughter) *and how can you keep an Aborigine,*
an Eskimo and our lives sort of . . . one thing . . .

Mike's main cause for concern seems to be that he does not understand the structure of the subject. The reasons for this are probably complex[6] but the fact remains that he cannot make sense of what he is doing. At the outset he had an idea of what Environmental Studies would probably be, but this was very soon confounded by the departure into 'Eskimos'. He criticizes the study of Eskimos on fairly utilitarian grounds (as he had previously criticized Religious Education):

> MIKE: *Well, that wouldn't help you in any job at all, not being a vicar,*
> *because you wouldn't want to learn about other religions, would*
> *you even . . .* (Appendix 1)

But this is a parameter that he does not apply to English. This to me is a paradox; as I look at it, the uselessness of building igloos seems analogous to the uselessness of discussing Andy Warhol. So why does Mike not say that English is 'no use to you'?

My conclusion is that for Mike, and perhaps for other pupils as well, the 'utility test' has to be seen in the context of all the other tests that pupils apply to teachers and their lessons. In the diagram I have attempted to put together the tests Mike applies along with tests I have derived from other pupils. I have set them out in linear form because, for the first two stages at least, it does work that way. Of course, I am not saying that pupils actually do evaluate their lessons this systematically. The diagram is primarily a model for me to make sense of the judgements that are made. It may seem at first sight that the tests passed by good teachers are very simple (not easy, but simple). For instance, can a teacher really go into a class and say, 'Oh yes, I understand you', and pass the test? Obviously not — the tests are more subtle than that. I think that in the assertion that a teacher 'understands' pupils we have a form of shorthand, signifying that the teacher is acceptable on a number of counts which are subsumed under the heading 'understanding'. For instance, the actions of a teacher who continually sets written work would not be classed as 'understanding' actions. The *things* that a teacher has to do to become an understanding teacher are very important and I will go on to discuss them in the next section.

I will end this section by mentioning briefly a survey being carried out by some sixth formers as part of their 'A' level Sociology course. The survey aimed to discover how pupils perceive and evaluate their teachers and lessons. The survey was still uncompleted when I left the school but a pilot study had been done on two groups of fourth years (none of them in 4X). One of the questions asked them to choose from a list of about thirty words and expressions those which described their favourite teacher (they could add words if they wanted). The words most frequently chosen were, first, 'has a sense of humour' and, second, 'understanding to pupils'. I felt this lent support to the conclusions I had reached from observation of other classes.

Figure 2 An evaluation scheme for teachers

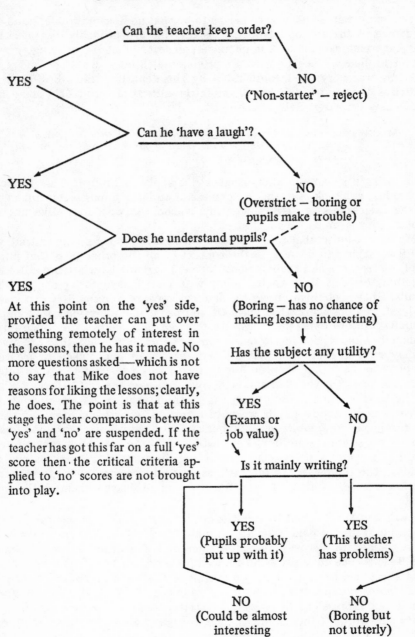

Can the teacher keep order?

YES

NO
('Non-starter' — reject)

Can he 'have a laugh'?

YES

NO
(Overstrict — boring or
pupils make trouble)

Does he understand pupils?

YES

At this point on the 'yes' side, provided the teacher can put over something remotely of interest in the lessons, then he has it made. No more questions asked—which is not to say that Mike does not have reasons for liking the lessons; clearly, he does. The point is that at this stage the clear comparisons between 'yes' and 'no' are suspended. If the teacher has got this far on a full 'yes' score then the critical criteria applied to 'no' scores are not brought into play.

NO
(Boring — has no chance of
making lessons interesting)

Has the subject any utility?

YES
(Exams or
job value)

NO

Is it mainly writing?

YES
(Pupils probably
put up with it)

YES
(This teacher
has problems)

NO
(Could be almost
interesting
occasionally)

NO
(Boring but
not utterly)

5. WORK AND BOREDOM

This is one of the hardest parts to write. This is because I am piecing together statements and ideas drawn from various situations and people and also because, as I mentioned in Section 2, I am sure that the rationale which pupils apply to activities in school is very different from any rationale that teachers are used to. In this section I attempt to highlight some of these differences. When it is also borne in mind how many teachers, teaching methods imply a complete ignorance of these differences, it can surely be left to the reader to imagine how they contribute to misunderstandings and confusions in the teaching process.

I include the transcript of a fairly lengthy section of a lesson (Appendix 1) because the evaluation of activities is considered throughout. The conversation ranges across a number of topics but it is nevertheless something to which the group returns repeatedly. The course of the lesson prior to the beginning of the transcript had been roughly as follows: the teacher had asked the class a number of questions to do with the way a teacher positions himself in the classroom, how desks are arranged and what these things might signify about the teacher and his understanding of his role. The responses from the class were not enthusiastic and I made a guess that they could see no point to the lesson. That is where the transcript starts. I want to examine three areas of the lesson and they are connected to three individual pupils and their views: first, Mike and his comments on the content of lessons; second, Phil on the subject of getting out of school; and third, Tony on the subject of having to come to school.

We have already seen how Mike attempted to make sense of the Environmental Studies course, how the change from Eskimos to Aborigines struck him as quite arbitrary and meaningless. In addition, when I presented him with an 'official' explanation for studying Eskimos he reluctantly replied that it sounded O.K. 'on paper'. He then added that practical comparisons can only be made on the basis of practical experience. So Mike has two problems: first, that no-one has ever told him, in terms that he can understand, why he is studying Eskimos and Aborigines, and second, when presented with my suggested 'teacher's' rationale for the course of study, he found it unacceptable. No wonder he is confused. He seems to be someone who needs a sensible rationale for his activities — I think that of all the pupils I spoke to, he spoke about motives and reasons more than any other. But for Environmental Studies he can find no rationale. Another statement where Mike shows the gap between his own construction of reality and those of his teachers is where he says of his teachers (Appendix 1):

> MIKE: . . . *you don't start at the beginning, you sort of start at the middle and* end *at the beginning and things like that. You get so confused.*

words which should surely be hung over the entrances of all Colleges of Education.

I must pause here to admit that I find Mike's words very disconcerting, and the thought that there might be others like him very worrying. For he is not a miscreant or a trouble maker. He is fairly strongly motivated to learn and seems from his statements very anxious to make sense of what he is doing so that he *can* learn. And yet the school is not explaining itself, even in its own terms, well enough for him to understand what is going on. Nobody told him enough about Classics for him to be able to distinguish it from what he knew about classical music; nobody told him that Environmental Studies was different from Society Science; nobody told him why he was studying oriental religions. If the school's courses are not making sense to someone as highly motivated as Mike, how must they be getting through to some of those who require more coaxing?

I am drawn by such evidence towards the conclusion that many pupils must be forced to evaluate their activities in school by some more intrinsic, rather than extrinsic, rationale. By this I mean that if pupils are unable to evaluate routine activities in school by reference to some philosophy encompassing an idea of relevance between those routine activities and 'the world outside', then they must evaluate them in the context of relationships to teachers and to each other, and in the context of their own preference for passing time. Perhaps an example will show what I am driving at.

Note-taking is an activity which some teachers include in their lessons. The meaning that teachers themselves give to note-taking may relate to views they hold about the need to store information for the future (perhaps in preparation for exams), or it may be concerned with beliefs the teacher has about the desirability of pupils practising written expression or even handwriting. There may even be one or two teachers who see it as a means of 'settling down' a class after some other activity. But if the teacher does not explain *his* reasons for the pupils' note-taking then I claim that they will make sense of it by reference to the teacher's personality ('Oh, he likes to give notes') or to verbal or other cues that the teacher gives. For instance, if the teacher says, 'We've got five minutes left so let's take some notes on what we've just done', then it is quite possible that the pupils will deduce that the teacher himself sees note-taking as a means of filling time. In the absence, then, of any such cues from the teacher, as I have said, the pupils will evaluate activities like note-taking according to how they enjoy it as a way of passing time. This will probably depend on how proficient they are at writing, how much they like writing, whether or not there is the possibility of doing other things which might be curtailed or hindered by note-taking (e.g. looking out of the window) or the desire to occupy one's hands, and so on. This would provide one explanation of why some pupils develop attachments to activities which teachers rate as having little or no value (e.g. decorating the margin of pages of written work).

This leads me on to Phil and the subject of preferences for different activities. But first I would like to make, partly for contrast but also for genuine illustrative reasons, some general propositions about the way most teachers evaluate activities in school and especially in the classroom. It is probably fair to say that most teachers have as the basis of their practical organization some form of philosophy which incorporates notions about *learning*. Many teachers would say that learning is a long-term process, and therefore the pattern of daily activities must be set in the context of a period of time stretching across a number of years, and also that this pattern must be seen as deriving its meaning partly from the future goal of the educated child. Therefore, from day to day, it is probably necessary to achieve a balance between different activities such as, say, writing and discussion, in order that the final product of the educated child should itself be a well balanced compound.

Now, for Phil and others like him I maintain that activities are not evaluated on the basis of such future goals as much as on other criteria like enjoyment and whether the activity makes sense in the present. I am in no position to be confident or precise in my suggestions of these criteria, but what I will do is piece together ideas from Phil and from other people to try to show how some preferences are made. Here are some of Phil's ideas summarized from Appendix 1:

(1) Work is better than school because you have more responsibility and because you get paid.

(2) Any school activity which takes you out of school is a good thing.

(3) Going on trips to new distant places is better than going to local places which you have already visited on trips.

To this I will add Tony's comment in Appendix 1 that the discussion activity is a good thing, being 'better than writing'. It is clear that the practical purposes behind such statements are different from those of most teachers. Using the above statements and others that I heard in school from pupils, I have made up a 'popularity table' of activities. As with my chart of 'teacher-tests' this does not aim to represent the views of any individual, although when I presented it to one group of fourth year pupils no-one disagreed with it substantially. The table starts with highly valued activities and proceeds to low:

(1) Not being at school. (This is, strictly speaking, not one activity but a residual category taking in such things as weekends, evenings, part-time jobs, absence from school through sickness or truancy.)[7]

(2) Going out on school trips: new places preferred.

(3) Film shows in school, or other 'events'.

(4) Classroom discussion.

(5) Listening to tapes in class.

(6) Reading in class.

(7) Writing in class.

This list is subject to modification at times, which affects the basic rating: each activity is rated as interesting or boring and this may cause a shift in preferences so that an interesting class discussion may be preferred to a boring film. Writing is not only bottom of the table but is also the only activity that is always referred to as 'work'. A distinction is commonly drawn between writing and talking, the former being work and the latter not work. This I believe is the basis of Ann's despairing: 'That means we'll have to *work!*' (Appendix 1) when she thought she would be taken for Social Studies by Mrs. T. (who is, incidentally, also the Geography teacher Ann refers to in Appendix 1).

To get another comment on the preferences of activities in school we should look at the statements from Tony (Appendix 1) concerning the fact that school is compulsory. This factor affects greatly how Tony sees the possibilities for choice within the school.

He says:

> TONY: *You've got to go to school. If I didn't come to this lesson they'd have me down the House Head's room and everything . . . 'Why didn't you turn up?' . . . I can't say: 'I was bored'.*

It is worth noting that in this dialogue the teacher does not accept Tony's distinction between work and school on the grounds of freedom (Tony says: 'you don't have to go to work, you can go on the dole or something like that'), though, literally speaking of course, he is quite correct: what other occasions are there in a person's life when they are compelled legally to take part in activities in this way for such lengths of time? For me, however, this is not the most significant factor in Tony's attitude. I would rather draw attention to the fact that he offers the compulsory nature of school as a reason for him to submit to all the procedures within school without much complaint. He says he cannot complain about the lessons. Throughout the lesson in Appendix 1 the teacher was trying to encourage critical comments about the processes within school, but with no success. Tony said that it was no use even going to another school, as one would only get the same lessons there. (Unknown to Tony, the Social Science department was co-operating with the Social Science department of a nearby school to produce printed resource material more economically for them both to use!) This was, for me, one of the most apparent expressions of the gap between teacher and pupil models. The teacher implies that changes can be made in the school structure, that individuals can act to improve their circumstances. Tony, on the other hand, says that you cannot change the school. I was frequently told by pupils of occasions when they had tried to express some opinion about the running of the school or tried to negotiate some improvement, only to have the attempt defined as naughty behaviour by the staff. I also frequently heard staff complaining to each other about the difficulties *they* experienced in getting the smallest thing in the school changed.

John also made statements like Tony's about the compulsory nature of school and I found one of them very worrying. It occurred in one of 4X's discussions about Education where the teacher had been asking some points about the use of Education to develop cultural values and national identity. The teacher had related how the British had exported their own Education system as part of the process of colonization during the British Empire, with the result that Africans in African schools would be learning English constitutional history. The teacher asked, rather rhetorically, what right the colonists had to do this and John replied as follows:

JOHN: *I hate school but I have to sit here and take it all, so I don't see why they shouldn't teach the Africans English history.*

I have no doubt that most teachers would think it extremely distasteful that John should see his own classroom experiences as being analogous to a process of subjugation. I hope that they would also worry that the compulsory nature of school might be helping develop attitudes of intolerance outside the school.

For John and Tony the fact of *having* to come to school seems to foster an attitude of total rejection and undiscriminating criticism of what goes on in school. This seems to be connected to the high rating given to any activity involving getting out of school. At times I thought that John did not care about anything that went on in school so long as it did not involve him, activities being rated according to how little they impinged on him.

This brings me back to the word 'boring'. I think many teachers have difficulty coping with the term as used by pupils. Aside from the tendency teachers have to see the use of the word as implying a *personal* criticism of them, I think the main problem is that teachers tend to evaluate their lessons according to the pedagogic content while pupils, as I have said before, evaluate the lesson by other criteria which have more to do with their own enjoyment. All very puzzling: if the Mikes of this world say a lesson is boring, it may be because they don't understand what the content of the lesson means; for the Phils it may be because they don't like writing; whereas the Johns may say it because they hate school.

I wish now to look more closely at the use of the term 'work' and I shall make some comparison between school and employment. I shall refer to them as 'schoolwork' and 'jobwork'. Pupils quite frequently made comparisons between the two. Ann said (Appendix 1), 'I think you ought to get wages for coming to school' and John said (Appendix 1), 'It would be better if schools sort of taught you a trade'. From these and other statements I suggest that some pupils think of school and jobwork in comparable terms. I can set out the comparison as follows:

(1) Their parents go to jobwork for a certain number of hours each day and the pupils go to school. In both cases it involves massing people together in specific places to perform common tasks.

(2) The organization of time in schools and factories is similar in some respects: 'work' interspersed with shorter periods of 'free' time. The 'work' is usually less enjoyable than the free time.

(3) The 'work' in both schools and factories involves the performance of routine activities which in both cases may be very repetitious and, insofar as it does not engage the individual's *own* preferred creative or recreative interests, may be boring, especially in view of the length of time spent on it.

The Social Studies department of the school had prepared some material in work packs for a course on the sociology of work. These packs began with the information that the pack was about 'work — not school work but *real* work, eight hours a day, five days a week . . . '. I maintain that for some pupils, like John and Tony, this is not seen as an important distinction between schoolwork and jobwork. Both are seen as similar as regards routine and boredom (though Phil did say that there was more responsibility at work, a belief which may be held by others). The *important* difference between school and jobwork is that the former is compulsory while the latter is not and that for jobwork you get paid money, an immediate reward for your activities, whereas in school you do not. Also, for many young people the entrance into work marks the change from childhood to manhood: *men* work.

It is not only in the Social Studies department that there are attempts to convey a definition of school which separates it from jobwork. In other schools I have often seen attempts to indicate to pupils that school is preferable to jobwork. Statements such as 'How do you think an employer would react to that sort of behaviour?' are made to show that a pupil has more freedom than an employee. But if the teachers in school fail to take note of the compulsory nature of school and its importance to pupils, then they will also fail to see that for some pupils an equally pertinent comment to the one above might be this one from a pupil: 'How do you think the workers would react to behaviour like *that* (from an employer)?' In addition to this, the school frequently contradicts itself about the alleged comparison with jobwork. In some contexts, usually when the staff demand adherence to some activity or standard of behaviour, it is stressed that school *is* work. One teacher in the Social Studies department would frequently chastise latecomers to school with a comment such as 'If I can get here on time why can't you?', which was frequently met with a reply from the pupil: 'But this is your job', to which the teacher would reply: 'It's *your* job as well'. Exit pupil mumbling, 'But you get paid for it'.

This sort of double-bind forms an authority trap which many schools fail to recognize. At home the pupils are under the authority of their parents who tell them they should go to school to 'work'. At school they have the *in loco parentis* authority presenting them with conflicting ideas about school and work, with power to compel them to accept certain forms of behaviour and certain activities. As the schools go about their business of developing patterns of behaviour which may be acceptable to employers it is possible that they are creating real confusion in the minds of their pupils, or at least those who are open to this sort of persuasion. On the one hand school is contrasted favourably with jobwork, and yet the word 'work' is used to describe school activities rated most highly by the school.

6. END

Perhaps the hardest thing about this paper is ending it. I could go on for a lot longer — I have many more tapes I could transcribe, many more comments I could make about their contents. I have much more polemic I could put at the end of each section. I will merely say that in this respect I have been persuaded by the schoolchildren: I will not make a generalized summary of the preceding pages! I assume that you will have made your own deductions and your own generalizations. Some readers may be concerned about the lack of consideration generally given to schoolchildren's views, while others may take my words as further evidence of the need to continue the struggle to mould young minds according to acceptable standards. I have my beliefs and you have yours. Let everybody make sense of my writing as he can, just as I have tried to make sense of my pupils' making sense of school. No doubt I have missed many points. No doubt I have 'got my facts wrong'. No doubt I have made deductions unwarranted by the evidence. But then I know you will too.

APPENDIX 1: TRANSCRIPT OF MOST OF A SOCIAL SCIENCE LESSON RECORDED ON 26.1.73 WITH 4X AND MR. TURNER

OBS: I get the impression some of you don't see why this is important.

PUPIL: Why are we doing it?

TONY: It's better than writing isn't it?
(*noise*)

OBS: Has anybody thought why Mr. Turner started talking about it?
(*noise*)

TEACHER: What was that?

PUPIL: I thought he was wasting time.
(*laughter*)

TEACHER: Well that was honest! O.K. Any other ideas on this?

MIKE: Why are we doing it? What difference does it make where he puts the desks?

TEACHER: I'll answer that in a minute.

MIKE: In any case you're not always in the same room with the same desks.

TEACHER: It's interesting to me that no-one said: why are you doing this?

OBS: You don't seem to worry that you don't understand what's going on?

TEACHER: Why don't you protest?

OBS: In any other part of your lives, if you're doing anything else, surely if you're bored or you don't understand what's going on or you're not deriving some sort of satisfaction from it, then you switch over to the other channel or you do something else . . .

TEACHER: You walk away.

OBS: . . . you don't buy it again or . . .

TONY: You can't do that at school, can you? You've got to go to school. If I didn't come to this lesson they'd have me down the House Head's room and everything . . . 'Why didn't you turn up?' . . . I can't say: 'I was bored'.

TEACHER: I've known people say that to me in my own tutor group. They say: 'Oh, X's lessons are boring'. Now whether they turn on the old excuses: you know, Mr. Turner, he's a sympathetic kind of stupid twit, he'll let us off if we say that, or whether they really mean it, is not that easy to tell. It's up to me to try and judge I suppose. I've had people say that to me.

TONY: Yes I know, but you get some teachers like, say, Mr. B. for instance. You go down to him and he'd say: 'Why didn't you go to that lesson?' You can't say: It was boring.

PUPIL: That's not the reason.

PUPIL: You don't have to come to this school . . . there's always another one.

TEACHER: What's the answer to that? What's the answer to that to be honest?

PUPIL: You ain't got one.

TONY: You still get the same lessons at that school. You get a different teacher but you get the same lessons.

TEACHER: I think that's the point . . . I mean the answer to that is: what difference is that going to make? — I mean I'll get bored there just like I get bored here. — I like this school better, I know it better — what's the point of moving?

OBS: . . . I prefer to be bored here . . .

TEACHER: Yes, I prefer to be bored here . . . it's nicer in other ways, perhaps. Go on, Ann . . . er . . . Alice.

ANN: In some lessons like . . . Geography last year that was good but this year it's boring . . .

TEACHER: Well, I mean . . .

ANN: . . . It's not *too* bad . . . she's a good teacher but she does drag on a bit.

TEACHER: You say nevertheless she's a good teacher. What do you mean: she's a hell of a bore but nevertheless she's a good teacher?

ANN: She is really . . .

TEACHER: Well, what do you mean?

ANN: Well . . . um . . . ah . . .

TEACHER: I mean is a good teacher an interesting one or something else . . . or both.

ANN: It depends. You can get a teacher . . . right, I've learned how to do quite a few things with her . . .
(*sarcastic hooting*)

TEACHER: Thank you gentlemen.
(*laughter*).

TEACHER: I know what you've been learning about obviously. Go on, Ann, anyway.

ANN: Well, she teaches you things but it's boring.

TEACHER: You mean, if you learn something from the teacher then that's a good teacher? . . . if you learn quite a lot from the teacher.

ANN: (*inaudible due to murmuring by class*)

TEACHER: This is about what's a good teacher and what's a bad teacher: something I think we might take up . . . um . . . you know next time. For the moment though I don't want to lose sight of the question Mike put: what are we doing this for now? . . . and I don't want to lose sight of the question. We still haven't really . . . I don't know . . . well . . . to my satisfaction . . . uh . . . to your satisfaction and mine. You know you just come . . . nobody asks me about anything and lots of others of you just sort of sit there and get on with it and nobody sort of says: 'Well, hang on, Mr. Turner, what are we doing this for?' You know: What about doing so and so?' or, you know, 'I don't want to do that', or you know . . . nobody sort of asked me a question or anything like that.

OBS: Well, if what Mike says is true: that in a way you come to expect not to understand . . . you know, I mean if you have other lessons where you don't understand then presumably you don't . . . they assume that some . . .

MIKE: If you ask: 'What are we doing this for?', you're thick, sort of thing. They sort of look at you and say: 'Well I've been doing this for three weeks now and you don't understand it'. But you don't start at the beginning, you sort of start in the middle and *end* at the beginning and things like that. You get so muddled up.

TEACHER: What do other people feel about this? I think Mike's got a point. I don't know . . . come on Keith what do you think about this? . . . or Eric or some people . . . some of the ladies . . . how do you feel about this?

(laughter at a comment made by a pupil)

No, I mean let's not make a laugh out of it. I mean I think it's damned important: you spend hours of your lives in a place that can be boring and you come to . . . you sort of say . . . take it . . . I can't think of any other time in your life . . . except perhaps in a job, and at least you're getting money out of it, where you go and you say I'm prepared to put up with being bored four or five hours a day you know . . . five days a week for ten or whatever it is years . . . I mean, God . . . I wouldn't . . . I'd say: 'To hell with it'. I'd chuck that for a start.

TONY: School . . . you've got to go to school but you don't have to go to work, you can go on the dole or something like that.

TEACHER: That's not much of a choice really I mean if you've got kids or a mortgage or all kinds of things . . . or not even that, you know . . . um, if you haven't got money then your life is going to be much duller . . .

ANN: I think you ought to get wages for coming to school.

TEACHER: Go on Phil.

PHIL: *(inaudible)*

TEACHER: Yeh, O.K. Well. Well, supposing we say that schools are important. Supposing we say the law's right: you've got to come . . . O.K. you can say that . . . O.K. you're in this school then what? I . . . you're still bored.

JOHN: It would be better if schools sort of taught you a trade.
(noise)

TEACHER: Go on Phil.

PHIL: When you're at work you've got more responsibility . . . like if you keep mucking about at school then your mum and dad'll say: 'Why do you keep playing about?', and then they'll say to you. 'If you're going to be like that at work you're not going to keep a job long. And another thing about work . . . you get paid for it.

TEACHER: So you need some kind of money just to . . .

PHIL: Like you go to work and you get paid for it . . . *(inaudible)*

TEACHER: I think it's another important point that if you get paid for it then, O.K., then you'd better go along with it and do it because there's some kind of reward . . . you get something out of it and yet school . . . am I right in thinking that at school, well, you've got to go and suffer it? . . . the boredom and all the rest of it and you don't get anything out of it?

TONY: Well you get something out of it . . . you must do.

OBS: What and why?

TONY: Well, even if it's only a game of football or a game of rugby you get something out of it don't you?

OBS: Yeh.

TEACHER: Well, teachers are obviously here because they hope to make you get something out of it but whether you think you do . . . or whether you really do . . . you know, may be a bit different . . . and I mean if you think you're not getting very much out of it, as much as you think you should then . . . well, I don't know what . . . O.K. so that's it, you know, sit here and that's it.
(*a few seconds' silence*)

MIKE: Well you learn some subjects but they ain't going to do you any good, are they! Like last year — was it last year? — I think we had to do R.E. or something, it was either last year or sometime . . .

TEACHER: Hang on, sorry, Ted, if you've got something to say let's all hear about it, O.K.? Go on . . .

MIKE: Well, that wouldn't help you in any job at all, not even being a vicar because you wouldn't want to learn about other religions, would you? . . . (*laughter*)

TEACHER: I can assure you that you couldn't be a vicar anyway, Mike . . . (*laughter*) . . . well, O.K. so you do Eastern religions or something like that and it's going to be sweet fanny adams use to you when you leave and so on, so why on earth do you do it?

PHIL: You have to.

TEACHER: O.K.

TONY: You've got no choice.

TEACHER: Have you really got no choice in what goes on in the place?

TONY: Well you've got it this year but you didn't get it last year or the year before.

TEACHER: O.K. for this year for example . . . O.K. before I ask if anyone wants to say something . . . in a minute . . . then I want to . . . you had a choice last year as to what sort of thing you did this

	year. We had a big thing with Mr. Wilkins and your tutors and all the rest of it you know . . . Go on Ann . . .
JEAN:	Well, you know it was absolutely no use . . . I mean I've ended up doing courses this year that are absolutely no use to me. Now I've decided what I want to do I've found out I'm doing the wrong subjects . . .
ANN:	Yeh, same as me.
JEAN:	. . . they gave you no help at all really.
OBS:	Sorry, can you spell that out. I mean what subjects are you doing and which ones would you prefer to be doing?
JEAN:	Well, I'm doing Literature because my English teacher told me I should but honest it's terrible: you get a set book and you have to read it whether you like it or not. It's pretty boring.
OBS:	What do you want to do when you leave?
JEAN:	Well I'm going into graphic design work.
TEACHER:	But I mean when . . . O.K. Let's go back to Phil.
PHIL:	I think all the good subjects get people who are keen and want to work.
TEACHER:	Do you think that happens?
PHIL:	Because the teachers are ready to trust them . . .
TEACHER:	Do other people feel that this happens for example, you know: all the trusties into the nice subjects and all the rest into the yuk subjects? Do you really think it happens like that?
ANN:	Here sir, last term Mr. Q. was away one week and we had this real old bag (*laughter*) . . .
TEACHER:	(*to* OBS) Censor that please.
ANN:	. . . and she made us write something about religion and we were having these big rows with her, telling her we'd given up religion and I said to her we didn't want to do it . . . (*inaudible*)
TEACHER:	Well, you see there are two questions still in my mind . . . you know it's easy to wander on with lots of interesting things . . . there are two big questions in my mind, we've brought up this idea of choice, and Tony says, well we've got some choice about this year and then people said, well, yeh, but that choice wasn't a very good one or it went wrong somehow. Ann said it went wrong or when it was it wasn't a good one for me. That's a choice of one subject or another or what combination of subjects . . . what about a choice about the lessons within a subject, you know: what happens in Social Science or what we do in R.E.

or what you do in . . . something or other. We were talking about a choice between one lesson and another . . . a little bit . . . you know, it's far from perfect, maybe.

MIKE: When we first come to this school and they told us what subjects we were going to do and I was really baffled because I didn't know what Classics was. I had no idea, and at one stage I thought it was classical music. (*light laughter*).

TEACHER: Yeh, O.K.

MIKE: They didn't tell you what you were going to do. It was just put on a plate. I went into Environmental Studies with my eyes shut and didn't know what that was going to be. I thought it was going to be almost identical to this . . .

TEACHER: Yeh.

MIKE: . . . Environmental Studies: I thought: well it's environment, so it's going to be about where you live but it isn't really. It's all sorts of things . . .

TEACHER: Hang on, hang on. You could easily go off onto a tangent about what Environmental Studies is or not . . . perhaps you should take that up with your Environmental Studies . . . perhaps you should take it up with them and say well, you know, it hasn't really turned out to be what I thought it was going to be . . . or um this is my idea of what I thought it was going to be about what's your idea?

MIKE: But we're doing *Eskimos!*

TEACHER: Maybe there's a reason for that. I don't know. I can think of reasons why it might be done but the point is you can't. So what are you going to do about it? . . . I mean.

OBS: Can I put a sort of slightly different question and that is that if you knew what the reason was why the teacher thinks it's a good thing to do Eskimos, would you then be happy doing Eskimos?
(*two replies of 'yes', one of 'no' from the class*)

OBS: Do you see what I mean?

MIKE: Not really, no.

OBS: Well, I mean, you say that you don't really know why you're doing Eskimos . . .

TEACHER: You're in the dark.

OBS: Well supposing . . . I mean for instance I'll make up a reason for why you're doing Eskimos. It may be the real reason, I don't know. Or maybe the reason the teachers give . . . you are doing Eskimos because Eskimos live in a particular type of environment which is an extreme one and it's interesting to be able to

	compare it with your own environment. Now . . . does that make sense?
MIKE:	Well it does yeh, on paper. (*laughter*)
TEACHER:	He's got the right expressions anyway!
MIKE:	. . . but it doesn't in a practical way because no-one here has ever lived in an igloo, I don't think, so they can't really compare it with us, can they?
OBS:	No, but that . . . sorry . . . well the rest of . . . to explain it a bit more, I'd go on to say: obviously we can't build you an igloo and give you the experience of being an Eskimo.
TEACHER:	I'm not even sure he'd want to if you could.
OBS:	Well quite, but what we can do is by films and worksheets and, you know, generally talking about it, tell you and, you know, enable you to learn about what the life of an Eskimo might be, so that you'd then got a bit knowledge in your head with which to compare your own life.
MIKE:	Yeh.
OBS:	Well, don't just say 'yeh'.
TEACHER:	You don't sound convinced. I mean that was sort of 'yeh, well thanks for the soft soap but you ain't fooled anybody'. That's what it sounded like.
MIKE:	We're doing Aborigines next week (*laughter*) and how can you keep an Aborigine, an Eskimo and our lives sort of . . . one thing.
TEACHER:	Shall I let you into a secret and sort of . . . he's been helping to prepare some of the materials for that . . .
OBS:	The Aborigines?
TEACHER:	The Aborigines . . . I mean . . . he's on the inside . . . he's got reasons for it you see . . . I mean some of the reasons he's got . . .
OBS:	I'll tell you, you've got a good film coming on Tuesday (*laughter*) a real good one.
TEACHER:	Go on Phil, you want to say something . . .
PHIL:	Another thing: Environmental studies turned out (*inaudible*) . . . I knew we'd be going on trips and that, and I thought right, that'll be all right. I never knew it'd be to places like (*names*) and that 'cos that's just the usual school places that we go to, isn't it?
TEACHER:	So it's sort of all the usual package but in a new cover, you know, it's the same old stuff but dressed up a bit?
PHIL:	Yes you know (*names of places*).

TEACHER: Honestly though our cons don't work, you know . . . : we're going to do some Sociology. We're going down to (*name*) to do it . . . I mean but it's Sociology, it's Social Science . . .

PHIL: It's getting away from school . . . that's one good thing . . .

TEACHER: Yeh, yeh.

OBS: I think it's about time you gave your reason . . . your answer to his question . . .

TEACHER: What is it . . . I can't remember the question now.

OBS: Why did you start off talking about the desks?

TEACHER: Why did I start off talking about the desks . . . what I was concerned with was to get at what kind of person a teacher is and what kind of jobs he's supposed to do . . . you think he's supposed to do . . . and whether what you think a teacher should do is the same as what he thinks he should do . . . and how a teacher shows . . . that he is a teacher. How do I prove it . . . I don't wear a gown or a thing to . . . like a policeman wears a uniform . . .

PUPIL: Silly isn't it?

TEACHER: (without a break) . . . or are there certain kinds of things . . . in your minds . . . that automatically go with being a teacher . . . and is that always right. I mean I could . . . I mean Mr Gannaway . . . I could introduce him you know as a local copper . . . or I could have introduced him as a brother or all kinds of things . . . I mean you weren't to know that he was a teacher and supposing that he just walked into a room and suddenly he started behaving like a teacher behaves . . .

PHIL: Well teachers don't . . .

TEACHER: Now in what way do teachers behave like teachers? Are there certain ways that sort of even without wearing 'TEACHER' you automatically . . . he's a teacher . . . just because of what he's doing . . . he clings to his desk . . . or whatever he does.

PUPIL: He'd start teaching you things.

JOHN: Because of his age.

TEACHER: Age? Here . . . !

JOHN: Well you wouldn't get a teacher old (*inaudible*).

TEACHER: Well yeh, between the age of twenty and sixty say . . . that's about forty years difference . . . that's not going to help you very much is it?

MIKE: Well you just know instantly . . .

TEACHER: Well how do you know instantly? You see that's what I'm trying to get at. How do you recognize a teacher because he hasn't got it written on his forehead.

OBS: For instance how can you tell . . . *can* you tell the difference between a teacher and a student teacher?
(*Calls of 'yes'*)

OBS: Yes? Well say how.

MIKE: A student is always trying to right things. A student always thinks that there's always something wrong and he's got to sort of put it right. He reckons he's going to change the world but when you get turned into a teacher . . .

TEACHER: (laughs) Missionaries! Missionaries!

MIKE: But when you get turned into a teacher then you realize that, well, you can't . . . and well, I get my money so I'll just . . . do my job. (*laughter*)

TEACHER: You can go, you can. That's not fair.

OBS: Sorry. Ann . . .

ANN: Are you a student?

OBS: I'm a student teacher.

TEACHER: No! You shouldn't have said that . . . you should ask them how . . .

OBS: Sorry.

ANN: No but I'll tell you why: you can trust a student.
(*laughter*)

TEACHER: Charming! Well thanks a lot . . . hang on, go on Tony, Tony . . .

TONY: Yeh. You're teaching and he's kind of like (*voice: 'watching'*) yeh, watching . . . and like watching the old master kind of thing picking up tips and things like that.

OBS: Have you noticed that difference this morning?

TONY: Yeh.

ANN: Sir, are you our Social Studies teacher.

TEACHER: You conned them, you fool you . . . !

OBS: What?

ANN: That means we *have* got Mrs. T.

OBS: No . . . Social S . . .

ANN: Studies . . . on Wednesday . . .

OBS: Yes.

ANN: You are our actual teacher?

OBS: On Wednesdays . . . for this term.

ANN: That means we haven't got Mrs. T. then . . .

TEACHER: You won't have Mrs. T. . . . not for Social Studies . . .

ANN: We will have . . .

OBS: She's covered it for this term . . .

TEACHER: Is that it? Oh.

ANN: Oh, that means we've got to work.

TEACHER: I'm only second in charge of this department and I didn't know. I'm supposed to be genned up on these things. I should have known that but I didn't know. Sorry.

PUPIL: (*referring to Social Studies*) Why have we got to see that film, it's so crappy.

TEACHER: I agree. I think it's bloody awful.

PUPIL: Some of the teachers like it . . . Mr. C. thinks it's awful . . . some of the others . . .

ANN: What film?

TEACHER: That television film.
(*noise*)

TEACHER: I said to my group too . . . I said I thought it was damned awful . . . the first time I saw it we saw that one as a preview . . .

ANN: Oh. (*to* OBS) Do that banana bit, sir.
(*laughter*)

TEACHER: I'm going to have words with him afterwards . . . put him . . .

OBS: Put me right.

TEACHER: Yeh. That's right, put him right.

ANN: He did it so well . . . he put his hand on the table . . . banana . . .

OBS: (*to* TEACHER) I was . . . we were talking about . . .

TEACHER: Go on, explain yourself.

OBS: On Wednesday we were talking about the first one that we'd seen the week before and I was reminding . . . I mean I thought they'd all remember the bit about the banana . . . because I thought it was the funniest bit in the film . . . and they'd forgotten it so I did a little imitation of it . . .

78

TEACHER: Did they get the message the second time around?

OBS: Yeh.
(pause)

TEACHER: So what I was getting at is . . . is there some way . . . just from what a person does you can say: aha he's a teacher? And some people think they can do this . . . they believe they can do this even when there's a person outside school, you know, on a bus or something and even I sometimes wonder, you know, that . . . I'm almost sort of . . . guilty of being a teacher with other people outside . . . you know, getting on a bus . . . instead of sort of um . . . watching all these mad twits getting on in a stupid crush . . . even from another school or adults I'm always . . . I mean I feel I want to say: 'Now let's get on tidily, shall we?' I feel I want to say it you know I feel I want to be a schoolteacher again. I'm so much a teacher in this school that it's almost as if I don't shut off outside.

PUPIL: Affects your brain.

TEACHER: Yeh, if you like . . . you know.

PUPIL: Sir, sometimes you can't spot teachers but certain people you can spot out in the street . . . like coppers you can spot . . .

TEACHER: Even if they're out of uniform?
(calls of 'Yeh)

PUPIL: They just stand and stare . . . all over the place.

APPENDIX 2: TRANSCRIPT OF PARTS OF A SOCIAL SCIENCE LESSON RECORDED ON 19.1.73 WITH 4X AND MR. TURNER

TEACHER: How close do you want a teacher to be to you? I mean . . . some teachers in this school like to be called by their christian names . . . I think Jane P is one . . . who has done this . . . I don't know how much.

PHIL: Jim R.

TEACHER: And Jim R. does it a bit . . . um I do it in the sixth form . . . you see, for myself I'm not sure how much I could do it with people younger than that, but I certainly do it with people in the sixth form. Would, you know, O.K., is this one way of doing it, calling a teacher by their christian name or what? *(inaudible murmur from someone)*

TONY: They're just Mr. or Mrs. aren't they?

TEACHER: My tutor group obviously knew me best of all. Supposing I came in one morning, or today, and said, 'Well look, we know each other pretty well, we get on pretty well . . . in fact I get on with this, with *you* lot (*referring now to 4X, many of whom are in the Teacher's tutor group*) one of the best classes I have in terms of getting on (*good natured sceptical groans from the class*) . . . no, I'm not soft soaping. I'm honest, that's not soft soap . . . it's just that we get on pretty well. Supposing I came in tomorrow morning and said, 'If you particularly want to you can call me Jerry if you really want to, I mean, you don't need to'.

PHIL: I think we would take advantage of it really because we're not used to it. In the sixth form people have grown up that little bit more and they wouldn't take advantage.

KEITH: I don't think you would be able to control us.

TEACHER: Why do you think that, Keith? I mean Phil talked about taking advantage cf it.

KEITH: I just mean we'd muck about.

MIKE: They wouldn't know what it meant, sort of thing, because if you said, 'Call me Jerry', it wouldn't be the same as 'Mr. Turner', would it? It wouldn't have the same sort of . . . wouldn't have the same sort of . . . I don't know . . .

TEACHER: Would it . . .

MIKE: It wouldn't give you such an authority.

PHIL: I think if we called you that we'd get the idea that you weren't as much a teacher as if we called you Mr. Turner.

TEACHER: Does it make me too close to you?

PHIL: Possibly.

OBS: Is it something you're prepared to accept from other teachers though?

KEITH: Mr. C. was calling the register once and for a laugh I called out, 'Yes, Donald', and he chucked me in the showers with all my clothes on. (*laughter from the class*) And um done his nut. He never called out my name on the register again. Jim R. used to say . . . (*inaudible*)

TEACHER: It was O.K. with Jim R. then?

PHIL: It's O.K. with some teachers.

OBS: You mean it's O.K. by you with some teachers?

KEITH: Well . . . yeh.

OBS: But not with others?

KEITH: Mick H. is another one as well.

TEACHER: What makes the difference?

TONY: Well, I think . . . you know . . . you need to be like . . . Miss L. She was young, kind of thing, and she was a step older than us, kind of thing, you know, out of our age group just another step. You know we used, well, just our table, kind of thing, used to call her Ellen or something like that. You know she never used to like it because she never liked her name. I think if you've got a young teacher you'll be all right but if you've got someone like, say (*interjections*: ANN: Mrs. Y! KEITH: Mr. Turner!) O.K., Mrs.Y. . . . you know, if you called her by her first name it just wouldn't seem right.

TEACHER: Go on, Ann.

ANN: Why don't you call *us* Miss Smith or something?

TEACHER: I wouldn't like it in a way because it would make things seem a bit cold . . . sort of unfriendly.

(*Later on in the same lesson*).

KEITH: It's easier to use a christian name on an English teacher than a Maths teacher.

PHIL: If I was going to call anyone by their christian name I would choose an English teacher because they've sort of got the right ideas . . .
(*inaudible*)

TEACHER: The subject seems to make a difference to you. I mean do certain subjects have reputations?

PHIL: Well, take a Maths teacher. Supposing someone said call a Maths teacher by their christian name you'd think: Well: Maths! But if you say English . . . well, it's more free, you know.

TEACHER: What's more free? Now this is interesting; this is something I've been collecting (?) for a while. What's more free?

PHIL: I don't know. It's just the sort of impression I get.

MIKE: English is sort of about what you think. But in Maths you can't. There's just sort of one answer and that answer's right. But in English you could have about four or five answers which are correct.

OBS: So you prefer English on account of that, do you?

MIKE: Oh yeh, because English is sort of more free . . . because in Maths if you get the answer right then your answer's the same as everyone else's but if they ask you in English what do you think of . . . uh . . . that Warhol bloke . . .

TEACHER: Oh yes, Andy Warhol.

MIKE: Someone might say 'he's great' and someone might say, 'he's stupid', but to you that answer's right.

Acknowledgements

I should like to thank all teachers and pupils who helped me so much and allowed me to disrupt the calm. Thanks also to the people at Goldsmiths' College who helped: Ian Hextall for his comments, Joan Whitehead and the others in her group for the discussions throughout the year which clarified my ideas. Finally, I must thank Julian Laite of the University of Manchester and Paul Atkinson of the University of Stirling for reading the paper and making many valuable suggestions.

Notes

1. I use this term to include all the contexts in which teachers talk to others in the profession. It includes Keddie's (1971) 'teacher' and 'educationalist' contexts.

2. Blishen (1969), p. 15:

> The prose used by some adolescents is heavy only because they believe that no idea can have weight unless it is expressed in the most ponderous phrases available. It is a kind of literary puppy fat and must be allowed for.

3. Earlier in the year I had visited another school for a few days and had spent one day going round with one class to all their lessons. By the end of the day I was near to hysteria. Every 40 minutes we had plodded about and, somehow, as the day wore on, each successive teacher seemed more and more like the previous one. I imagine it was only a deep-seated professionalism that prevented me from shrieking at the French teacher who took the last lesson of the day.

4. Appendix 1 is an example of this. There were about 25 pupils in the class but, even if we consider all the statements labelled 'pupil' (thus labelled on the transcript because I could not distinguish on the tape who was talking) as being from separate pupils, there are still only twelve or thirteen pupils 'taking part' in the discussion.

5. In the Staff Handbook of the school, a manual designed to help new staff, especially novices, there is a section on the conduct of classes and Tutor Groups which contains the following:

> The first task therefore is to achieve the right relationship between the teacher and the class. The relationship should eventually grow to a point when informality and friendliness is the normal atmosphere. Before that can be achieved formality and strictness are necessary. (Underlined in text.) A teacher should never continue to talk in a new class if one child so much as fidgets with a pencil or is inattentive.

6. One reason might be that the Environmental Studies course is fairly new both in the school and for Mike, who has now only in the fourth year been able to choose to take the subject. It may be that the content of new courses takes a few years to acquire respectability in the school, among both staff and pupils.

7. School holidays are a special case — the long ones can give rise to boredom in certain circumstances, e.g. friends away on holiday with their parents. Perhaps the top of the table should read: 'Not being in school — provided you have things to occupy you'.

82

References

Blishen, E., ed., 1969, *The School I'd Like,* Penguin, Harmondsworth.

Holt, J., 1965, *How Children Fail,* Pitman, London.

Keddie, N., 1971, 'Classroom knowledge', in M. F. D. Young, ed., *Knowledge and Control,* Collier Macmillan, London, 1971.

Lévi-Strauss, C., 1955, 'The structural study of myth', *Journal of American Folklore,* p. 68.

Kohl, H., 1969, *The Open Classroom.* Review Books, New York.

Lévi-Strauss, C., 1958, *Anthropologie Structurale,* Plon, Paris.

4. Pupils' expectations of their teachers

By Roy Nash

Editorial introduction

Nash discusses some of the characteristics which pupils expect of their teachers: that they should keep order, explain things carefully, that they should not be boring, not have favourites, and so on. He illustrates how a teacher who does not live up to his pupils' strong and well-defined expectations can run into discipline problems and difficulties in trying to innovate in a traditional school.

Note the methodology and the nature of the data. First, Nash uses a quasi-experimental interview technique to elicit from children the concepts they use to think and talk about teachers. Second, these data are discursively related to data collected by observation in the classroom. Much of the paper simply comprises, then, quoted classroom incidents and quotes from pupils talking about their teachers. On the one hand, such relatively 'raw' data are useful in providing a rapid insight into the classroom scene. On the other hand, such data are amenable to many kinds of conceptual analysis, besides the discursive analysis which Nash gives them.

The reader should be aware that Nash is more explicitly concerned than the other contributors to draw conclusions about how teachers *ought to* behave. The other papers are concerned centrally to develop a descriptive language for classroom events, whilst largely leaving the reader to draw his own conclusions from the description of the passing classroom scene. Some readers may here prefer to take and develop Nash's methodology and observations, whilst ignoring his prescriptive conclusions.

M.S.

During the last few years, research in education has become concerned with the problem of 'expectancies': the idea that teachers' beliefs about pupils may act as self-fulfilling prophecies. Rosenthal and Jacobson (1968) describe how children mentioned to their teachers as 'spurters' showed greater gains in measured IQ than a control group. Although this pioneer study was seriously criticized by Thorndike (1968) and Snow (1969), the results were startling enough to promote further research. Recently, Pidgeon (1970) and Barker-Lunn (1970) have both reported findings which, though by no means conclusive, do suggest that this phenomenon may be important. However, almost all research so far has been based on indirect survey methods rather than on direct observation. Its empirical nature has also meant that relevant theoretical frameworks have been ignored. Moreover researchers have paid no attention to the obvious reciprocal hypothesis that the expectations that pupils have of teachers may be an important influence on their behaviour. Although there have been investigations of the qualities pupils like to see in their teachers, the analysis has rarely been carried beyond the level of simple description. Taylor (1962), for example, analysed children's essays on the 'Good Teacher' and formed a scale to measure the favourable qualities most often mentioned. The composite scale comprised the following traits: helpful, patient, firm, encouraging, friendly. Similar conclusions were reached by Evans (1962) who summed up previous research in this area rather neatly:

> Children like teachers who are kind, friendly, cheerful, patient, helpful, fair, have a sense of humour, show understanding of children's problems, allow plenty of pupil activity and at the same time maintain order. They dislike teachers who use sarcasm, are domineering and have favourites, who punish to secure discipline, fail to provide for the needs of individual pupils and have disagreeable personality peculiarities.

One may think these findings unremarkable: it would be more than odd if this were not the case. But they become more interesting when it is understood that these findings are not merely a description of children's likes and dislikes about teachers, but are a formulation of the rules of conduct which they lay down for them. Morrison and McIntyre (1969) are the first (within the mainstream tradition of British educational research) to realize that these attitudes and expectations become norms. They write:

> that children in British schools commonly expect their teacher to act as policeman and judge; a teacher who ignores this and behaves as if his task were simply to instruct or as if he will be accepted as a friend, counsellor and stimulator of ideas, is not likely to be perceived as he perceives himself. He will rather be categorized by pupils as 'soft' and incompetent, and be given little respect.

Although only lately come to the consciousness of the empirically minded, this idea is a commonplace of interaction psychology. For example, the way in which children's expectations of their teachers become normative has bcen specifically discussed by Geer (1968). She argues that the class transforms what the teacher says and does into rules for him to follow. Rules which he must not change and which he must apply to all pupils. Following Waller (1932), Becker (1952) and Geer (1968), in thinking of the classroom as a setting for social action, Nash (1971, 1972) has shown that within every classroom there is a high consensus of opinion among teachers and pupils about the relative abilities of the members of the class. It is suggested that these findings support the interactionist theory that children are continually engaged in forming a self-concept and in developing consistent patterns of behaviour appropriate to this self-concept. The firmer these patterns of behaviour become the more unshakeable the perceptual models of them held by others will be, and the more power their expectations will have in confirming the actors' behaviour.

This interactionist model enables us to go beyond the mere collection of children's views on the behaviour of their teachers and begin to analyse their status as determinants of teacher action. We need to study the 'taken for granted' rules children formulate for their teachers. One way in which members' rules tend to become normative has been discussed by Waller and Hill (1951). They suggest that regular patterns will be perceived as rule-bound because innovations by either actor upset the other's expectations and thus prompt him to correct the deviation from the expected norm. Schutz (1967) reminds us that the logic of the everyday thinking we are here studying will be inconsistent, incoherent and only partially clear. Nevertheless it has for these members the appearance of a sufficient coherence, clarity and consistency to provide a reasonable chance of understanding and being understood.

In this study a fairly structured technique for holding conversations with children was adopted. The procedure employed was a modification of the traditional elicitation routine invented by Kelly (1955) for use with his repertory grid technique. Each child in a class of thirty-four twelve-year olds in their first term at secondary school* was seen individually and presented with a set of cards, each bearing the name of one of his teachers. He was asked to sort the cards into two sets, (a) teachers he 'got on with' and (b) teachers he did not 'get on with'. This done, one card from each set was shown to the child and he was asked to explain in what ways those teachers behaved differently. Ideally, the child may say, for example, 'well, Miss X (whom he gets on with) and Mrs. Y (whom he does not get on with) are different because Miss X helps you more. Mrs. Y just walks up and down'. Thus the bipolar construct *behaves helpfully–behaves unhelpfully* would be obtained. The procedure was repeated until the child had finished what he had to say. He was not in any way asked to force his thoughts into a clear and consistent set of bipolar constructs. Rather he was encouraged to enlarge on the teachers' behaviour and to discuss and compare them as he liked. The aim was to use the elicitation procedure as an aid to keep the conversation focused on the characteristics of his

---

*The study was carried out in a Scottish school. Readers in England might check out these pupils' perceptions in other settings. Ed., *M.S.*

teachers. In this it was very successful. The conversations were tape-recorded and later transcribed. The transcript of one conversation is presented in the Appendix at the end of this chapter.

On analysis, six common constructs were found. Very often, seemingly identical constructs appeared to be given different verbal labels. This is inevitable, but it does seem fair to regard many differently expressed constructs as being essentially the same. It is a matter of fine judgement to decide whether some of the bracketed alternatives given below are true alternatives or whether they are, in fact, descriptions of different aspects of teacher behaviour. The six constructs were:

(1) *Keeps order — unable to keep order*
(strict — soft) (punishes you — doesn't punish you)
(2) *Teaches you — doesn't teach you*
(keeps you busy — doesn't keep you busy) (lets you get on — just talks)
(3) *Explains — doesn't explain*
(helps you — doesn't help you) (can be understood — can't be understood)
(4) *Interesting — boring*
(good — dull) (unusual — ordinary) (different — same)
(5) *Fair — unfair*
(no favourites — has favourites) (consistent — inconsistent) (fair — picks on people)
(6) *Friendly — unfriendly*
(nice/kind — unkind) (talks gently — shouts) (has a laugh — gets on at you)

These constructs clearly show that the pupils' view of what is appropriate teacher behaviour and what is not, is well developed. The discussion below illustrates with representative comments how children use these constructs in their conversation about teachers.

(1) *Keeps order — unable to keep order*
It is interesting that both Geer (1968) and Morrison and McIntyre (1969) give as examples of the normative nature of children's rules those they formulate about the teacher's disciplinary functions. These children, too, were certain that the teacher has an obligation to keep order. The following comments are representative:

(a) *Mrs. K keeps the class in order but Mrs. A just lets them speak and doesn't keep them in order like Mrs. K — She gives them the belt if they misbehave. Mrs. A just sends them out of the room.*

(b) *I don't like her that much because, well, she should be stricter. And she says* please be quiet *— and I like Mrs. K better — she gives you a good laugh sometimes.*

(c) *Mrs. K is stricter . . . Because say we're reading a book like Patrick Kentigern as we're doing now, if we talk she'll say, 'right, put the books away', and you're enjoying yourself and she has to put the books away and you're doing English — which not many people like doing.*

(d) *Mrs. A is not strict enough, Mrs. K she makes you work — she gives you reading and all this kind of thing. Mrs. A just lets you do anything you really want and she isn't strict enough . . . Well, she'll tell you to be quiet and you don't be quiet and she'll tell you to be quiet again — but if it was Mrs. K she wouldn't let you do that . . . Well, Mrs. A is soft. She just says, 'I'll give you one more warning'; I think there's a lot of noise because she doesn't belt them.*

(e) *Instead of giving people the belt Mrs. A says 'Stand up', or something; 'Who's speaking?', or something like that. And if there's anybody speaking they don't get the belt.*

The children were here voicing the opinions of almost the entire class. Everyone was generally agreed that teachers should be able to keep order. Pupils who were well-behaved considered that the teacher should keep the noisy ones quiet so that they could work in peace. This is no more than one would expect. However, somewhat less obviously the noisy children also believed that teachers should keep them quiet. These children commonly blamed the teacher for 'being soft' and thus failing to keep them under control. Clearly, as Morrison and McIntyre (1969) say, the teacher who thinks he can opt out of this particular requirement of the job, or believes he can relegate it to an unimportant part of his role, is likely to be quickly disillusioned. Without the checks they expect, the class will soon become so rowdy that only wholesale repression will suffice to quieten them, a repression incidentally for which he will gain no respect. The pupils will simply believe that he should have been more strict in the first place.

(2) *Teaches you — doesn't teach you*

After getting the discipline right, the teacher is expected to have a fairly coherent idea of what real teaching is. The extracts will illustrate this conception:

(a) *Mrs. K — she gives us stories and Mrs. F she makes us write a lot. She does teach you more.*

(b) *Well, with her you learn things. About plants and science.*

(c) *Mrs. K, she gives you good work and that and Mrs. L and Mr. B and Mr. M give you good maths to get on with . . . Well, so you can get on with it instead of just sitting about.*

(d) *Well, she's all right, but she doesn't give us enough work to do really. She just gives you stories and that and, well, you're not learning anything and it's — you just have to sit back and you get bored.*

(e) *She's good. She teaches us about copper sulphate and you learn a lot.*

(f) *Mrs. L always gives you things to do and sometimes — well, you do learn things from Mrs. L.*

(g) *Well, I like woodwork. He teaches you how to make boats and all things you would need.*

Clearly the teacher is expected to teach well-defined and specific subjects. These children tend not to regard discussion as real work: they do not think it demands an essential part of the teacher's skills and they feel they learn little from it. This suggests that the teacher who attempts to encourage discussion, and strives to break down the barriers between subjects, needs to be careful to give the impression that she is still 'learning' them 'things'.

(3) *Explains things — doesn't explain things.*

(a) *Say you got stuck on a certain sum and he explains it out in detail to you, but with Mr. G, I think he'd say, 'Well, it's simple. Work it out for yourself'.*

(b) *Mr. D shows you if you get it wrong — tells you what to do. So does Mr. M. But he (Mr. B) just tells you to open the page and go on with it. Don't tell you much.*

(c) *She just tells us about Greece and we have to write about it and take dictation and you just ask what she said and she'll say, 'just work it out for yourselves and think'.*

(d) *Mr. M just gives you more attention than Mr. B does — well, if you — you just need to ask him something and he'll teach you, but you — Mr. B — he comes along and says, 'What do you think?', and every sum you have to try and figure out for yourself, but Mr. M gives you more attention than Mr. B does.*

(e) *Well, she describes things more better than Mrs. L and she explains what to do and Mrs. L just gives it to you, and I'd rather have Mrs. K.*

(f) *With Mr. M he explains things first on the board — where Mr. B gives you things out of books and he canna explain the same as Mr. M. does on the board. A lot of people get stuck with Mr. B but Mr. M when you do it — well he helps you to learn.*

Evidently, children do expect to be helped and to have difficulties explained to them. Specifically, they expect the teacher to be patient and not to shrug off his teaching responsibilities by telling them to work things out for themselves when they ask for help. The children feel that the teacher is employed to *teach*. If he does not they will think the worse of him for that.

(4) *Interesting — boring*

A further important demand pupils make of their teachers is that they should not bore them. The extracts are representative of this feeling:

(a) *This one takes you out places. Out into the playground and she takes you up Arthur's Seat and down to Inch Burn. And Mrs. A keeps you to work all the time — and reading.*

(b) *Well, sometimes, say, well — she gives us an exercise and we've done it and we've got to wait until the rest catch up. I just like to get on with some work.*

(c) *She doesn't give us enough interesting work. Mrs. K she does give us stories out of the book — and it doesn't make any sense.*

(d) *Well, everybody — you ken, they stand there and nobody listens because they don't really like French. She could give you different things because you do the same things as last week.*

(e) *It's awful boring with Mrs. A — well, in — she stops reading the story and that and she's telling you and you don't really want to listen and you start talking.*

(f) *Mrs. A she can't get you interested in it but Mrs. K she can get you interested more.*

These quotations show that pupils appreciate the teacher who can make his lessons flow and knows how to put the subject across in a way that makes sense. They do not like the teacher who continually interrupts the lesson to put what often appear as disruptive questions. Lessons which are disturbed and difficult to understand are perceived as boring. Quotations (d) and (e) suggest that the pupils' perceptions of a teacher as boring and uninteresting do alter their behaviour. And because the pupils' behaviour changes so does that of the teacher. If a teacher's lessons are always the same the pupils become bored, therefore they talk or mess about, the teacher interrupts the flow of the lesson to quieten them, her exhortations prove ineffectual, the pupils perceive her as 'soft', and so on.

(5) *Fair — unfair*

Though it is important to be strict, it is just as important to be fair. The following are representative extracts:

(a) *Mrs. E, she's too strict — say you're in a group and somebody talks, she'd most likely give the whole group the belt, and she'd shout and one person talking she'd give the whole class lines.*

(b) *Well, for the slightest thing you're getting into trouble. One time somebody said something funny and everybody started laughing and then she just took everybody she saw laughing and just gave them the belt and I dinna think that was all that fair. And Mrs. K — I dunno — she only punishes you when there is a reason — a good reason.*

(c) *And if you do anything in Mr. M's room he'll give you a proper row but he won't give you the belt the first time. But Mrs. E she gives you the belt for almost everything.*

(d) *Well, Mrs. K's fair and that. Sometimes it is interesting. She gives you time to talk and that.*

(e) *Well, I dinna like her much. She seems to be the same as the other teachers kinda — some of them seem to be all right, fair and that. But other teachers — Mrs. J, if everybody in the other class is making a noise, well, she'll look at me and she'll give me the blame while everybody else is doing it too.*

(f) *I like Mr. M because he talks to you gently all the time; and Mr. G he laughs with you and then gives you a row for laughing at him.*

Obviously there are certain rules of behaviour that pupils expect from the teacher. He should give you a second chance or a fair warning. But then he should be strict. He should allow a certain amount of quiet talking, particularly towards the end of the period when most people have finished their work. He should not insist on complete silence throughout the whole lesson. He should not joke and then punish children for laughing. He should not pick on pupils or have favourites. These are standards that the teacher is required to live up to. The novice teacher, for example, can easily fall foul of these expectations. He may give too many warnings or not take action until it is too late. The action he does take may then be perceived as over-severe; a panic six strokes of the belt to the whole of the back row instead of one stroke to the responsible boy in the corner. Inexperience at spotting culprits is not considered an excuse for indiscriminate punishment. Nor is it fair to punish one offender unless all the others are equally punished. These are almost impossible conditions for the novice teacher, especially if he thinks that ignoring initial instances of misbehaviour is a good way of deterring further instances. It is not.

(6) *Friendly — unfriendly*

Friendliness is something of a bonus. Children seem not to *expect* it: but they are grateful when they receive it. The extracts which follow are representative of the behaviour of teachers that children perceived as friendly.

(a) *I like her. She gives you a good laugh sometimes.*

(b) *Mrs. K's nice — well, she sort of — I think she likes children really.*

(c) *Well, I like Mrs. K because, well, you ken, she talks to you — just like Mr. W does — she doesn't give you the belt for anything.*

(d) *Mrs. J, yes, I like her, because, well, all the people I like, you ken, they talk to you, and then, well, you can understand them. And it's like my mum, you can understand her, but sometimes with my dad you can't because he gets on at you all the time. And that's what I like about Mrs. K.*

(e) *He's quite a nice teacher. He sort of likes you, I think. He doesn't shout and bawl all the time. And he gives you work to do.*

(f) Mrs. K never shouts and Mrs. E is always shouting. The least little movement and she's always shouting and telling you to be quiet. I don't think she likes teaching and children.

The teacher most liked by the children is the one who is quiet and friendly, the one who can talk easily with them and share the occasional joke. Many children of this age do become easily upset and made nervous by the shouting which they hear not only from the over-strict domineering teacher, but also from many novice teachers. And although it can reasonably be argued that it is the children's exploitation of the new teacher's inexperience which provokes his loud reaction, the pupils, as we have seen, blame him.

One may conclude that the expectations the children have of their teachers are very powerful. It certainly seems that they have a considerable influence on the behaviour of the teacher. It is clear that the teachers the children did not 'get on with' were those who did not keep the rules. With some teachers the misunderstanding was particularly tragic. Several times I have observed liberal-minded teachers who, although they cared deeply for their pupils, were unable to gain even minimum cooperation from them, because they would not follow recognized ways of getting control over the class. Because these teachers were felt to have broken the rules they were considered fair game and were treated unmercifully. It does seem difficult for the liberal-minded teacher in a conventionally run school to avoid being construed by her pupils as 'soft'. Most such teachers are forced, after a very short time, to begin to punish children and to be more formal and distant in their relations with them.

One way to see how much easier the teacher makes her task by acting in line with the expectations of her pupils, is to show how two different teachers react to a 'trying out' process by children of the same class. Mrs. C and Mrs. A are both young women, fairly new to teaching, and they both taught English to the class I studied. Their effectiveness with this class was very different.

Mrs. C was quiet and effective in her management of discipline. She never used the belt. The following incident, taken from field notes made at the time, was the most serious challenge she experienced:

All reading. Silence. Nothing to write about for minutes. Heads down. A little restlessness from Alec and George. *What's the matter boys?* This settles it. *Why are you talking? Have you finished? Yes,* says Alec. *Well, you'd better read on.* (Silence for about two minutes.) *You're still talking. Stand out there.* To Alec: *Take the book with you.* He replies, *I've finished.* Mrs. C looks at him. *Carry on where you left off. Right down in the corner.* She speaks very quietly. Alec walks over to the corner. The class look unaffected. They are all concentrating on their reading. Everything is very still.

Alec was a bright boy with a rather strong tendency to make a fuss when he became bored or thought the teacher 'soft'. He went too far with the abrupt, *'I've finished'*, but Mrs. C refused to rise, which might have given him support from the class, and Alec was left standing in the corner. The effectiveness of Mrs. C's response lies in her ability to spot immediately the implied threat to her maintenance of discipline in Alec's response. The moment seemed very important and the notes may be glossed at this point. Most members of the class were aware of the interaction between Mrs. C and Alec and they perceived it as a confrontation. The behaviour they expect of a teacher is to recognize and deal with such a challenge. Mrs. C shows that she perceives Alec's behaviour as the class perceive it, as a threat, and demonstrates the effectiveness of her control by her quiet insistence on isolating him in the corner as a punishment. The class take in this meaning. To them it is another indication that Mrs. C 'knows the ropes'. She cannot be 'messed about'.

Mrs. A's response to a similar 'trying on' by the class is very different. It was quite clear that Mrs. A very much disliked resorting to corporal punishment or even punishment of any kind. Her approach to teaching was fundamentally progressive but it was difficult for her to translate her ideas into practice. Mrs. A wanted her pupils to internalize the value system held. She wanted them to work out of interest in what they were doing and to be quiet from a realization that noise disturbs their classmates. Mrs. A often made this philosophy explicit. 'Class, I do not like these bad manners. When anybody is speaking or reading we will have quietness then they'll do the same for you'. The class clearly didn't believe this and they perhaps knew themselves better than Mrs. A did. Because of this attitude Mrs. A allowed a freedom of comment unprecedented in this school and habitually ignored remarks obviously meant to challenge her authority. The following field note extract provides a good example:

> Teacher reads the poem. Emily and the other girls near her call for another poem. *We want 'Rats', Miss. Page 62. Wait a minute,* says the teacher, *Do you think 'My Sister' is as good as 'My Father'?* William calls out, *Don't know — never met your father.* Teacher ignores this. But she gives up the attempt to ask questions.

This was the usual fate of Mrs. A's attempts to question the class. The boys especially were so very disruptive that Mrs. A would quickly move on to written work which could be more closely supervised. Because Mrs. A refused to act as the class expected a teacher to act, in that she declined to check provocative comments and neither defined nor enforced clear limits to their behaviour, they soon became almost completely out of hand. The following notes adequately demonstrate this:

> Alec and William are chattering and dancing up and down on their seats. Mrs. A calls out the names of pupils who are not present. She dusts the board. William chats to Irene. Alec is messing about. Great noise. Irene, William, Alec and Rosemary chatter together. *Perth, you are not doing very well this afternoon.* William is moved to the other side of the room. *Wasn't me talking,* he says. *You've been talking on and off all afternoon! Wasn't me,* he says again. *Get over there and*

don't answer back. He goes. Mrs. A quietens the class a little. *You know what this is?* she asks holding up her belt. Mrs. A wants to do a lesson on Blishen's *The School that I'd Like.* There is great noise. *You must be quiet or you won't get anything to do. You'll just get boring work.* (The lesson proceeds for ten minutes). Mrs. A calls for attention. *Listen! Listen!* It is impossible to hear. Mrs. A gives up. *If there are any more comments you'll just get dictation.* George and Judy call out. Jim is giggling. Someone (William?) is making a noise like a cuckoo. *If there are any more of these noises, I'll pick out the people and even if it isn't the right ones I'll belt them. And you'll get dictation.* This doesn't quieten them. People call *Unfair* and *Wasn't me* and so on. Alec, Kathleen and Helen chant *dic tic tation corporation.* Mrs. A is getting pretty flustered and starts to write names up on the board. She writes up Eileen's name. William is still hooting from time to time. Mrs. A is definitely getting very cross. She catches Hamish hooting. Kathleen yells, *Belt him, Miss. Belt him good.* Uproar again.

Mrs. A never really succeeded in quietening the class during that lesson. Admittedly this was one of the class's bad days, but episodes like this were very frequent in Mrs. A's classes. To an observer the ineffectual threats seemed to be treated with open contempt by most of the children. Her determination to control William achieved results for only a few minutes because the same firmness was not applied to the rest of the class. It should also be noted that when the situation got really out of hand even timid and inoffensive children like Hamish would join in. It hardly needs to be emphasized that these were the very ones to be caught. Kathleen clamours joyously for him to be belted because she is delighted to see a 'good' child in trouble. In fact, Mrs. A only once belted a boy from this class. Here is the record:

Alec comes in. He spills the pile of books he is carrying all over the floor. Everyone laughs and cheers. Except Mrs. A. She gets out her belt. *What's that for?* asks Eileen. *That's nothing to do with you. It wasn't an accident.* 'It was an accident Miss. I tripped on a board there'. The floor is dead level. Mrs. A ignores him. Alec holds his palms upwards. Mrs. A turns him to face the class and belts him just once. Alec returns to his seat holding his hand.

It would be wrong to assume from this account that Mrs. A was an ineffective teacher. Most people would agree that faced with this class the style she adopted was unsuitable, but this is not to say that with other classes or perhaps in other schools her methods and philosophy would be more helpful. But even Mrs. A herself would not deny, I think, that this class gave her a hard time. I suggest that the fundamental reason for this was Mrs. A's insistence on teaching, or trying to teach, in a style which was quite outside the experience and expectations of her pupils.

It is because the classroom is rarely seen as a setting for social action that so many novice teachers have such difficulty. Most of the so-called practical training offered to teachers has no more scientific status than a tip for the Derby. Trainee teachers are told variously to: 'project the voice', 'make your lessons interesting', 'isolate the rowdy ones', 'clamp down on the first day', and so on. More to the point would be to teach student teachers to learn the members' rules. The 'trying on' process described so well by Waller (1932) and Geer (1968) and in several 'non-fiction novels' by school teachers, for example Blishen (1955), has a vital importance. It means 'Do you know the rule?', 'Are you prepared to follow them?' If the teacher does not, or will not, then in a very real sense he is not a proper teacher. Therefore, there is no need to listen to him or try to learn from him. He has no *bona fides*. There is a dilemma for teachers who know the rules but do not like them. Many 'progressive' teachers do not believe it should be part of their role to check the class for noise; they feel the children should regulate their own behaviour in this respect. Unfortunately, it may take a long time to establish the new idea as the norm. It is a matter of renegotiating the contract between teacher and pupils. A new class is not a clean slate passively waiting for the teacher to inscribe his will on it. It is an ongoing social system with very definite expectations about appropriate teacher behaviour. If these are not confirmed the pupils will protest and the renegotiated patterns of behaviour may not prove to be just what the teacher intended.

The six distinct characteristics are a powerful agent working against change in the classroom. Changes initiated by a group of teachers who are in the majority in the school probably can overcome the existing expectations and create new ones. But the lone teacher seeking to innovate in a traditional school is likely to fail uncomfortably.

One other point has to be made. In many of these expectations pupils have implicitly recognized a passive conception of their role. For example, the children think they should be kept in order. They do not believe they should be given the opportunity to control their own behaviour. Again they say that they should be 'taught things'. They do not demand to be given the opportunity to find things out for themselves. In some ways this seems to be particularly disturbing. The conception of teacher behaviour they consider correct is the one that deliberately restricts their own autonomy and their range of purposeful action. If the experience of school does generate such limiting self-definitions it is surely not wholly achieving its aims.

APPENDIX

The following is a transcript of a structural conversation with one of the boys aged 12 in this class. William has sorted out a set of cards, each bearing the name of one of his teachers, into two groups: (a) a group he 'gets on with' and (b) a group he doesn't 'get on with'.

RN: These are in order?

W: That's first.

RN: That's first.

W: And that's the last.

RN: Um. Fantastic. Let's write them all down to begin with. The ones you get on with. Mr. G, Mr. H, Mr. C, Miss E, Mrs. L, and Mr. B. Right. So let's take these as people you get on with pretty well. O.K.? And these as people you don't get on with very well at all. O.K.? Would that be fair enough to say that?

W: Yes.

RN: O.K. Well, what I want you to do — what can you tell me about the differences between these two teachers? (*showing cards of Mr. G and Mrs. A*). Do you see any differences in them?

W: Yes. She hardly talks to us and she dinna come up to your desk and say, 'How are you getting on?', and that. Mr. G comes round and looks at your paintings and like Mrs. L, here, she comes round to see your experiments — Mr. G, he has fun with you, no other teacher more or less has fun with you.

RN: Yes, what do you mean fun, William?

W: Well, he comes up to you and talks to you. He says, 'What would happen if you lived in these days?', and all this. And, 'What would you be like if you had no clothes on?'.

RN: Does he? That's the sort of joke he has with you, is it?

W: Yes, he takes the mickey as we say. Takes a lot of fun.

RN: So it's fun being in his classes?

W: Yes.

RN: What about these? (*Handing him cards of Mrs. L and Miss E*) You were saying something about Mrs. L coming and looking at your experiments.

W: If you call her she comes, she says, 'Wait a minute', and then she comes up. She doesn't — like Mrs. E says — she doesn't say, 'That's good writing', or 'Oh, that's a good one, how about focusing it up?', or something like that. Or doing something else to it. Mrs. E doesn't do that. She just tells you to do something and you've got to do it.

RN: Great. What about these teachers? (*handing cards of Mr. C and Mr. D*).

W: Well, he (Mr. C) only checks you a few times and he has a good laugh with you. And he helps you paint, if you're not a good drawer he draws a picture and you paint it.

RN: Right, who else is there? You've got Mr. H. What does he teach?

W: Music.

RN: Ah, yes.

W: He's pretty good. If you want, say you want such and such a song he'll play it for you and that. He's good.

RN: Fine, now what about these? (*handing cards of Mrs. A and Mrs. E*).

W: Oh, she — you just — er — ask for a loan of a pencil and she comes out and you get three of the belt for that, for absolutely asking for a pencil.

RN: No other teacher's like that?

W: No other teacher's like that.

RN: Why do you think she's like that?

W: Don't know, it's just — she does that.

RN: O.K. How do you get on with Mrs. A? What's she like?

W: Oh, I get on pretty well with her.

RN: And Mrs. J, here, how do you get on with Mrs. J?

W: Well, I sometimes get on with her and I sometimes don't.

RN: Do these two teachers (Mrs. A and Mrs. J) have any differences? Or anything in common?

W: Well, they're both about the same — like Mrs. J might be — no writing at all one day and then maybe you're slogging away at writing the — another day. Mrs. A she keeps you like that as well, sometimes she just has fun with you, tells you poems and that but sometimes she might get strict and give us writing and that — she's sometimes strict.

RN: You say she's sometimes strict?

W: Yes, sometimes.

RN: Very often?

W: Not very often — but sometimes.

RN: Let's see if we can see any differences between Mrs. K and Mrs. A. What would you say the differences between them were?

W: Mrs. K is stricter.

RN: What do you mean stricter? What does she do?

W: Because say we're reading a book like Patrick Kentigern as we're doing now, if we talk she'll say, 'Right, put the books away', and you've got to put the books away and you're enjoying yourself and she has to put the books away and you're doing English — which not many people like doing. Mrs. A doesn't do that. If you start talking she just tells you to be quiet or gives you stricter work or something.

RN: But very often people are not quiet whatever the work is in her class.

W: I think she should give you lines or the belt or if you're naughty or that or anything like that they should take you out at the end of the period and should give you about four of the belt maybe that would quieten them down — or maybe send you to Mr. T. Because he's got a very good belt.

RN: Fine. Are there any differences between people that we haven't mentioned?

W: No — some things are — it's really good. Art and History are good, so's Music. They're all interesting subjects.

RN: Are they interesting in themselves or are they interesting because of the people who teach them?

W: In themselves I suppose. Because History is about the clothes and you get this thing printed into your book — it's a sort of ink thing — and you colour it in and he hardly checks you and if you're quiet he gives you more stuff and it's more fun if you're quiet.

RN: Yes . . .

W: Mr. G's only got to say, 'Be quiet', and you're quiet because it's that interesting a subject.

RN: Um. We haven't mentioned Mrs. F?

W: It's not really interesting. These (Mrs. E and Mrs. W) they don't like me very much.

RN: How can you tell that? I'm not saying they don't, but what makes you think that?

W: Well, last week, for instance, we got lines instead of library because of me and John we just walked into the class whispering and we sat down and we got our books and that and she said, 'Oh, it's no use taking your books out because you are going to do lines', and ever since then she's been checking us. We went into the classroom today and she said, 'Remember, no talking', to me and John. She'll do that next week probably if I come in with John; 'Remember, no talking'.

RN: O.K. Fine. We've done that all all right. Thanks.

Acknowledgements

The research was carried out while the author was at the Centre for Research in the Educational Sciences, University of Edinburgh, and in receipt of an SSRC award. The paper was first published in *Research in Education* and the author is grateful to the editor for permission to include it in this volume.

References

Barker-Lunn, J. C., 1970, *Streaming in the Primary School*, National Foundation for Educational Research, Slough.

98

Becker, H. S., 1952, 'Social class variations in the teacher–pupil relationship', *Journal of Educational Sociology*, **25**, 8.

Blishen, E., 1955, *Roaring Boys*, Thames and Hudson, London.

Evans, K. M., 1962, *Sociometry and Education*, Routledge & Kegan Paul, London.

Geer, B., 1968, 'Teaching', in *School and Society: a Sociological Reader*, Routledge & Kegan Paul, London.

Kelly, G. A., 1955, *The Psychology of Personal Constructs*, Norton, New York.

Mead, G. H., 1934, *Mind, Self and Society*, University of Chicago Press, Chicago.

Morrison, A. and D. McIntyre, 1969, *Teachers and Teaching*, Penguin, Harmondsworth.

Nash, R., 1971, 'Camouflage in the Classroom', *New Society*, 24 April 1971.

Nash, R., 1972, 'Measuring teacher attitudes', *Educational Research*, **2**, 14, pp. 141–146.

Pidgeon, D. A., 1970, *Expectation and Pupil Performance*, National Foundation for Educational Research, Slough.

Rosenthal, R. and L. Jacobson, 1968, *Pygmalion in the Classroom*, Holt, Rinehart & Winston, New York.

Schutz, A., 1967, *The Phenomenology of the Social World*, Northwestern University Press, Chicago.

Snow, R., 1969, 'Review of *Pygmalion in the Classroom* by Rosenthal and Jacobson', *Contemporary Psychology*, **14**, pp. 197–199.

Taylor, P. H., 1962, 'Children's evaluations of the characteristics of a good teacher', *British Journal of Educational Psychology*, **32**, pp. 258–266.

Thorndike, R. L., 1968, 'Review of *Pygmalion in the Classroom* by Rosenthal and Jacobson', *A.E.R.A. Journal*, **V**, 4, pp. 708–711.

Walter, W., 1932/65, *The Sociology of Teaching*, Wiley, New York.

Waller, W. and R. Hill, 1951, *The Family*, The Dryden Press, New York.

PART 3

Teacher–Pupil Interaction and Classroom Talk

All the papers in the book use the concept of 'social interaction'. The four papers in this section explore different concepts for describing and explaining communication and talk in the classroom.

5. Beyond Flanders' fields:
The relationship of subject matter and individuality to classroom style

By Sara Delamont

Editorial introduction

Delamont examines how the individual teacher's personal style and subject matter affect classroom interaction. She argues that such complex, individual effects are central to classroom life, but that they cannot be tapped by orthodox research means.

The paper develops the argument put forward by Delamont and Hamilton in the first chapter. Systematic observation schedules can provide convenient data on certain aspects of classroom interaction; they can show, for example, that different teachers have different 'profiles', i.e. different overall characteristic ways of teaching. But such an observation technique can never show *why* teachers differ on such measures. Such questions are, by definition, beyond the scope of the method.

Delamont argues that to answer such questions requires data on teachers' styles of self-presentation, i.e. on the messages which are conveyed by their 'personal front' (to use Goffman's term) and by their classroom settings. To disentangle such individual characteristics necessarily requires research methods which allow categories and concepts to emerge *during* the research. (The categories of a systematic observation schedule are *pre*-specified and unchangeable).

Delamont begins therefore by presenting systematic observation data on the teachers, but then argues for supplementing these data by data collected by 'anthropological' techniques: long-term unstructured observation plus formal and informal interviewing. Systematic data thus form a quantifiable basis which can be filled out and strengthened by qualitative data of different kinds.

Delamont's work is also useful in providing descriptive information on a type of institution which has very rarely been observed in detail: a private girls' school. Educational research has, paradoxically, failed to provide even basic ethnographic descriptions of the range of classroom settings in British schools. On this theme, contrast the radically different contexts experienced by the girls studied by Delamont and Furlong.

M.S.

In this collection of papers we are all concerned with what happens in classrooms: within the four walls that normally enclose the teacher's private domain. For a variety of reasons, outlined in Chapter 1, we all believe that this invasion of the teacher's traditional privacy is a necessary step towards meaningful descriptions and analyses of teaching and learning. In this paper I examine some of the effects of the individual teacher's 'personality', and of the subject matter being taught, upon classroom interaction. I argue that these are among the key elements in the dynamic process of classroom interaction and that they cannot, because of their individualistic nature, be tapped by any of the orthodox methods of educational research. New methods of studying them must be found. In particular I examine the use of one systematic observation technique[1] and its place in the ethnography of the classroom.

The main part of the paper falls into two sections. The first deals with this observation technique, its strengths, weaknesses and limitations, and presents some general findings from a sample of teachers. The second section is an intensive study of four teachers, using a variety of unstructured observational material. The rest of this introductory statement sets out the general research strategy, and describes the school where the main research was done.

It is almost a truism that despite all the features common to all classroom situations, the relationship between an individual teacher and a particular class is a unique one.[2] Individual schools may also generate their own characteristics and subcultures that have pervasive effects within the classroom. This paper deals with one very specific aspect of classroom life — the differences between teachers as individuals — and with a rather more general aspect — the effects of the subject matter being taught.

To study either of these aspects successfully it is necessary to 'filter out' the more general factors and to focus on the more specific features. This 'filtering out' is often a difficult process. In many British schools the individual and personal determinants of the classroom situation are swamped by such overriding problems as rapid turnover of teaching staff and a wide disparity between the outlook and values of the staff and their pupils. In a school serving mainly custodial functions much time will be spent in disciplinary matters, and it would be difficult to concentrate on systematic variations between subjects, or on the characteristics of the teachers other than their ability as disciplinarians. Both Hargreaves (1967) and Lacey (1970) found that social class and streaming were such predominant factors in the social relations within the schools studied that individual differences became insignificant. To avoid these problems I deliberately chose a school, St. Luke's, in which there was full scope for examining individual variations.

St. Luke's School

There were three main reasons why St. Luke's was ideally suited for a study of small, subtle variations — its history, its intake and its internal organization. The school was founded a century ago, by feminist pioneers, and has a long distinguished record as a girls' public school of the traditional kind'.[3] The girls who attend St. Luke's are all from the professional and managerial classes and are bright enough to have passed a stiff entrance examination.[4] The internal organization of the school avoids both the polarization commonly produced by rigid streaming (by teaching in flexible 'sets') and the divisions associated with narrow subject specialization (by giving all the pupils a broad, basic curriculum).[5]

The joint effects of the history of the school and the type of pupil at St. Luke's mean that the atmosphere, though highly academic, is relaxed. The pupils share with the teachers, and their parents, similar ideas about what the school is trying to achieve, and agree that those goals are worthwhile.[6] Some girls are very academically motivated, others less so, but all are prepared to work diligently; disciplinary rules are internalized and lessons are devoted to scholastic matters. Thus relieved of order maintenance problems or of generating interest in bored or antagonistic pupils, the teachers are free to teach their subjects and to organize their material as they see fit (within the syllabus laid down for public examinations).

The broadly based curriculum and flexible 'sets' mean that the girls are not rigidly separated into arts and science specialists or into 'A' or 'B' streamers, but mix freely. As a result, the informal friendship group or cliques which exist are not mutually hostile, as are those described by Hargreaves and Lacey. Instead, all the girls in each age-group are friendly and form small groups on the basis of common hobbies or interests, rather than polarizing into hostile subcultures.[7]

In short, St. Luke's is a very uniform school. The girls, clothed identically, all with similar home backgrounds, have similar outlooks on the school. They are taught all their major subjects by highly qualified women,[8] nearly always in the same situation: seated in rows in a classroom facing the front while one person talks and the rest listen. Within this framework it is possible to investigate the variations between subjects and between the lessons of different teachers which would not be visible in a school which did not exhibit this regularity. In the following section one way of discovering these variations is discussed.

FIAC DATA ON THE CLASSROOM

In this section, data collected in the classroom using Flanders' Interaction Analysis Categories (FIAC) are presented within a critical framework. Chapter 1 of this book argued the merits and demerits of such systems in general terms — here a specific case study is discussed.

As part of a wider study of pupil behaviour and attitudes in different classroom contexts, I undertook eight weeks' fieldwork at St. Luke's. Systematic observation of classrooms was undertaken using Flanders' categories (as shown in Figure 1, Chapter1); these data were embedded in 'anthropological' observation and interviews of teachers and pupils. The relationships between the two types of data were of theoretical and methodological interest to me. In addition, both aid the understanding of classroom life at St. Luke's.

As Hamilton and I have argued in Chapter 1, the origins and history of systematic observation research in classrooms have resulted in certain assumptions being implicitly embodied in the techniques. The major aim of much of the work done with systematic techniques has been to produce immediately useful, *practical* results, rather than to do 'pure' research. The researchers are particularly interested in improving 'teacher effectiveness' and the use of observation methods in teacher training. (See, for example, Biddle and Ellena (1964), Flanders (1970) and Wragg (1971)). This has two main consequences that concern us here: the desire to improve teaching *within* the *status quo* of the traditional classroom, rather than to question its basic premises, and the aim of establishing 'norms' for teacher behaviour rather than of looking at each teacher as an individual.

Flanders's system examined

An examination of ten categories making up FIAC (shown in Figure 1, Chapter 1) reveals certain assumptions about classroom interaction which underlie them, some of which are made explicit by Flanders himself while others, of equal importance, have remained implicit. The assumptions made explicit by Flanders include two points which need mentioning here. First, the system is designed for classifying *interaction* — which is here defined as *public* talk involving more than one person. Thus FIAC is not intended to suit lessons where one person reads aloud or lectures the whole time, or classes where the pupils do a lot of silent seat-work or practical work singly or in groups and where public talk is limited. Obviously, FIAC can be used to classify the public talk which does occur in such lessons, but the picture which is produced is necessarily limited. I have used the FIAC system in Science lessons, and during Needlework, Art and P.E. lessons, and it can be used in modern primary classes, but these situations are probably better served by systems designed to cope with the mixture of public and private interaction.

The second set of assumptions is related to the concentration on teacher-talk in the design of the categories. Flanders does discuss the explicit reasons for this bias: he explains that FIAC is intended as a method for studying teaching styles, that research has shown teacher-talk to be the predominant element in classroom interaction and that, 'since the teacher has more authority than any pupil', his communications are the 'most potent single factor' in establishing the tone of the interaction[9] (Flanders, 1970, pp. 35–36).

The first two points are unexceptionable, but the third carries a load of implicit meaning, which can best be understood by reference to the psychological background of the studies, as discussed in Chapter 1. We can see why the FIAC system places such stress on the 'emotional climate' of the lesson — on whether the pupil's ideas and feelings are accepted or rejected by the teacher. In essence, Flanders believes that schoolchildren and students will learn more, and be happier, if their teachers behave 'democratically' or 'integratively'.

FIAC data

These, then, are some of the assumptions which underlie the systematic technique used in this research; now to describe how it is used and how the data are analysed. FIAC is a time-sampling system; that is, the observer classifies the interaction into one of the ten categories at regular intervals, rather than waiting for specific events to occur.[10] At the end of a lesson the observer has a string of numbers, representing the categories into which the behaviour was classified: these form the raw data base for analysis. These data can be manipulated in a variety of ways, by hand, or via sophisticated computer programs, and provide information on gross and minute aspects of the coded behaviour. Flanders has devoted much of a large book (Flanders, 1970) to the possibilities of handling FIAC data, and an excursion into data handling here would be superfluous. In this paper it is sufficient to select the indices of comparison between teachers which I have found most useful.

Before studying the FIAC data on the four teachers who are the main focus of this paper, it is necessary to relate their FIAC 'profiles' to those of a larger number of teachers. This 'embedding' will show whether the four are within the range of their colleagues' profiles and can be considered as 'ordinary' teachers. I have collected data on thirty teachers in Scottish girls' schools. Here, eighteen academic staff are used, from St. Luke's and one other school, the Laurels, which was in the same city, had an intake similar in terms of class and I.Q., and similar staff and curricula.

In both schools I collected FIAC data in my first few weeks in the field, before I knew the pupils by name and the teachers as individual personalities. For the first period of the fieldwork in any school then, I sat and coded interaction like an automaton, without using the unstructured methods and interviews to 'corrupt' the ratings.[11] This follows Flanders's own advice (1970, p. 35): 'The trained observer acts like an automatic device, albeit highly discriminating, and codes without hesitation at the instant an event is recognized'.

Results

The simplest method of comparing teachers using FIAC is to calculate what percentage of the interaction is spent in teacher-talk (TT), pupil-talk (PT) and in silence or confusion (SC). Table 1 shows the teachers ranked in descending order of percentage teacher-talk, with Flanders's figures for the 'average teacher' included for reference.[12]

An examination of Table 1 shows first that my sample of teachers are distributed approximately equally on both sides of Flanders's 'average', and show therefore a reasonable cross-section of 'normal' teaching behaviours. A second feature of the table is the tendency for teachers of similar subjects to cluster together.

Table 1. Percentage of teacher-talk recorded for eighteen Scottish teachers

Rank order	Teacher*	TT (%)
1	History A	82·2
2	Geography B	81·7
3	History B	80·3
4	Biology A	79·6
5	English B	78·1
6	Physics A	76·7
7	Chemistry A	73·2
8	Physics C	72·8
9	Chemistry B	71·6
10	Flanders's average	68·0
11	Geography A	66·5
12	Maths A	64·8
13	Latin A	62·6
14	Maths B	62·3
15	French C	62·0
16	English A	61·2
17	Biology C	60·1
18	French B	57·7
19	Latin B	50·0

* 'A' indicates teacher of top set at St. Luke's.
'B' indicates teacher of lower set at St. Luke's.
'C' indicates teacher from The Laurels.

Flanders has suggested that the age and sex of the teacher, the subject matter, and the age and maturity of the pupils, are all important influences upon the pattern of interaction revealed by FIAC. Here the subject matter can be seen to influence the percentage of the interaction time spent in teacher-talk. (Many of the features mentioned by Flanders were, of course, controlled in this study, where both teachers and pupils were female and where the same pupils were followed throughout the study). The History and Geography staff talk the most, followed by the Science teachers, while the Language staff have below-average percentages.

Of course this is not a perfect pattern — Geography A and Biology C are markedly different from their subject colleagues, but otherwise the 'fit' is remarkable. The cases of Maths and English are interesting. The two Maths teachers are close to each other but they do not 'belong' with the Science teachers — instead they seem to belong with the linguists, on this particular measure at least. The English teachers are clearly distinct from each other, English A has a score which makes her appear to be teaching a language, while English B's position places her firmly with the History and Science staff. Thus FIAC counts in the lessons have shown an interesting fact about Maths teaching at St. Luke's, and spotlighted a clear difference between the two English staff.

The overall distribution of subjects in Table 1 is not unexpected.

Teachers of both modern and classical languages are partly concerned that their pupils should speak the language, as well as using written work to test their comprehension, and the analysis of language lessons therefore shows that the teacher speaks rather less, and the pupils rather more, than in most other classes (cf. Flanders, 1970; Wragg, 1972). The predominance of teacher-talk in three of the History and Geography lessons may well be due to the heavily factual nature of the 'O' grade syllabuses, leading the staff to concentrate on covering the subject matter by lecturing, rather than by discussion or question-and-answer sessions. The Science lessons, which show almost as high a proportion of teacher-talk, occupy an inter- mediate position between History and the languages. They also reveal one of the inherent limitations of using FIAC in certain types of classroom, mentioned earlier in this section. The majority of the Science teachers appear to be talking for approximately three-quarters of the lesson. In fact this means they talk for three-quarters of the time *devoted to public interaction.* Unlike most academic subjects at St. Luke's, much of any Science lesson is practical work, where private interaction is usual.[13] The FIAC data show us that the teachers talk a good deal in the public periods of the lessons. We need other methods to find out what the rest of the lesson is like.

However, before discussing other methods, I examine some of the more detailed analyses possible with FIAC data. In his early work, Flanders made extensive use of the distinction between teachers whose influence over their classes was *indirect*, that is, based on praise, acceptance and use of the pupils' ideas, and those whose style was more *directive*, based on lecturing, directions and criticism. (See Flanders, 1964, 1965). Since then he has developed a variety of comparative ratios of finer discrimina- tion; and it is three of these which I use here. The Teacher Response Ratio (TRR) compares the proportions of teacher-responses to pupil-talk which are accepting and rejecting; the Teacher Question Ratio (TQR) compares the amount of questioning and lecturing in the teacher's speech; and the Pupil Initiation Ratio (PIR) concerns the relative proportions of pupil-talk which is spontaneous as against solicited.[14]

Table 2 shows the same teachers ranked according to their scores on the three ratios. In column one, the top teacher has the highest proportion of accepting reactions to pupil contributions: in column two, the highest ratio questions to lecturing; in column three, the highest proportion of spontaneous pupil-talk to solicited pupil-talk.

A superficial examination of the three rank orders shown in Table 2 gives one the impression of chaos. The subject taught is no longer the guiding principle, and no other organizing feature is apparent. Faced with such data the researcher interested in the *norms* of teacher behaviour is in difficulties. Not so the social scientist who studies individual classroom regimes — for her the anomalies revealed by Table 2 are the ideal starting point for an investigation of unique characteristics. Any teacher, or pair of teachers, can be studied in great detail, and attempts made to understand

Table 2. Rank orders of eighteen Scottish teachers on three FIAC
ratios: Teacher Response, Teacher
Questions and Pupil Initiation

Rank	TRR	TQR	PIR
1	History B	Latin B	Physics A
2	Geography B	French B	History B
3	English A	French C	Biology A
4	Biology A	Chemistry A	Geography B
5	Maths A	English A	History A
6	Physics A	Maths A	Geography A
7	History A	Chemistry B	Chemistry B
8	French B	History B	Biology C
9	Geography A	Geography B	English A
10	French C	Biology C	Maths A
11	Chemistry B	History A	Maths B
12	Chemistry A	English B	English B
13	Physics C	Geography A	French B
14	English B	Physics C	Physics C
15	Latin A	Latin A	Chemistry A
16	Latin B	Physics A	Latin B
17	Biology C	Maths B	Latin A
18	Maths B	Biology A	French C

the underlying reasons for their place in the FIAC rankings. We might
ask why the two Maths teachers are so similar in the proportions of pupil
initiation they receive, yet so different in the proportions of questioning
and acceptance of student ideas in their speech. Alternatively, we might
investigate why History B and Geography B ranked higher on all the ratios
than the 'A' set teachers of the same subjects. Many other anomalies could
be investigated.

In this paper I concentrate on four teachers: the two Latin staff and
two scientists, Physics A and Biology A. Table 2 shows that the two Latin
teachers — whom we will call Miss Iliad (Latin A) and Miss Odyssey
(Latin B) — are similar in the proportions of acceptance in their reactions
to pupil-talk and in the low proportions of pupil initiated speech they
receive, but very different in the proportion of questioning to lecturing
in their speech.

I choose the two Science teachers, Physics A (Mrs. Cavendish) and
Biology A (Mrs. Linnaeus) for study, not because they differ from each
other, but because they are so unlike the other scientists on all counts.
Table 2 shows that Mrs. Cavendish and Mrs. Linnaeus have lower proportions of questioning to lecturing and higher proportions of pupil initiation
than their subject colleagues. The most outstanding difference between
them and the other scientists is shown in the first column, where Mrs.
Cavendish and Mrs. Linnaeus are in the top half of the list — that is, they
accept and use a high proportion of pupil contributions — while all the
other Science staff are in the lower half of the rank order.

Thus, the two Science teachers discussed in depth in the following section are interesting because they differ markedly from their subject colleagues; the two Latin teachers arouse our interest because they appear so similar in two respects yet so different from each other in the third.

Both types of question are beyond the scope of the FIAC system to answer. It would be possible to examine the data and discover exactly *how* each of the four structured their lessons in minute detail, but this would only provide further evidence about the *form* the differences take. To understand *why* the FIAC scores look so different it is necessary to turn to other kinds of data.

Information is needed here about the less quantifiable aspects of the teachers' style and self-presentation, on the nature of the syllabus and the teachers' attitudes to it, and on the pupils' interpretations of the teachers' intentions and their feelings about them. These data are, of necessity, individualistic and idiosyncratic; they cannot be collected with systematic, predetermined schedules; they demand unstructured methods, where the observer can pick up the important features in each teaching situation whether or not they are the same in each case. In other words, unstructured observation is essential, and, to be confident that one has picked up the aspects of a situation which are important to the participants, both formal and informal interviews are necessary.

Obviously data of this type, collected by unstructured observation, have several drawbacks, including a tendency to become unwieldy. (These drawbacks are discussed at length in McCall and Simmons (1969) and in the work of Becker and his coworkers (1961, 1968)). To mitigate the unwieldiness, some unifying themes have been selected to structure the data. These themes *crystallize* the differences between the four teachers, as well as illuminating the interesting questions raised by the numerical analysis of classroom behaviour. The themes chosen are those which appeared most frequently in both formal and informal conversation with the girls: that is, the factors which were important in characterizing each teacher's individuality for the pupils and those which seemed particularly illuminating to the observer during the fieldwork period.

The following section deals with some of these themes in relation to the four teachers already mentioned: the Physics teacher, Mrs. Cavendish, the Biology teacher, Mrs. Linnaeus, and two Latin teachers, Miss Iliad and Miss Odyssey.

THEMES IN TEACHER INDIVIDUALITY

In this section four main themes are used to organize the presentation of the teachers as individuals: the physical setting they created, their personal appearance, their pupils' opinions of them and extracts of dialogue from lessons. The first two perspectives are closely related, although the information about the physical settings is drawn from my field-notes, while that on personal appearance is largely drawn from conversations with the pupils. The third perspective comes from interviews with the girls: the fourth, from detailed notes taken in the classroom.

Setting and personal front

The first two themes can best be explained using ideas drawn from Goffman's (1959) parallels between everyday behaviour and dramatic performance. There Goffman included the ideas of 'setting' and 'personal front' which incorporate my first two themes in a way which is particularly relevant to the study of teachers. Goffman maintains that the physical setting in which a performance takes place is an essential element in defining the situation for the observers of an act. He explains his use of the term as follows:

> First, there is the 'setting', involving furniture, decor, physical layout, and other background items which supply the scenery and stage props for the spate of human action played out before, within, or upon it. A setting tends to stay put, geographically speaking, so that those who would use a particular setting as part of their performance cannot begin their act until they have brought themselves to the appropriate place and must terminate their performance when they leave it. (p. 22)

Goffman goes on to relate the physical setting to his notion of 'personal front' as follows:

> If we take the term 'setting' to refer to the scenic parts of expressive equipment, one may take the term 'personal front' to refer to the other items of expressive equipment, the items that we most intimately identify with the performer himself and that we naturally expect will follow the performer wherever he goes. As part of the personal front we may include: insignia of office or rank; clothing; sex, age, and racial characteristics; size and looks; posture; speech patterns; facial expressions; bodily gestures; and the like. (p. 24)

The internal organization of St. Luke's makes the concept of the physical setting particularly appropriate. There, established teachers[15] have their own rooms, to which all their different classes come. This room becomes the teacher's own territory, a fixed physical setting where she can arrange her equipment and add her own embellishments to the basic school furniture and fittings. This setting provides a stable, personal background for her teaching performance. In contrast, the new, or part-time, teacher has to teach all her classes in other people's rooms, performing each time against someone else's setting, thus heightening her sense of newness, impermanence or 'marginality'.

The appropriateness of the concept at St. Luke's, and its use as an indication of differences in teaching performance between individuals, was apparent from the early days of my fieldwork. The particular difference between Miss Iliad and Miss Odyssey, the proportion of questioning to lecturing, is not directly related to their physical settings, yet these give some clues to it. However, setting does reveal a key element in the pattern of differences between Mrs. Linnaeus and Mrs. Cavendish and their Science colleagues. The relative importance of setting in the explanation of differences in teaching behaviour changes from one group of teachers to another.

The personal fronts displayed by the staff at St. Luke's form the staple ingredients of pupils' discussion of the teachers as individuals. Several of the characteristics listed by Goffman are obviously irrelevant: all the staff are of similar sex and race and no insignia of office or rank are worn by any of the teaching staff. The characteristics considered important by the girls are age, marital status, speech patterns and gestures and, most important, clothing. All the clothes-consciousness of the adolescent girl in a school with a uniform is concentrated on the styles of dress and general appearance of the teachers. In contrast to the physical setting, the personal front 'put on' by Miss Iliad and Miss Odyssey reveals a good deal about the differences in their teaching behaviour, while that of the scientists is less helpful. The two themes together are particularly illuminating for both sets of questions about teaching styles.

The two Latin staff

If we consider the physical settings in which the two Latin staff taught, the most noticeable fact is Miss Odyssey's lack of a fixed base. She is only in her second term at St. Luke's and therefore has to move all round the building. In fact, each of the five lessons per week with my sample took place in a different room, none of them even belonging to other language specialists. Miss Odyssey habitually arrives at the venue of her next lesson *with* the pupils, instead of being installed in the setting, ready to begin when they arrive — though this adds considerable strength to a teaching performance. The impression thus created — that Miss Odyssey is not a real, *permanent* member of the staff — is often heightened by admissions on her part that she does not know where her next lesson is due to take place and intends to rely on meeting the pupils in the corridor and following them to the appropriate room.

In complete contrast, Miss Iliad has a firmly fixed setting with a strong personal style. She has been at St. Luke's for twenty years and is the senior Classics teacher. Hers is the only class which is entered and left by silent files of pupils, rather than chattering groups. Miss Iliad is always there waiting for the girls to arrive. My fieldwork notes, taken during one of the first lessons I observed in her room, describe the room:

> Miss Iliad's room is in the extreme end of the North wing — it's very cold — there are a lot of windows, and I think the radiators are off. The pastel walls are bare — only a photo of the Parthenon frieze round the top of two walls, 3 framed pics. of classical sculptures. Notice boards have nothing but official notices — one or two charity posters.

Most classroom notice boards carry things put up by the pupils — such as their paintings, cuttings from magazines and, where their form mistress is sympathetic, pin-ups of pop stars or footballers. Many teachers add cuttings about their subject, prints and calendars of their own. Posters on metrication, decimalization and other such topics are also common. Miss Iliad's room is very impersonal.

From these small pieces of information about the settings we can deduce something about the teaching styles of these two different individuals. Miss Iliad's surroundings are clearly well-ordered, well-defined and traditional. Miss Odyssey has no fixed setting, and appears transitory, inefficient and ill-defined (particularly by being lost in the school buildings — a very unteacherlike activity). If we go on to consider their relative personal appearances, the contrast between the two staff is accentuated.

Miss Odyssey is always fashionably dressed, wearing the sort of clothes that the girls themselves might choose for everyday dress. In addition to her academic books and papers, she usually carries a shopping basket with her knitting in it — the knitting is even brought out at slack moments in lessons. The most noticeable symbol of her marginality is a large engagement ring (she duly left St. Luke's in the middle of the academic year to get married).[16] Her manner of conducting lessons is informal. She often gives work to be done by pairs of girls, or by the group, cooperatively, and allows informal chatter, both between girls and to her, on all topics which arise, whether related to Latin or not. Her posture and gestures reveal her informal attitude — she sits at the front in a relaxed, even 'sloppy', fashion or perches on the edge of pupils' desks.

Miss Iliad rarely sits down, conducting most of her lessons standing at the front of the class. When she does sit, she marks books industriously; she does not relax. She dresses in the classic tweeds common to the older staff at St. Luke's — in the sort of clothes the girls expect to find teachers wearing if they belong to the same generation as their mothers, or even their grandmothers. Latin lessons with Miss Iliad are formal; only one person speaks at a time, work is done orally or alone rather than cooperatively, tests and exercises are frequent, and everyone has to 'sit up and pay attention'.

An event which occurred at the beginning of one of Miss Odyssey's lessons is revealing about her relationship with her class. My field notes read as follows:

> Miss O arrives to find Monica selling me raffle tickets for a school charity. Monica unabashed, turned to her and piped up, *Will you buy a raffle ticket — Miss Delamont's just bought three.* Miss O laughed and did.

The only equivalent event involving Miss Iliad which came to my ears throughout my fieldwork was an incident described to me by Charmian: 'I once took her something in Greek I wanted translated and she positively beamed at me. A great occasion!' Charmian's very expression shows how unusual such informal contacts were.

In summary, the first two themes, the physical setting and the personal front, show clear differences between the two Latin staff. Miss Iliad is a formal traditionalist in dress and behaviour and gives a well-organized, precise performance. Miss Odyssey is an informal modernist, who gives an undefined, imprecise performance. (Not all older teachers give precise performances of course, nor all modern teachers woolly ones — several of the established staff at St. Luke's gave imprecise performances and several of the newly trained teachers had very clear-cut ones).

Before being able to understand exactly why they differ in one aspect of verbal teaching behaviour — questioning — two more themes are needed, but these first two have given a picture of two *individuals* in a way the FIAC data cannot. The second pair of themes bring the subject matter back to the forefront and explain the similarities and the differences in the speech patterns of the two individual teachers.

Subject matter and personal style

The information available about Miss Iliad and Miss Odyssey concerns their methods of teaching girls who had opted to take 'O' grade Latin in a year's time. Miss Iliad's group includes all the girls likely to take the subject beyond that level, Miss Odyssey's group those who are not. Both mistresses are covering similar grammar and translation passages and both are faced with the same problem of relative emphasis within the subject. Translation from Latin into English is a two-stage process; first, there must be a precise 'construe' of the Latin words, then a version must be produced in good, idiomatic English. These two stages demand very different types of thinking; the construe demands strictly logical, precise thought, the second stage demands fluent literacy. The same dilemma faces all translators, but is particularly associated with Latin scholarship. The paradoxical mixture of pedantry and literacy is a strong tradition in the subject.[17] The problem faces anyone concerned with the study of Latin, whether she is an eminent authority or a schoolgirl, and is particularly acute for the teacher, because she has to teach girls who have yet to gain the technical ability to translate accurately,without stifling their literacy. The decisions which different Latin teachers make about the relative stress to be placed on the two skills are among the most important distinguishing factors among individuals and strongly affect the pupils' perceptions of the nature of the subject.

The opinions expressed by the sample from St. Luke's about what Latin was, how they were taught and whether Miss Iliad and Miss Odyssey were 'good' — i.e. appropriate Latin teachers — are very revealing.[18] These perceptions (together with our fourth theme—extracts of dialogue) produce a rounded picture of the two mistresses which explains how and why their FIAC scores differed.

Pupil perceptions

The most noticeable point about the interview data on the two Latin teachers (apart from the fact that they are perceived very differently) is that, whereas Miss Iliad's class are in complete agreement about her, Miss Odyssey's group have a wide range of opinions about her. In other words, Miss Iliad, as one might expect from her self-presentation, has created a stable image of herself amongst her pupils, while Miss Odyssey, again as one might predict, has not. Miss Iliad is seen by all her class as 'a really good teacher' and 'someone who makes us work', 'frightening', 'cross', 'strict', 'efficient'. Every girl in the group produced all these descriptions, or close synonyms of them, spontaneously during an interview. When asked to expand, typical comments are as follows:

> She makes you learn very, very hard — I suppose it's good, she really gets you to learn it.

> She's quite efficient . . . about preps and things like that . . . and can keep order . . . in class, it's to do with being older, she's had more experience.

> She's . . . well, she didn't frighten . . . doesn't frighten me, but I think she does some people . . . she tends to get cross if you can't do something . . . She doesn't show favouritism . . . very formal.

> She's very . . . aahh . . . insists on conscientious learning and ahh . . . and you have to sit up in her classes and listen and you can't possibly do anything else like drawing . . . and when she's just being quiet and you know you ought to have remembered it, or heard it, and you weren't listening . . . it's so frightening . . . it's too awful for words . . . especially . . . and you can't remember the first person singular of amo if you're really frightened.

> She's especially well organized . . . keeps you working all the time . . . she doesn't let you stop for a minute . . . you don't keep looking at your watch for the end of the lesson . . . you don't have time . . . Feel that your parents are getting their money's worth anyway.

> She sticks to Classics and how you're doing. Rather shut in by Classics . . .

> Really have to work, do your work thoroughly, or she gets annoyed with you . . . you know where you stand . . . she's firm — but fair . . .

In these comments, a common view is being expressed. All the pupils have similar comments to make about Miss Iliad. Miss Odyssey's pupils have no such universal perception of their teacher. The only unanimous verdict about Miss Odyssey is: 'She's easily led astray'. There is no general agreement about her position on the common dimensions used to describe teachers — I was told that she was strict and easy-going, pleasant and unpleasant, efficient and inefficient, a good teacher and a bad one. Even close friends in the group do not agree about her. Some comments follow:

> She's easily led astray . . . quite enjoys it as long as it's not too obvious we're leading her . . . she's not afraid to make . . . to admit she doesn't know something — she's quite open about it . . . just toddles off to the library and looks it up in the dictionary.

> She'll wander off the subject. If you lead her on to another track she's quite happy to talk about it.

> She's not a good teacher . . . she can't get her subject across . . . she knows it, but . . . to a certain extent she's two-faced . . . at least not exactly . . . I like her . . . I didn't at first but I got to like her . . . she's so sort of reserved . . . she's not fond of working . . . she has other things on her mind — like marriage.

*She's unmarried . . . usually a married one has more understanding . . .
she's neither scatty nor well-organized — kind of in-between . . . I don't
know, she's funny — she acts as if she's taught for years.*

*Not like the older ones — you can waste as much time as you want
. . . I think she quite enjoys it too . . .*

She really get you at it . . .

She's quite cheery . . . and she makes me work . . .

The comments made about Miss Iliad are clear-cut. Everyone knows what
she is like and, though not exceptionally articulate, the quotations are easy
to follow. Those made about Miss Odyssey are muddled. All the girls are
telling me different things, and some of them seem very unsure what they
themselves think are her salient characteristics.

Classroom extracts

The fourth theme, extracts from lessons taught by the two teachers, makes
clear the source of these disparate perceptions and finally 'explains' the
FIAC data as well. The first extract comes from field notes taken in a
typical lesson of Miss Iliad's.[19] Language lessons were particularly easy to
take notes in. I adopted the simple expedient of ignoring all the speech
in the foreign language, thus giving me time to write down the parts of
the dialogue which took place in English. This extract comes from a point
some way into the lesson, when corrections were completed and the translation of a Latin passage had begun.

MISS I: (Tells the girl at the front of the left-hand row, Katherine,
            to translate the first sentence).

KATHERINE: (Reads out the Latin correctly. Then hesitates . . .) *The
            noble consul swore . . .* (She stops).

MISS I: *Take the verb next.*

KATHERINE: (Still does not speak).

MISS I: *It's part of* progredior — *Yes, Jill?*

JILL: *To advance or progress or go forward.*

MISS I: (Accepts that. Tells Evelyn to give the principal parts).

EVELYN: Progredior, progredi, progressus sum — *deponent verb.*

MISS I: *Yes. Finish the sentence. Selina.*

SELINA: *The noble consul swore to advance towards the captured
            city . . .* (pauses) . . . *and to relieve their allies.*

MISS I: (Accepts this. Tells Charmian to go on).

CHARMIAN: (Reads the sentence falteringly. Two errors. Corrected).

MISS I: *Right. Now translate it. Take the verb first. What case is* civibus?

CHARMIAN: *Ablative.*

MISS I: *Rubbish.* (Reprimands her. Selina volunteers).

SELINA: *It's dative — dependent on the verb.*

MISS I: (Accepts this. Reminds them of grammar rule). *Must remember verbs which take the dative. Which are they? Alexandra?*

ALEXANDRA: (Reels off the appropriate list).

MISS I: (Accepts this). *Now finish the sentence, Charmian.*

The extract is long enough to show a surprising amount about the interaction normal in Miss Iliad's class. She usually goes round the class asking for a sentence from each girl in turn, using voluntary contributions only to correct other girls' errors. Factual accuracy is at a premium and detailed attention to small points necessary. Miss Iliad is clearly in control and demands the pupils' contributions, which need very precise answers. A comparison between that extract from my notes and the following one from a lesson of Miss Odyssey's is interesting. This extract starts from much nearer the beginning of a lesson. Miss Odyssey rarely spent the early minutes going over homework — she merely returned it.

LORNA: *Can we finish that Latin crossword today?*

MISS O: *Not until we've finished that translation passage we started yesterday. If we have any time left . . .* (Silences pupil protests. Asks Nancy to start).

NANCY: *I wasn't sure of this bit. Is it 'The old man, knowing that he was about to die, called out to his son'?*

MISS O: (Quibbles over 'called *out*').

NANCY: *It is called* for

MISS O: (Accepts this. Asks Monica to continue).

MONICA: *Hearing of his father's illness, the son left the town and set out . . .* (pauses) *. . . towards his father's farm.*

MISS O: (Queries the translation 'hearing of his father's illness'. Asks for volunteered improvement).

LORNA: (Volunteers, without raising her hand). *I had, 'when he heard about his father's illness'.*

MISS O: (Accepts this as an improvement). *You could say, 'When he heard that his father was ill'.*

BELINDA: (Waving her hand — waits to be asked). *I had, when he heard that his father was sick unto death', would that do?* (Everyone laughs, including Miss Odyssey).

MISS O: (Suggests it is too 'theatrical' or 'biblical', but doesn't reject it as wrong).

Some differences are immediately apparent. Whereas Miss Iliad drills her Group, going round the class *demanding* an answer from each girl in turn, Miss Odyssey *asks* individuals to speak. In Miss Iliad's class volunteers are only used to correct other pupils' mistakes, while Miss Odyssey has girls putting forward their own interpretations of the sentence of their own free will. Both extracts show concern with the niceties of Latin–English translation, but the concern in Miss Odyssey's class is expressed more in terms of the idiomatic 'feel' of the English than as a matter of factual incorrectness. Miss Odyssey's interaction is generally less formal, and less ritualized than Miss Iliad's.

The greater informality of Miss Odyssey's relationship with her pupils was vividly translated later in that lesson. All the girls were stuck the same clue in the crossword and it was not a word Miss Odyssey knew 'offhand' either. Lorna suggested that she should 'go and look it up in the library' and Nancy that she should 'ask Miss Iliad — *she's* bound to know'. Both suggestions were greeted by Miss Odyssey with laughter.

In contrast, Miss Iliad's class sometimes gave the impression of behaving like a well-drilled army. Every time a new word occurred in a passage every girl automatically drew out a vocabulary book and entered the word, without any explicit instruction or acknowledgement.

In summary, I would suggest that the main difference between Miss Iliad and Miss Odyssey is that Miss Iliad concentrated more on grammatical accuracy with her pre- 'O' grade classes, and left encouraging the idiomatic aspects until later in their school careers, while Miss Odyssey, who was newly trained, was more concerned with a balance right from the beginning.[20]

The differences between the two teachers' FIAC profiles is now clear. Both teachers accept the pupil responses — they use the translations or grammar and praise correct answers. Latin, under the present syllabuses, is not a subject where much affective comment is generated at this level,[21] and so neither teacher has much 'pupil feeling' to accept or reject. Thus it is not surprising that their ratios of accepting and rejecting reactions are similar. Neither mistress leaves much scope for pupil initiation — most pupil contributions are responses to questions and are within well-defined limits, so it is not surprising that their pupil-initiation ratios are similar. However, Miss Iliad 'drills' her class in such a way that most of her speech is in the form of definite statements or commands which the girls obey, while Miss Odyssey phrases most of her contributions in the form of questions, which the girls answer. Hence the big difference between them which FIAC revealed — the proportion of questioning to lecturing — is an indication of a whole attitude to the teaching of Latin. The high ratio of questioning to lecturing which characterizes Miss Odyssey is closely related to her discursive, idiomatic 'angle' on her subject[22] and to her marginality and undefined self-presentation. The low proportion of questioning which characterizes Miss Iliad's teaching is equally due to her emphasis on factual accuracy and 'drill and practice' and her stable, well-defined self-presentation. Thus the four themes come together, to amplify, explain and humanize the systematic data on the two Latin teachers, who are similar in many ways because they both teach the same syllabus — yet who differ profoundly in their philosophies of teaching their subject.

The two Science staff and their colleagues

A different question was raised by the FIAC data on the Science staff. I wondered why two of the Science mistresses, Mrs. Linnaeus (Biology A) and Mrs. Cavendish (Physics A), were so unlike their subject colleagues on all the FIAC ratios considered.[23] These two have lower proportions of questioning, higher proportions of pupil-initiation and vastly greater proportions of use and acceptance of pupil contributions than the other scientists. Again the four themes: physical setting, personal front, pupils' opinions and extracts from lessons — all themes concerning the teacher as an individual — together with information on the nature of the curricula, will be used to explain the anomalies in the systematic data.

The academic content of the Science syllabuses is very different from that of Latin, particularly since the introduction of the new S.C.E. curricula, with their emphasis on experimental method, guided discovery, and other 'Nuffield-type' changes in the learning patterns desired. (See Hamilton's paper, in this volume). This has consequences for the school's organization of the teaching and for the structure of the lessons. For example, Science lessons at St. Luke's occupy two forty-minute periods together, to allow sufficient time for the practical work; whereas other academic subjects have only single periods at a time. The experimental, practical basis of the subject also means that all Science lessons have to take place in a laboratory — no Science teacher ever finds herself teaching in a totally inappropriate setting as Miss Odyssey has to.

Physical setting

All the Science staff I studied at both schools have their own labs; that is, each individual has a fixed physical setting for her performance. Although all the labs are traditional in their basic structure — that is, they all have benches and stools, sinks and gas taps, and cupboards full of equipment — some staff have impressed their personal styles, and their speciality, upon the basic design.

In particular, the Biology teacher, Mrs. Linnaeus, has her lab in a new wing of the school, stamped firmly with her personality and speciality. The lab is light and airy, with long benches for writing and side benches for doing experiments. The side benches also carry a range of display cases and bits of apparatus: stick insects, tropical fish, frog spawn and mounted Victorian birds and mammals jostle for space with dozens of pot-plants and experiments 'in progress'. On the notice boards Mrs. Linnaeus has pinned cuttings from the 'serious' Sunday papers on biological topics: evolution, pollution, animal behaviour and the brain.

Mrs. Cavendish's lab, though equally personal, is very different. In the older part of the building, it is small, cramped, dark and slightly stuffy. The benches are small, yet have to be used for practical work and writing. The side benches are packed solid with equipment, but here it is all electrical and mechanical: wires, plugs, voltmeters, balances, trolley-boards and ticker-tape machines. The electrical wires and plugs and other small items of apparatus are all stored in old chocolate boxes, a strangely domestic touch.

In contrast to these highly characteristic rooms, the other Science staff have very impersonal labs, with nothing on the walls but tables of atomic weights, and with all the apparatus tidily in cupboards. Mrs. Linnaeus and Mrs. Cavendish are unusual in that, despite the impersonal, scientific nature of their basic room structures, each has etched an idiosyncratic, personal style upon that structure. In Mrs. Linnaeus's room everything from the sunshine to the notice boards seems to emphasize *life*; in Mrs. Cavendish's the electrical and technical have been tamed and made homely by their arrangement and storage.

Personal front

These, then, are their distinctive physical settings. In terms of our second theme, the personal front, the two teachers are also different from their colleagues. Both Mrs. Cavendish and Mrs. Linnaeus are, or have been, married, and are known to have teenage children. All the other scientists are single, except the youngest (Chemistry A) who got married during my fieldwork period though, unlike Miss Odyssey, she did not leave St. Luke's in consequence.[24] Mrs. Linnaeus and Mrs. Cavendish are therefore perceived as 'mothers' as well as teachers, which none of their colleagues could be.[25]

In matters of dress, only Mrs. Cavendish appears unusual, as Mrs. Linnaeus wears very similar clothes to those chosen by her colleagues. Mrs. Cavendish, as well as being very plump, in a subject area staffed by very thin women, dresses in a more casual manner and chooses much brighter, more vividly coloured clothes than the other staff of her age. She also wears her lab coat throughout the school, even sitting through the lunch hour in it, which no-one else does. In this way she brings her Science (albeit a 'clean' one in that her coat is rarely stained with chemicals, vegetable dyes or blood, the usual pollutants) out into the school. Thus she domesticates her science by taking homely things into the lab and by bringing the lab out into the rest of the school.

The Science department is entirely staffed by well-established teachers who have been there for at least five years. All of them have evolved settled personae and performances, and the nature of the subject matter and emphasis of the syllabuses means that all Science lessons have a basic, structural similarity. In general, a lesson in Physics, Chemistry or Biology begins with a short résumé of the previous session's work followed by a brief discussion of the problems to be tackled in that day's class and how the relevant experiments are to be done. Then, forty to sixty minutes are spent in practical work, usually done by the girls working in small groups but occasionally by the teacher. Classes end with public discussion of results and the associated theory, during which the girls tidy up and write about the experiments. Within this basic structure considerable variety is apparent between the various presentations of self and subject given by the different teachers.

As we might expect from their FIAC profiles, Mrs. Cavendish and Mrs. Linnaeus differ from the 'normal' pattern of Science teaching at that level, in that type of school.[26] All the other Science staff studied keep their lessons moving along at a brisk pace and obviously 'stage-manage' the experimental work in a no-nonsense fashion. Some, like the two Chemistry staff at St. Luke's and Physics C, rely heavily on duplicated worksheets to structure their classes, while others, like Biology C, put 'guide-lines' and 'timetables' on the blackboard. All the others give an impression of obvious efficiency, much pre-structuring, and control over events. Neither Mrs. Linnaeus nor Mrs. Cavendish conducts her lessons like that at all; each has an approach of her own.

The other Science staff I observed are brisk; they move rapidly about the lab, speak quickly, rattle off instructions, 'drill' their classes in the basic facts and frequently urge speed to their pupils. Mrs. Linnaeus always acts as if she and her class have plenty of time; she drifts round the lab, pausing frequently to chat informally with girls, moves and speaks slowly, rarely tests and never drills them. She never seems to hurry or be flustered. During my fieldwork the class were covering photosynthesis, but she often stopped to discuss other topics which arose — on one occasion some rats being dissected by the sixth form which were in the lab, on another her son's gerbils, which she had brought to school for a younger class to study.

In contrast to this smooth, languid mood, Mrs. Cavendish's lessons appear rushed and disorganized. The girls are often unsure about which experiments they are doing and ask an endless stream of questions about procedure. Practical work sometimes overruns, clearing-up has to be hurried, and no discussion of results is possible until the next lesson. Mrs. Cavendish is always bustling round the room, alternately joking with the girls and yelling instructions over the noise. If the normal pattern is brisk, stage-managed discovery, Mrs. Cavendish's classes seem abnormally chaotic. She never tests or drills the group and rarely gives them any coherent information about the experimental work. Her contributions to the lesson are mainly shouts for 'order' and explanations of the mathematical and theoretical aspects of the subject.

In summary, the first two themes, the physical setting and the personal front, show that the two Science staff who have 'peculiar' FIAC profiles are also unlike their colleagues in other ways. Whereas the two Latin teachers were shown to vary in the degree to which they were established at St. Luke's, here the differences are more matters of personal choice of style among experienced, well-qualified teachers.

We have a picture of a group of unmarried, unmotherly Science teachers, who inhabit impersonal settings and run their teaching performances efficiently against that background. In contrast we have two teachers who have chosen deliberately to diverge from that pattern.[27] Both have created very personal settings. Both stand aside and let their lessons develop; one giving an impression of disinterested tolerance, the other of uncontrollable muddle. The introduction of the next two themes, the pupils' opinions and extracts from lessons, show exactly how these two unusual teachers interacted in different ways from their colleagues.[28]

Pupil views of Science

Girls taught by Mrs. Linnaeus and Mrs. Cavendish produced unusually detailed comments on those subjects and how they are taught. It seems that the abnormal self-presentations and teaching strategies of these staff have led the pupils to think about the nature of the subject matter and how it could be put across, in far more depth than they habitually would. Because these classes are peculiar, the girls do not assume that they or I could take them for granted — instead they made explicit to me that new reactions were necessary. This is precisely the result which both Mrs. Linnaeus and Mrs. Cavendish hoped to achieve.

Both women told me privately that they were trying to change their pupils' 'attitudes of thought' towards Science. Both are explicitly attempting to change the girls' work-styles, because of the new syllabuses, and so both consciously teach in a way that rewarded rather different pupil behaviours from those which the class had grown to expect in Science lessons. For example, in conversation one day Mrs. Linnaeus told me she had had to 'wean' her classes away from dictated notes and experiments copied from the board. She said that the first classes to face the new syllabus, who were aged seventeen at the time of my study, had been particular unhappy about her new emphasis, while later groups had found it easier to make the shift.[29]

The two mistresses have not, however, been equally successful in convincing the girls of the correctness of their new approaches. Mrs. Linnaeus's methods are generally considered to be effective and acceptable, if 'odd', while Mrs. Cavendish is seen as failing to achieve her own aims. A few comments from pupils will illustrate the point. First a quote from one girl, Philippa, who told me that Mrs. Linnaeus taught 'in a roundabout way'. I asked her to explain what she meant by this and she went on:

PHILIPPA: *Well she'll say 'do this and then we'll work out a conclusion to it' and she'll explain why this is that — and you finally get — you don't realize quite why you're doing it, and then you suddenly see why, and all the experiments make sense*

> *It really makes you think for yourself — and then . . .*
> *apparently the 'O' grade paper really . . . there's nothing*
> *you've actually done before, and . . . it's completely under-*
> *standing. She makes you make up your own notes . . .*

ME: *Do you mind making your own notes?*

PHILIPPA: *Well it's more difficult to make up your own, but I can see*
it may be a help later because I sort of remember them
better when I read them through — I remember them much
better if I've made them myself — but you can't be sure
if you've done anything wrong. She never really corrects
them . . . you might have something wrong and then . . .
learn it wrong.

This characterization was produced by all the girls Mrs. Linnaeus teaches, though not always in such detail, nor with as much 'balance'. Alexandra told me that Mrs. Linnaeus 'didn't give us much help — she should give us more help', and Monica that 'she doesn't seem very interested in *teaching* us'. The process of adjustment to a different set of teaching strategies was described by Henrietta:

> *I think Mrs. Linnaeus . . . last year when we first had her I couldn't stand*
> *it — but this year . . . it's made me remember things we've done. If she'd*
> *spoon-fed us we'd be learning things we've done but it wouldn't mean*
> *we'd understand it. If I understand something . . . It means I don't have*
> *to learn it — and I wouldn't voluntarily learn any fact.*

Mrs. Linnaeus teaches a large, mixed-ability group, which included some of the most and the least able girls in my sample. All the girls agree about the way in which she teaches, but there is a discrepancy between their other perceptions of her. The brighter girls see her as more 'friendly', 'helpful' and 'easy-going', the less bright as more 'aloof', 'unhelpful' and 'stricter'. The negative perceptions of Mrs. Linnaeus all come from the members of one clique; their main complaint is that she was 'only interested in the bright ones' or 'in those who can get the experiments to work'. They do not say that Mrs. Linnaeus is anything but a good teacher, merely that she is personally cool towards them.

Mrs. Cavendish teaches only twenty girls, all of whom are potential university entrants.[30] The one description which they all apply to her is 'muddling'. In addition, she is seen as 'disorganized', 'friendly', 'someone you can be at ease with', 'unable to explain things', 'cheerful', 'experienced' and 'not shut in'. In summary they feel she is a nice, clever person who is *unable* to teach. This is the usual form that condemnation of a teacher takes, 'she knows her stuff but she can't get it across'. It is very rare for a girl to suggest that the teacher does not know her subject (though one girl said of one teacher outside this sample 'she knows her facts, but she's not what I call an intellectual'). The girls vary in the extent to which they found Mrs. Cavendish's teaching manageable. Rosalind was very worried by it:

ROSALIND: *I don't think she's any good — she doesn't give any notes, and when she explains things she goes so fast that you can't really follow, and if you ask her to explain again she just says exactly the same thing — and . . . I mean that doesn't really help.*

ME: *Does anyone find her easy to learn from?*

ROSALIND: *No — well no-one I know anyway.*

Another girl, Tessa, expressed a much more cheerful attitude:

TESSA: *She and Mrs. Linnaeus both get off the subject when they're talking — people like Henrietta lead them off . . . Mrs. Linnaeus is always expecting you to do extra work in the holidays — Mrs. Cavendish doesn't give us much prep. She gets us muddled up sometimes. She'll give us something and we'll get it, and someone doesn't, and she'll work it up on the board and she works it differently and you get a bit muddled.*

ME: *How do you feel about doing the experiments?*

TESSA: *Sometimes they seem a bit stupid when you're doing them — but the results are O.K.*

Henrietta has some insight into Mrs. Cavendish's intentions:

Mrs. Cavendish can't explain anything . . . will tell you about unnecessary detail. She can't explain things — we just want basic facts — everyone is lost except Charmian. It may well make us more independent but . . .

Charmian, a girl regarded by the staff as 'outstandingly gifted mathematically', is commonly believed by the pupils to be the only person who understands Mrs. Cavendish. Her comments were as follows:

I think she makes simple things complicated — you have to — oooh — I think — you do things . . . I think if you're given enough things to do yourself you'll learn physics quite well that way but . . . oooh — it's more Teach Yourself Physics — with the experiments . . . The book's a jolly good one, and you have to understand from that. Once I've worked out how, why a thing is what it is, then I'm all right'.

It is interesting that none of the girls realize that Mrs. Cavendish deliberately acts as she does.

The pupils' opinions about the other Science staff they had known and about the two Chemistry teachers are rather colourless compared to those expressed about Mrs. Linnaeus and Mrs. Cavendish. The two chemists are both popular, and held to be good teachers, but as they are 'normal', no-one had much to say. A few typical remarks follow:

As long as you understand things Chemistry is easy, just learning the stencils — but she's (Chem. B) quite good at explaining things when you don't. (Alexandra)

(Chem. B) is much more interested in us — in a way — she takes more trouble to explain things — prefer her to Mrs. Linnaeus. (Gale)

(Chem. A) explains things more than Mrs. Cavendish — you learn more from her . . . with Physics it's more Maths, equations . . . but Chemistry there's more learning things. (Belinda)

(Chem. A) and Mrs. Linnaeus are better at explaining things than Mrs. Cavendish . . . Maybe I just find Chemistry and Biology easier . . . (Chem. A) expects a lot from you — or says she does — in a way it's quite encouraging. (Angela)

(Chem. A) has sort of orderly lessons — you don't get shouting . . . well you do get calling out — the subject is orderly. She knows what she's doing. (Tessa)

The girls' opinions give the two Chemistry teachers credit for being better at explanations, more orderly and in better control. The main difference between Mrs. Linnaeus and Mrs. Cavendish is that the former manages to get her subject across while the latter does not. However, the quote from Angela given above shows an important point — the relative difficulty of the syllabuses and the stress they cause. All the girls seemed to find the Biology within their grasp, and most the Chemistry, while the Physics syllabus is perceived by the school to be taxing, all the group find it hard and some are profoundly miserable about it.

Extracts from Science lessons

The extent to which the girls are or are not 'on top' of the work is shown clearly by the fourth theme, extracts from the lessons. First, an incident from one of Mrs. Linnaeus's classes:

(Lessons 6 and 7, Wednesday, Week 4). The class are coming to the end of 'doing' photosynthesis. Most girls are tidying up or writing up. Mrs. L wants to do the classic sunlight and silver paper experiment — shouts for quiet and announces the last experiment . . . [31]

SHARON:	*Good!*
MRS. L:	(Ignores Sharon, explains why they are doing it). *If we cover leaves with silver foil for a few days what will happen to them?*
ZOE:	*You'll get starch in the holes and not anywhere else.*
MRS. L:	(Accepts that — states it formally as an hypothesis — asks for volunteers to come and cut and cover leaves). *You can cut your initials out if you like, then if it works you'll see your initials outlined in iodine.*

(Mary, Karen and Janice volunteer and come to the front to get on with it. The others revert to own activities. Michelle puts up her hand).

MICHELLE:	*Mrs. Linnaeus, I don't see how that will prove it — it could be all sorts of other things we don't know anything about.*
MRS. L:	(Asks her to expand her question — explain what she doesn't see).
MICHELLE:	*Well you said if there was starch in the bare patches it would mean there was . . . it was because of the light, but*

> *it could be the chemicals in the foil, or something we know nothing about.*

SHARON: (Butts in). *Of course it'll prove it, we wouldn't be wasting our time doing the experiment if it didn't.*

MRS. L: *I don't think that's a very good reason Sharon . . .* (laughs) (Goes into great detail about experimental design, the atomic structure of carbohydrates, and other things in an attempt to satisfy Michelle. Only one or two others bother to listen). (Meanwhile I overhear Sharon and Clare talking).

CLARE: *Why are you drawing, Sharon? You can't have finished writing up all three experiments already!*

SHARON: *I have. I just put one out in full, then 2, about CO_2, method the same, result the opposite, conclusion obvious. Number 3, about sunlight, ditto.*

CLARE: *You can't just put that!*

SHARON: *Why not? I know what it means.*

This extract shows the nature of the relationship between Mrs. Linnaeus and her pupils to be informal and reveals the emphasis of deduction. It shows that Mrs. Linnaeus is not hurried, she stops to explain something to Michelle which is of little interest to the others. The reaction to Sharon's remark about time-wasting is interesting. Mrs. Linnaeus does not ignore it, like the earlier interjection of 'good'. Instead she laughs at it, signalling both that time is not so precious that they cannot waste some, and that she disapproves of explicit statements about her stage-management of their discoveries. The total extract gives us some idea of what Philippa meant by 'roundabout' teaching.

A similar strategy is intended to run through Mrs. Cavendish's classes, but the result is a more disjointed lesson, with the girls frequently unsure of what they are trying to discover, or how to do it. This fragmentary quality affected the notes I took, in that dialogues of more than a few sentences rarely took place, and the notes appear 'bitty'! The following is an extract from an ordinary lesson:

(Lessons 4 and 5, Tuesday, Week 4). Mrs. C sums up last week's experiments — in answer to queries from Fleur. Tessa and Lorraine write down this summary — though they were present at the lesson (Fleur wasn't). Tessa moves to check summary with Jackie on next bench. Mrs. C asks simple question on basics — Eleanor answers right — Mrs. C gives longish explanation of calculating acceleration.

Girls then get out equipment (ticker-tape machines) to re-do the experiment. Tessa, Mary and Fleur work near me — they discuss lax (lacrosse) teams — Mary says she's left the next table (where she is supposed to work) *'cos they're trying to muddle me up'.*

I move to next table where Charmian and Henrietta are explaining acceleration to Karen — then Angela comes to Karen for help and is passed on to Charmian for a repeat performance.

Throughout my field-notes on physics lessons there are similar episodes. For example, the following week I wrote:

Lessons 4 and 5, Tuesday, Week 5). Mrs. C starts lesson by announcing. *Last week you discovered an important relationship.* Greeted by ironic laughs. Ignores this and gives explanation of relationship between force and mass. After answering three questions, giving reassurance to Penny, Henrietta and Karen, she gets out the Newton balances, all stored in chocolate boxes. Henrietta asks, *What do you do with all the chocolates?* Mrs. C demonstrates an experiment. (Later) Getting out equipment for an experiment started last time. Chorus of, *It didn't work.* After two experiments class still unsure of what they are doing and why. She gives detailed explanation again. Then says *A time will come* [when they will understand it]. A chorus of ironic echoes of her sentiment.

Tessa, Lorraine and Fleur muddle around for some time with apparatus — eventually work out what they are meant to be doing from book and commonsense. Henrietta, Charmian and Michelle — much more together — have actually got some figures out of it.

In a typical lesson Mrs. Cavendish would ask someone to volunteer a recapitulation, explanation or deduction of some point which should have been apparent from a completed experiment, and no-one would be able to do so. Either no-one could work out the mathematics necessary for the deduction, or the experiment had failed, or they had simply misunderstood the possible conclusions. Mrs. Cavendish would then be forced to explain everything again, set them to repeat the experiment, or prove the mathematics again, and then the purpose of the exercise would 'dawn' on enough of the group for her to move on to the next area.

Once these extracts are examined, and compared with the information carried by the other themes, setting, personal front and pupils' opinions, the differences in FIAC profiles become explicable. Mrs. Linnaeus and Mrs. Cavendish are shown by FIAC data to have lower proportions of questioning to lecturing than the 'ordinary' Science staff, and higher proportions of pupil initiation and acceptance of pupil contributions. The first two differences are clearly interrelated; most Science teachers regularly hold drill and practice sessions orally with their classes to check comprehension of basic facts, while Mrs. Linnaeus and Mrs. Cavendish never did. Drill sessions, as long as they are conducted by asking questions and not by demanding answers, produce high proportions of questions and lower amounts of pupil initiated speech.

Mrs. Cavendish and Mrs. Linnaeus have adopted the 'guided discovery' philosophy so wholeheartedly that they have chosen teaching strategies particularly appropriate to it. They feel that it is better for the pupils to keep their own private records of the work done, monitor their own knowledge and understanding and discover their own 'blank spots' and ask about them, rather than have the teacher mark their notes or quiz them about their grasp of the material. For example, throughout my fieldwork, neither Mrs. Linnaeus nor Mrs. Cavendish took in their pupils main notebooks to look at them, nor suggested what should go down in them. Thus, Sharon is able to record her experiments in the unorthodox manner revealed in the Biology extract without interference. Mrs. Linnaeus gave one test on photosynthesis at the close of the topic, a test based on reasoning. Mrs. Cavendish never tested. Given this attitude of theirs, it is not surprising to find that they ask fewer questions and receive more pupil initiations — and indeed that they have high ratios of use and acceptance of pupil contributions as against rejection of them. Minimizing the amount of oral drill interaction implies replacing it with more pupil-initiated sequences and Flanders (1970) has shown, in numerous studies, that these are only likely to occur if pupils' ideas are readily accepted and used.

The FIAC data, therefore, though necessarily incomplete because of the nature of all Science lessons under the new syllabuses, does reveal evidence of the results of two different schools of thought among Science teachers about the proper amounts of guiding and discovering. One school of thought believes in a good deal of pre-structuring, and in using the non-practical parts of their lessons to check, by means of oral drill and frequent tests, that the right discoveries have been made and assimilated. Others, represented here by Mrs. Linnaeus and Mrs. Cavendish, believe in less interference in the discovery process, hide their structuring and rely on informal, pupil initiated interaction to emphasize points.

Once again the FIAC system has tapped differences in teachers' speech patterns which are closely related to their whole approach to the teaching of their subjects.

CONCLUSION

This paper was designed to demonstrate some of the strengths and weaknesses of a particular observation technique — one which has become enormously popular in recent years. All kinds of systematic observation technique are becoming more widespread, and the other authors in this collection are, on the whole, sceptical about their value and validity. This paper is intended to be a statement of my own attitude — namely that systematic techniques in general, and FIAC in particular, can be sensitive research tools, but that they are immeasurably strengthened by the addition of data collected by other, unstructured types of observation.[32]

Acknowledgements

The data presented here are based on research undertaken for a Ph.D. at the University of Edinburgh (Delamont, 1973). I wish to thank the Social Science Research Council and the Scottish Council for Research in Education for financial support from 1968 to 1973. The ideas in this paper have been discussed with my co-authors of this book, and I am grateful for their comments, although they bear no responsibility for the final version. Paul Atkinson, Margo Galloway and Jim Howe were my mainstays while I wrote the paper; Gerry Bernbaum and Tom Whiteside cheered me through the final stages. Finally I wish to express my gratitude to the staff and pupils of St. Luke's', who must remain anonymous.

Notes

1. Throughout this paper I use the term 'systematic technique' to apply to all observation systems which are based on predetermined schedules and which *aim* to satisfy Medley and Mitzel's (1963, p. 250) definition: 'procedures which use systematic observations of classroom behaviour to obtain *reliable and valid measurements* of differences in the typical behaviours which occur in different classrooms, or in different situations in the same classroom', (emphasis mine). I have doubts about the desirability of these as aims for observation systems; but all the well-established ones are designed with this intention and it seems reasonable to define and classify them accordingly. (See the seventy-nine systems anthologized in Simon and Boyer (1970)).

2. See Jackson (1968) for a study of some of the features common to all classrooms, and Smith and Geoffrey (1968) for a study of the unique features of one relationship.

3. In other words St. Luke's has spent a century preparing the daughters of the professional classes to enter the professions themselves. The education provided is of a traditional kind, based on 'chalk and talk' and angled towards the classics, pure science or foreign languages, designed to lead to Oxbridge at best, or one of the older Scottish universities. The school boasts a list of distinguished old girls, illustrious governors and a long waiting list; it is confident that the recent trend back to careers for women will ensure its continuance in its established role. (The research described here was carried out in 1969–71, but I have used the ethnographic present in this account).

4. All but one girl in my sample had a father with an occupation classified in the top section of the Registrar General's scheme, and all but one had had an I.Q. of over 110 when last tested (at age 12).

5. All the girls take the same basic course, Maths, English, French, History and Geography, in addition to two or three subjects drawn from a list of options. For most girls the choices available, both in terms of the number of subjects and the flexibility of the possible combinations, is unusually broad, even for a Scottish school. (See, for example, Pont and Butcher (1968) and Morrison and McIntyre (1969)).

6. Most of the goals publicly expressed by the school (e.g. in the prospectus, rules, motto etc.) are concerned with a broad liberal education and high academic standards — unlike the majority of the schools studied by Wober (1971). The teachers express similar sentiments in informal conversations, the parents are paying for sound educations, and the girls want intellectual satisfaction and/or qualifications for jobs and higher education — an unusually compatible set of expectations.

7. When constructing the sociometric pattern of the sample, I found six cliques and three isolates. Each clique had common interests which held it together, but questions about dislikes in the year were greeted with statements to the effect that 'I'm friends with all our year' and 'I think we're all friendly in our year'. The hostility between cliques described by many writers (Coleman, 1962; Hargreaves, 1967; Sugarman, 1970; Lacey, 1970) was not apparent at St. Luke's.

8. All the staff at St. Luke's, bar one, have honours degrees, and three have Ph.D.s. Exactly half have been, or are, married, and the average time they have been at the school is 5·6 years, though several have been there for twenty years and several are new. Stability of staffing without stagnation expresses the situation best.

9. In some ways then, FIAC could be seen as a more expensive way of discovering what Walberg calls the 'classroom climate' — the atmosphere in the classroom, which Walberg and his collaborators 'tap' with their Learning Environment Inventory (Walberg and Anderson, 1967).

10. The observer using the FIAC system makes a classification of the interaction every three seconds, which means that a single forty-minute period can produce up to eight hundred tallies.

11. As stated above, I spent eight weeks doing fieldwork at St. Luke's. Flanders advises (1970, p. 100) spending six to eight lessons with each individual teacher. I

collected FIAC data on all the teachers until I had used the technique in eight lessons. This took the first fortnight in the case of subjects with a large place in the curriculum, the first three to four weeks in the case of minority subjects. As soon as I had a reasonable sample of teaching behaviour I switched to unstructured observation aided by informal and formal interviewing for the remainder of my fieldwork period.

12. In my research with FIAC at St. Luke's and The Laurels, I found the percentage of teacher-talk varied from 57·7 to 82·2 with a mean of 70·3. The percentage of interaction spent in pupil-talk varied from 9·0 to 35·1, with a mean of 20·1 while the residual category occupied between 2·0 and 28·6 with a mean of 9·2.

13. In an eighty-minute double period, up to an hour was normally spent in practical work, with private talk between teacher and pupil but little public interaction, apart from occasional teacher statements about common problems and shouts for quiet.

14. These ratios are defined and explained on pages 102–4 of Flanders (1970). Briefly, the TRR is derived by adding totals in categories 1, 2 and 3, multiplying that total by 100 and dividing by the total of categories 1, 2, 3, 6 and 7. The TQR is derived by multiplying the total in category 4 by 100 and dividing by the sum of categories 4 and 5. The PIR is derived by multiplying category 9 by 100 and dividing by the sum of categories 8 and 9.

15. In this context, 'established teachers' were all full-time staff in their second and subsequent years at the school, and any teacher on three-quarters or seven-eighths time who was a form mistress. The deputy head had a room, but was not a form mistress, otherwise classrooms reflected something of their resident teacher and the resident form, except in rare cases like Miss Iliad's.

16. Young staff leaving the girls' public schools to get married were a common complaint among the head teachers interviewed by Wober (1971) — 'one head commented "they *come* with a great big diamond ring, and only wait till they can put the deposit on the bungalow"'. At St. Luke's it is rare for a teacher to leave when she marries, rather than staying till she starts her family — of the half-dozen staff who had married within the eighteen months surrounding my fieldwork period Miss Odyssey was the only one to leave on her marriage.

17. This paradox is interesting in the light of Liam Hudson's (1966) finding that bright classicists at school level are usually convergers rather than divergers like other arts specialists. One wonders if they have been attracted by the logical thinking involved in the first stage and, if so, how they managed the literary aspect when it became more prominent at advanced levels of study.

18. The pupils' opinions of their staff were collected by talking to them informally during my fieldwork and by means of formal, structured interviews outside the school once it was over. In the formal interviews I elicited their perceptions by means of triads — that is, by presenting each girl with the names of three members of staff at a time and asking for ways in which they were similar and different both as teachers and as people.

19. The reader will be able to see immediately that these extracts are drawn from field-notes, rather than from transcripts of tape recordings. This means that they are superficially more fluent than transcripts would be, because I ignored false starts and hesitations etc., yet also incomplete, in that they concentrate on the pupils contributions and omit the exact words used by the teacher in favour of recording their sense. In summary, these extracts are of little use to the linguist, but retain enough of the atmosphere to give the reader a glimpse of life in that classroom.

20. The introduction of new Nuffield-type syllabuses for Latin might well change the balance between the two aspects necessary at school level — and one might predict that these two staff members would react differently to such syllabuses.

21. At more advanced levels, appreciation of literature particularly poetry would alter this lack of affective comment, as might new syllabuses (see Note 20).

22. The emphasis on idiomatic 'fit' is probably related to the degree to which the girls

feel able to 'have a go'. In Miss Odyssey's lesson a girl admits she is not sure, while in Miss Iliad's they 'clam up' when stuck.

23. The generalizations about 'subject colleagues' in this section refer to the two Chemistry staff at St. Luke's and to the teachers referred to in the tables as Physics C and Biology C, who taught at The Laurels. As the only one teacher of Biology and Physics taught my sample at St. Luke's, I included the two from The Laurels to show that the differences in FIAC scores and personal style were not due to a Chemistry/other dichotomy. What I have to say is mainly concerned with the two Chemistry staff who taught my sample, but none of it is inapplicable to the two from The Laurels.

24. Chemistry A's marriage did not make her status transitory because apart from staying at the school (where she was already well-established) she married a man who taught many of the girls' brothers.

25. Mrs. Cavendish had teenage daughters and could discuss girls' clothes and preoccupations. Mrs. Linnaeus had a son who dated a girl in a junior form and was the subject of much cheerful gossip.

26. By 'normal' I mean only the pattern I found usual among science teachers of bright, middle-class fifteen-year-olds throughout the city.

27. It should be stressed that both teachers told me at some length that they deliberately aimed to create the atmospheres they did create — that their styles were conscious. This may seem hard to believe in the case of Mrs. Cavendish, but she saw herself as preparing girls for university science courses, where they would have little or no help from staff in the lab. The head of the Science department told me that she allowed Mrs. Cavendish to continue teaching in her own way — despite the distress it caused with junior forms — because the girls who had gone to read Science at universities were always coming back and telling her how grateful they were for Mrs. Cavendish's attitude. Apparently they found university Science easy to manage after her teaching, and could see that the difficulties which other students faced were due to their more structured teaching at school.

28. The interview quotes given are all from St. Luke's girls, where comparisons could be made. The comments about the Chemistry staff are similar to those made by girls from The Laurels about their Science staff.

29. The reader should not think that the Chemistry staff were not developing new angles on their syllabuses as conscientiously — in fact they spent much time discussing changes they might try or had implemented. However, their efforts had gone on creating work-sheets and devising multiple-choice tests, which the girls found easier to assimilate with their other work.

30. The policy at St. Luke's was that only girls who were good at Maths could take Physics in the third year — others had the opportunity to do the 'O' grade in their sixth year.

31. Leaves are covered in silver foil with small holes in it. After a week or so the leaves are tested for chlorophyll, which should be found only in the parts of the leaves exposed to sunlight via the holes in the foil.

32. Personally I feel also that the uses of systematic observation techniques are limited in research, but very useful in teacher-training where their pre-structuring of the observation makes them usable by students and supervisors. (See, for example Stones and Morris (1972)).

References

Becker, H. S. et al., 1961, Boys in White, University of Chicago Press, Chicago.

Becker, H. S. et al., 1968, Making the Grade, Wiley, New York.

Biddle, B. J. and W. J. Ellena (eds.), 1964, Contemporary Research on Teacher Effectiveness, Holt, Rinehart and Winston, New York.

Coleman, J. S., 1962, The Adolescent Society, Free Press, Glencoe.

Delamont, S., 1973, *Academic Conformity Observed: Studies in the Classroom,* unpublished Ph. D. thesis, University of Edinburgh.

Flanders, N. A., 1964, 'Some relationships among teacher influence, pupil attitudes, and achievement', in Biddle and Ellena (1964).

Flanders, N. A., 1965, *Interaction Analysis in the Classroom: A Manual for Observers,* School of Education, University of Michigan.

Flanders, N. A., 1970, *Analyzing Teaching Behavior,* Addison-Wesley, New York.

Goffman, E., 1959, *The Presentation of Self in Everyday Life,* Doubleday Anchor, Garden City, New York; Penguin, Harmondsworth, 1971.

Hargreaves, D. H., 1967, *Social Relations in a Secondary School,* Routledge, London.

Hudson, L., 1966, *Contrary Imaginations,* Methuen, London.

Jackson, P. W., 1968, *Life in Classrooms,* Holt, Rinehart and Winston, New York.

Lacey, C., 1970, *Hightown Grammar,* The University Press, Manchester.

McCall, G. J. and J. L. Simmons (eds.), 1969, *Issues in Participant Observation,* Addison-Wesley, New York.

Medley, D. M. and H. E. Mitzel, 1963, 'Measuring classroom behavior by systematic observation', in N. L. Gage (ed.), *Handbook of Research on Teaching,* Rand McNally, Chicago.

Morrison, A. and D. McIntyre, 1969, *Teachers and Teaching,* Penguin, Harmondsworth.

Pont, H. B. and H. J. Butcher, 1968, 'Choice of course and subject specialization in seventeen Scottish secondary schools', *Scottish Educational Studies,* **1,** 2.

Simon, A. and G. E. Boyer (eds.), 1968, *Mirrors for Behavior,* Research for Better Schools, Philadelphia.

Simon, A. and G. E. Boyer (eds.), 1970, *Mirrors for Behavior II,* Research for Better Schools, Philadelphia.

Smith, L. M. and W. Geoffrey, 1968, *The Complexities of an Urban Classroom,* Holt, Rinehart and Winston, New York.

Stones, E. and S. Morris, 1972, *Teaching Practice,* Methuen, London.

Sugarman, B., 1970, 'Classroom friends and leaders', *New Society,* Jan 22nd, 1970.

Walberg, H. J. and G. J. Anderson, 1967, *The Learning Environment Inventory,* unpublished mimeo, University of Harvard.

Wober, M., 1971, *English Girls' Boarding Schools,* Allen Lane, London.

Wragg, E. C., 1971, 'Interaction analysis in Great Britain', *Classroom Interaction Newsletter,* **7,** 1.

Wragg, E. C., 1972, *An Analysis of the Verbal Classroom Interaction between Graduate Student Teachers and Children,* unpublished Ph. D. thesis, University of Exeter.

6. Strawberries

By Rob Walker and Clem Adelman

Editorial introduction

One theme which runs through all the papers in the book is the inherent complexity of meanings communicated in the classroom. This paper by Walker and Adelman reveals an aspect of this complexity. Without spoiling the product, one can say that its theme is that talk, which is rich in bizarre meanings and hidden jokes, can express important facets of classroom life.

Two methodological points: First, such meanings are accessible only to a researcher who has been present in the classroom over a long period, not only observing but also talking to teachers and pupils. The paper therefore provides striking illustration of one crucial type of classroom phenomenon which is simply not accessible to non-observational research — or even perhaps to short-term participant observation. Second, Walker and Adelman (like all the other authors) are here dealing with an area for which there is no ready-made research instrument available. To apply to the talk some form of 'coding' for example, would be to code the phenomenon under study out of existence. Their approach in this and in other work has been to follow up a hunch by developing *appropriate* techniques to handle what seems important. (See Walker and Adelman (1972) and Adelman and Walker (1974) for a description of a stop-frame cinematographic technique developed for long-term participant observation of informal classrooms).

On a substantive level, the paper shows the serious import of humour. Almost no work has been done on the social functions of jokes and humour — for example, as a means of social control, of displaying social solidarity or of communicating covertly on a taboo topic. There are very few studies of how humour is *used* by people in everyday situations (compared with studies of, say, the 'psychology of humour' — abstracted from all social context and from *observations* of spontaneous wit). Torode's paper, in this volume, includes some interesting further examples of how pupils can *use* jokes to challenge a teacher's frame of reference or how a teacher can set up a fantasy situation as a means of social control.

Social control has itself been insufficiently studied. We simply do not know what range of ways teachers use for keeping their pupils in line: orders, threats, warnings, pleas, reasonings, explanations — or jokes.

M.S.

TEACHER: *Wilson we'll have to put you away if you don't change your ways and do your homework.*
Is that all you've done?

BOY: *Strawberries, strawberries.* (Laughter)

BOY: *And that's er, what do you call it? What you 'ave for breakfast.*

TEACHER: *What you have for breakfast?*

BOY: *Sometimes. Oranges — what d'you call 'em? Red things.*

TEACHER: *What you have for breakfast?*

BOY: *Sometimes.*

TEACHER: *Oh — it is — it isn't a living thing this?*

BOY: *No.*

TEACHER: *Strawberry.*

BOY: *Yes.*

TEACHER: *You have strawberries for breakfast?*

BOY: *Yeah.*

TEACHER: *Do you really?*

One incidental effect of the many and much-publicized recent attempts at educational innovation in this country has been a growing interest in the possibilities and problems involved in doing classroom observational research.[1] Claims of reform have inevitably assumed that at the very least process variables have been altered — that methods of classroom management and lesson organization, teachers' values and attitudes, and the roles and relationships of teachers and children have been changed. The instrument of change is sometimes identified as one of the variety of projects funded by Nuffield and the Schools Council, but may also be an overall plan created by a local authority (as with 'The Leicestershire plan'), an individual school that has achieved a 'progressive' reputation, or a more diffuse change like 'Modern Infant School Methods'. From a research point of view this kind of reform can be seen as putting the general principles of educational theory to the test, so creating for observational research in classrooms the problem of how theory is reconciled with practice.

We believe that a potential major use for observational research is in locating and describing the manifestations of different forms of educational change at the classroom level. This becomes a necessity since, before any reforms can be evaluated in terms of outcomes, it is necessary to establish just how, and how effectively, they have succeeded in transforming existing educational practices. For observational research the prescriptions of reformers represent a series of starting points for research.

From available field reports,[2] it appears that all too often innovations are managed as surface features in the life of schools. They are mobilized to impress visitors (and visiting researchers), to further individual careers, to raise the status of schools and departments within schools, and to release money from local authority funds. Despite surface appearances they cannot often be said to reflect any deeper level of change. There is no shortage of claims being made for or against particular reforms and the situation is complex since those you might expect to be most confident (for example, in the Schools Council), often appear (at the time of writing) to be the most cynical. But generally, if observational research is to relate to the significant policy issues in the field of educational reform it has to develop ways of proceeding that account for what innovations are attempting to accomplish. Above all this means that it needs to take the teacher and resources as major elements in its analysis.

This paper represents a preliminary attempt to do classroom observational research whilst keeping the concerns of the innovating teacher and curriculum developer uppermost in our minds. Its scope falls somewhere between the concerns of the academic researcher and the practitioner. Our hope is that it overlaps to some extent with both.

In our research we have attempted to use observational methods and techniques to look in some detail at the realities of teaching in a number of secondary schools which appear to have successfully changed some aspect of the educational process at the classroom level. We have looked both at schools that have adopted and developed particular curriculum projects and at schools that appear to have achieved overall organizational change. In all cases the observations have been made intensively over short periods (continuously from half a day to two weeks), but in many cases they have been continued intermittently over longer periods (up to five years in some cases). Our material has case-studied particular teachers and their classes and has involved the collection of over seventy hours of film recordings and a further forty hours of audio-recordings of lessons, as well as observational notes, teachers' notes, lesson plans and worksheets, and over one hundred hours of interviews with teachers, students and children.

Starting with long-term participant observational studies of the kind pioneered by Louis Smith, we have attempted to develop recording systems and research methods which condense the period of fieldwork. The technical details of the recording systems have been published elsewhere,[3] but briefly consist of audio-visual records which can be used continuously for long-run sequences of events (e.g. for a whole week). The research methods consist mainly of using these participant recordings[4] as a basis from which to collect alternative perceptions and definitions of situations.

INITIAL PROBLEMS

In attempting to use previously developed observational checklists and category systems[5] to assess the extent and impact of changes in the educational process at the level of classroom interaction we have been struck repeatedly by three assumptions that seem to limit the applicability of available methods and techniques to our material.

(1) Not only is the teacher's role seen as central in the classroom (which seems to us a fair assumption), but varieties in pupil role within and between classrooms are scarcely considered. It seems to us that in different classrooms children adopt quite different roles and identities and these determine to a considerable extent the kind of interactions that are possible within that setting. The image of the teacher that emerges from much established research is therefore of a *performer,* who relates to the children he, or she, teaches only in terms of a restricted and rather mechanistic relationship. What strikes us about the teachers we have studied is the warmth and individuality of their relationships with children. They are not all strong 'personalities' in the performance sense, but they all have strong personal *relationships* with the children they teach; this significant sociological distinction does not, however, seem to be accounted for in the established research repertoire.

(2) This leads us to the second difficulty, which is that the social context assumed by most available research methods as the predominant context for teacher–pupil interaction is one where one person (and usually it is the teacher) talks at a time and where everyone else takes an audience role. This simply does not fit with our material, where such contexts are rare and usually brief.

We should stress that this is not simply a technical difficulty of being able to hear what is said, as some researchers have suggested. As it is the professed objective of many innovating schemes to incorporate child–child talk into the normal flow of communication, it follows that any observational system that looks *only* at talk which is transacted via the teacher will produce a misleading picture of the lesson in relation to its rationale.

In the light of recent developments in the social sciences it would seem that any research design that leaps from teacher-talk to learned outcomes in the child as though they were discrete and easily connected variables, ignores both the complex interrelation of language and thought *and* the difficulties inherent in the attempt to communicate through talk. Our assumption is that radical changes in the contexts of talk involve different qualities of communication and these ultimately engage different identities in their participants.

(3) Related to both these assumptions in established research are particular concepts of language, talk and communication. Above all is the idea that communication through talk is a relatively straightforward, transparent, unambiguous, almost mechanical, process. In the classroom it involves a rather narrow range of meanings which have to be communicated more or less in sequence and which the teacher can either broadcast in monologue, or attempt to elicit from the children in the attempt to

induce 'learning'. This image is contradicted by our recordings, where talk is seen to be a highly complex, problematic activity, rich in contradictory and bizarre meanings and frequently fraught with difficulties and confusions.

In this paper we want to look a little more closely at these general assumptions, using illustrative material from our own fieldwork. We will start with the third point first, looking at some of the different levels of meaning involved in apparently straightforward classroom talk. This will lead us to consider some of the ways in which children are able to realize identities in different kinds of classroom context and finally to a discussion of the identity of the teacher in different forms of classroom social system.

THE MEANINGS COMMUNICATED BY TALK

We want to discuss two problems that emerged from our fieldwork when we attempted to use teacher–pupil talk as documenting particular lessons and providing a basis on which to compare different teachers and different lessons.

The first problem concerns the inherent complexity of the meanings communicated by talk; a good place to start developing this idea is to look at jokes. Early on in our research we studied one classroom quite intensively (three days a week for a term). The class was a bottom stream fourth-year group in a boys secondary modern school in one of the London boroughs. The teacher whose lessons we observed had a particularly strong and positive relationship with the class which often expressed itself through jokes. Some examples make this clear.

1. Working through text exercises in English.

   A: (Reading aloud from his book) *Business is brisk when this is roaring
       . . . ? Trade.*

   T: *Roaring trade. I don't quite know the origin of this. It may be —*

   B: *Lion tamer.*

   T: Lion tamer? (Pause) *Roaring trade.* (Pause) *Oh, very witty, very
      witty.*

We can think of this as quite pure 'wit' since the meanings are quite accessible. Sometimes, however, jokes depend more strongly on intonation, phrasing or the use of looks, pauses and gestures. In the next example for instance, the joke is not quite apparent from a first glance at a transcript.

2. Again in English.

   T: *What is a couplet? If it's got 'et' on the end, it means what?*

   A: *A little.*

   T: *Little what?*

   A: *Couple.*

T: *A little couple, or a little pair. A little pair of couple of . . .* (looking hard at C) *. . . sentences or expressions.* (Pause)

C: *We know.* (Laughter)

What both these jokes reveal is a quality of indeterminacy in the sequence of meanings shared by the participants. One reason both jokes are seen as funny is that they provide unexpected and bizarre shifts of meaning in what seems, superficially, to be a highly determinate series of events. It is as though the talk itself simultaneously carries a whole series of different levels of meaning which most of the time are dominated by relatively surface 'commonsense' interpretations. The jokes function as sparks which short-circuit the insulation between commonsense meanings and the other possibilities inherent in the talk.

It is partly because jokes make it possible to communicate two kinds of meaning simultaneously that they are often used by teachers (and children) to invade aspects of personal identity that are not, strictly speaking, legitimate areas of classroom discourse. For example:

3. At the start of a lesson.

T: *Right, will you all sit down.*
Plumb, I can't tell whether you are sitting down or not. (Laughter)

4. During English.

T: *Personification is when you take something which hasn't got a body, or something visible* (pause) *something abstract, and you sort of clothe it in flesh or being. You make a person out of it. In primary school when they have these sort of plays, like about the Good Fairy. They have someone who comes in and says, 'I am the Fairy of Truth, and whoever follows me will do well'. And this person is the personification of truth. Then you get someone come in and say, 'I am wickedness . . . ' You remember these things? Alan, which one were you?* (Pause) *'I am appetite?'* (Laughter)

Now these jokes rely for their effect on the fact that participants have access to personal knowledge of the boys involved. Unless you know that Plumb is the smallest in the class, and that this is something of a class joke, and likewise that Alan is the greediest, then the jokes are not really funny.

All the jokes we have quoted so far were available to us as observers in the class. However, quite a lot of the things the class found very funny, we did not 'get'. We had to ask people afterwards what the joke was. For example, one lesson the teacher was listening to the boys read through short essays that they had written for homework on the subject of 'Prisons'. After one boy, Wilson, had finished reading out his rather obviously skimped piece of work the teacher sighed and said, rather crossly:

T: *Wilson, we'll have to put you away if you don't change your ways and do your homework. Is that all you've done?*

B: *Strawberries, strawberries.* (Laughter)

When we asked why this was funny, we were told that one of the teacher's favourite expressions was that their work was 'Like strawberries — good as far as it goes, but it doesn't last nearly long enough'.

The remark, 'Strawberries, strawberries', might seem amusing, but trivial, because essentially it functions as a diversion, peripheral to the main stream of the lesson. Alternatively it might be seen as revealing the underlying means of social control in this class — the class is signalling to the teacher that they know what he wants and the quoting of the rule becomes a joke. Here we want to use the incident because it seems to us that it dramatizes and highlights an important quality in the way talk is used to communicate meanings in long-term situations like school classrooms. For meanings are not simply dictionary labels attached to words which we 'learn'; the words themselves have associations and particular, personal meanings not readily accessible to those outside the immediate experience of the group. As outsiders, when we look at lesson transcripts, what we tend to see is the bare bones of meaning — the universals freely available within our culture — not the full richness of talk, which is what makes a relationship valuable and unique to its participants. What we miss is the subcultural experience of the group and its associated private and personal meanings — in short, its restricted code.[6]

It is important to emphasize that the culture of a class of this kind of private, but shared, world of meaning applies not only to words and phrases but also to events. Particular incidents become part of shared memory ('Ooh sir, do you remember that time when . . . ') and this shared memory is not always distant or apart from the 'content' of lessons. An example of it operating locally and being inextricably linked with the content of the lesson is the 'fish incident'.

In the summer term the team agreed to coordinate their work around a series of themes, each running for two or three weeks. At the time of the incidents we are reporting here the theme was 'The Sea', and in the art room a number of projects had been started. The art teacher observed that nearly all the children were producing conventional, stylized images of fish which bore little resemblance to the real thing. In order to correct this she came in one afternoon with a selection of wet fish from the fishmongers — a herring, a plaice, some mackerel, some shrimps and so on. This led to a wide variety of activities — weighing and measuring different fish, making dissections, examining anatomical features, shapes, textures and colours.

Later the same week the children met for a class discussion and individually recorded their impressions for the afternoon spent investigating fish. At this point we became aware of certain themes related to the emotional experience of touching the fish, and why some children were more sensitive about this than others. Another theme related to the curious anatomy of the plaice and how it came to be like that.

When the observer and the teacher tried to reconstruct the events that first revealed these themes we found that it was only possible to do so in vague terms. For example, one incident we located as crucial in the development of both these themes was an incident involving a group of children examining a plaice. Some of the girls in the group were squeamish and said it smelled too strong. One of the braver girls offered to wash it in the sink. The sink became blocked and filled with water. Under the running tap the fish became slippery and slipped out of the girl's hand into the water. As it did so it simulated the curious undulating motion that flat fish exhibit when swimming, this caused some excitement as it was repeated several times, leading to a discussion with the teacher about what was happening.

At the time of the incident this seemed a fairly trivial activity causing a minor discipline problem for the teacher. Given the fact that so many interesting things were going on in the room it did not seem salient and was not recorded in any great detail by the observer. In the light of later discussions and later activities, however, this 'trivial' incident emerged as an event of some significance. Not only was the content explicated in some detail in later discussions (for example, in discussing the probable evolutionary history of the plaice, and in considering the problem of recording and describing movement), but it was also used by both teacher and children as a marker 'Do you remember Miss, when we was at the sink with the plaice . . . '). Though the event contained the germs of these meanings at the time of action, it was only in retrospect that it was seen by both observer and participants to contain these meanings themselves.[7]

The second problem we want to describe which emerged from using teacher–child talk as data, we first encountered when we tried extending our observations to other classrooms. In Jim Binham's class the context of teacher–pupil talk during lessons is predominantly formal — that is to say that when someone is talking everyone else listens. Talk becomes the medium through which experience is shared and shaped. Technically, when we come to record and transcribe this sort of talk it tends to come out in a form very like a conventional playscript, somewhat surprisingly since linguists often point out that 'we don't really talk like that'. But it has a distinct series of themes, or story line, it is written in relatively self-contained 'lines', and it can be understood relatively free of its context.

When we tried extending our observations we turned to classes where the context of teacher–pupil talk was predominantly informal — that is to say where for most of the lesson the teacher talked only to small groups or individual children and where this talk was not readily accessible to the rest of the class. Technically, such classes are more difficult to observe, more seems to be going on in them at any one moment and they demand radio-microphone equipment in order to 'listen in' to the teacher's conversations with children.

However, what we found when we reduced talk from a variety of such informal classroom situations to transcript, was that there were considerable differences between them. Our initial hypothesis was that there would be a strong correlation between the situation and the type of talk — that in formal situations we would find one kind of talk, and in informal situations another.

In some ways this is true — it does seem as though there is a way of talking generally characteristic of the formal situation and another way found mainly in informal situations. The former tends to come out in transcript as clean-cut, almost Socratic, dialogue, readily reducible to a 'playscript' format, and also tends to have patterns of intonation, pausing and characteristic routines. The latter, in contrast, is often fragmented, difficult to follow and complicated in transcript, full of false starts and interruptions and people talking through and over each other. In fact it is often so unlike a playscript that it is virtually impossible to understand in transcript and even a tape-recording needs to be heard in conjunction with a visual recording, because, without knowing who is talking to whom, what activities are involved, and what the total situation is like, much of what is said makes little sense.

However, this distinction does not hold completely. It is possible to find formal situations which exhibit forms of talk similar to those usually found in informal situations (especially when some group consensus is being sought). Also it is possible to find situations which appear to be informal but where the talk is more typical of formal situations. Such incidents seem particularly common in schools that are tentatively trying out new curricula but are reluctant to involve themselves in anything that demands changes in the teacher's role.

In other words the observer cannot draw conclusions about the quality of teacher–pupil relationships either from observation of the communication structure or from analysis of teacher–child talk. It is necessary to inspect teacher–pupil talk *in relation to its overall context.*

CHILDREN'S CLASSROOM IDENTITIES

In Jim Binham's class the same group are together for long periods of time and teacher–pupil talk occurs mainly within formal situations. The jokes we quoted illustrate how, in this class, the meanings communicated by talk are inherently indeterminate. Although the lessons seem straightforward and tightly 'scripted', there is plenty of scope for 'ad-libbing', for departing from the intended meanings through humour.

In this kind of classroom social system it is obvious that certain children will develop the skill and imagination not only to create jokes but also to create an identity[8] within the class where others will accept them as 'jokers'. In other words they are not just seen as having a quick sense of humour: they are expected to be funny.[9]

So, in sustained formal classroom situations, although teacher–pupil talk is mainly public, and meanings are therefore shared, it is possible for pupils to create individual identities for themselves within the class through their ability to play complex verbal games. Their identity is dependent on their skill (or, in some cases, lack of skill) in stamping their individuality on quite a narrow range of talk involving specialized styles and registers.[10]

In a class that has been together with the same teacher for a long time, each child can create a distinct identity which gives to teacher–pupil talk the quality of cryptic shorthand. The culture of the class becomes so strong, the meanings it assigns to particular items of talk so rich, that the talk itself becomes almost inaccessible to an outsider. ('Strawberries, strawberries').

To give a further example, we often heard Jim Binham use phrases like, 'Come on Jones, get on with your work or we'll have to see what you're wearing won't we?'. He later explained this to us by saying that when he taught the class in their first year in the school some of them used to giggle a lot. He had made a joke out of this by saying something like, I know what your trouble is, you've still got your woolly knickers on, haven't you?'. Over time this had become contracted and absorbed into the culture of the class, so that its meaning was no longer accessible to an outsider hearing only the words.

Some of the jokes we have quoted are clearly being used by the teacher as a means of social control.[11] But another way of looking at them is as challenges by the pupils to what Bernstein calls the 'frame'.[12] For the teacher jokes have a two-edged quality: they allow him access to the children's identities in a direct, intimate way, but they also allow the children some control over talk, and that can give them some measure of control over the process of defining 'classroom knowledge'. Jokes like the Lion Tamer joke can have the effect of challenging the frame because they push back the boundary between the intended meanings of the lesson and meanings drawn from outside the lesson. Pupils who become skilled at joking can therefore create positions where, to a limited extent, they can take over control of lesson content.

So far we have talked about the relationship between jokes and identity in formal situations. In classrooms where the social context of teacher–pupil talk is predominantly informal, it is much more difficult for teachers to create the kind of classroom culture we have described. When learning and teaching are 'individualized' the social structure of meanings centres more strongly on friendship groups than on whole classes. Teacher–pupil talk becomes localized to the group of children that work together; other children do not share in what they say, nor (for the most part) do they seem interested.

The classroom identities that emerged in Jim Binham's class (and the joker is only one of many) were created and sustained by an audience. But in informal situations audiences are virtually non-existent — everyone is a performer. This means that children cannot develop viable social identities through the creation of expectations amongst an audience of listeners. They have to project themselves fairly continuously through talk, face-to-face with the teacher, and this requires different skills and realizes different kinds of identity.

Perhaps here it is clear why we use Ward Goodenough's term 'identity' rather than the more usual term 'role'.[13] In the formal situation *social* identities are involved — that is to say, parts are played and expectations created in an audience which sustain the part. But in informal situations *personal* identities are involved which are not specialized parts in an organic social structure so much as qualities unique to individual encounters between teacher and child.

The child in an informal situation can use jokes in talking to the teacher, but such encounters rapidly develop into joking relationships. That is to say the child is able to create and sustain an identity by projecting himself through a unique relationship with the teacher not shared by other children in the class.

In an attempt to illustrate this we want to look at the relationships which two children in the same class (a mixed, unstreamed class in a comprehensive school) have with their teacher in a predominantly informal situation. All the incidents quoted are taken from the same integrated studies lesson. First we want to look at one of the girls in the class, Karen.

K: *Colin, can you send that letter off please?* (2·4 laugh)[14]

C: *Watch it* (3·2 um) *That letter.*

K: *Yes that letter.*

C: *Tell you what Karen, I'll make certain it is sent off* (2·4 um)

K: *Miracles.*

C: *You know the science area?*

K: *Wonders'll never cease. Oh I'm not going over there.*

C: *You know my room in the science area?* (2·2)

K: *Yes*

C: *If you go over there — with that key you'll find my case on the floor —*

GIRLS: *Oh that's too lovely. Oh Colin.*

C: *Bring it over — your letter's in it.*

C: *You've just done what?*

K: *I've written it in me own words.*

C: *Oh well, providing you're making* (0·2) *it very brief.*

K: *Oh yes now you tell me.*

C: *You seem to have torn it up again — you're good at this aren't you. You're so* impatient *Karen* (2·0 um)

C: *. . . and you want a bloomin' envelope. You can't find it? It's in here* (5·6) *Excuse me girls, could you conceivably let me — let me get to my* (0·4) *drawer. Thanks. Come on could you get out of the way* (4·2). *Next time you want to go there Karen —*

K: *Where?*

C: *— it's that one there. All right?*

K: *Oh you said the second one in on the left-hand side on —*

C: *I meant the right-hand side.*

K: *Oh!*

C: *The second one down — all right? (1·2) No the only thing you're going to need next is going to be the address, isn't it?*

K: *You (0·6) you. Oh!*

C: *Relax — I was about to give you the address — OK?*

K: *I don't know why I waste my breath! (2·4)*

Even without the intonation and phrasing it is clear that the talk here is of quite a different quality to that given in earlier extracts. In many ways it is much more like everyday conversation. What strikes us about the relationship between Colin and Karen is the way she seems to be constantly playing minor variations on the theme of him as likeable but inefficient. It is as though she is able to create an individual identity for herself out of the stream of classroom events by the use of fluent repartee to manage incidents in a way that keeps Colin within the image she has defined for him. She therefore creates an identity for herself, not as a public figure in the class, but through her ability to use talk to maintain her definition of situation and so to sustain a unique relationship with Colin. Her identity is dependent on her image of him and her ability to make it stick when she talks to him.

Karen is one of a group of girls who work together and have a constant joking relationship with Colin.[15] Karen creates her identity within the frame, but Benny, the second child we want to look at, is socially isolated and constantly challenges Colin's taken-for-granted assumptions.

C: *Benny (0·8) I've heard too much of you for the past five minutes, wandering around the room — what are you doing? (1·8)*

B: *Me? (0·2) I'm doing writing (0·8)*

C: *I can see you're doing writing but what are you doing (1·0)*

C: *Come on — what's this here?*

B: *Bird.*

C: *Well what bird is it?*

B: *Ooh (4·0)*

C: *Well come on you put it here — what is it? (1·6)*

B: *Giant Beak.*

C: *No it's got a name Benny.*

B: *Well it's got a beak 'n'it?*

C: *Yes, but what's its name?*

B: *Well it's one of them i'n'it?*

C: *It's the Hornbill, good.*

B: *Hornbill.*

C: *Now make certain next time you know what it is. What's this one up here? (0·6) This big bird? (0·6)*

B: *The Hornbill it?*

C: That's *the Hornbill. Now 'it' is the beginning of that sentence.*

C: *These are things they eat are they?*

B: *Yes (0·4)*

C: *Right. What are they?* What's that?

B: *Worm (1·2)*

C: *Caterpillar.*

B: *Caterpillar (1·0) One of them — bugs that grow on trees (2·2)*

C: *Greenfly? (2·4) Is that what you mean? Is that what it's called?*

B: *Yeah (0·8)*

C: *Right.*

B: *And that's er, (2·2) what do you call it? What you 'ave for breakfast.*

C: *What you have for breakfast? (0·6)*

B: *Sometimes (1·6) Oranges — what d'you call 'em? (1·4) Red things (1·6)*

C: *That you have for breakfast? (0·6)*

B: *Sometimes.*

C: *Oh — it is — it isn't a living thing this?*

B: *No.*

C: *Strawberry.*

B: *Yes (1·0)*

C: *You have strawberries for breakfast?*

B: *Yeah.*

C: *Do you really?*

Compare his conversations with Karen. When Colin talks to Benny his speech is slower and his intonation generally more measured (with some exceptions — see those marked). Benny's remarks are often so unexpected that they demand a considerable amount of remedying and filling-in to sustain the encounter. Whatever the reasons for Benny's curious way of talking (and they seem in part to be due to perceptual difficulties), their effect is to put Colin in a situation where he thinks carefully before he speaks and where he expects Benny to come up with the unexpected and bizarre. He knows that he does not understand Benny; when he talks to him he expects difficulties of understanding and this in itself gives them a relationship different to that of other children in the class. In fact Benny so undercuts Colin's system of meanings that he is able to effectively reverse roles, as in the end of the sequence quoted where Benny has Colin groping for the word 'strawberry' in a way very similar to the way teachers often make children guess words.

TEACHER'S CLASSROOM IDENTITIES

The teacher in the formal situation is constantly on stage: he learns how to become and remain a centre of attention for long periods of time while 'controlling' his audience. And, as he performs, he develops a strong social identity which may appear 'larger than life' because he is able to insulate it from his personal identity.

The teacher in an informal situation may be invisible to all but a few children for most of the lesson. When he, or she, does talk to a child it is usually an occasion for stepping back from the task for appraisal, redirection or light relief, rather than for searching questions to be publicly answered. His identity is personal rather than positional; he seems much the same person inside the classroom as out of it.

We hope that it is clear from what we have said that we see the teacher's classroom identity, not simply as the expression of individual 'personality' or style, but as a critical element in a complex social system. At the level of description we have adopted, the teacher's 'classroom identity' does not exist independently of the identities of the pupils; they are organically related.

The question then arises as to the different functions that friendship and work groups can play in alternative forms of classroom social system and the constraints that these can exert on the identity of the teacher. (This reverses the causal relationship implicit or explicit in much of the established research, which attempts to relate personality attributes of the teacher to qualities of classroom interaction).

As far as we can tell from available research reports most sociometric studies that have been made of secondary school classrooms, have been restricted to what we have called 'formal' situations. In these situations the sociometric data seems to tap information about relationships that exist under the surface of (and even counter to) those observed during classroom interaction. They relate to subcultures which are part of the child's world outside the classroom, and only the iceberg tip of which enter the normal course of the lesson.*

However, in informal situations those subcultural relationships become part of the lesson itself. Friendship groups become an important element in the organization of schoolwork — both through the division of labour

---

* Furlong, in this volume, starts from this point about sociometric studies and develops it fully. Ed., M. S.

and through the differentiation and allocation of tasks. The teacher in an informal situation does not encounter friendship groups as a hidden agendum, but as part of the surface structure of the situation. In a sense he is trapped in them, for they *are* the social system of the class within which he has to work and he can do little to change them.

It follows that some of the main problems of this kind of teaching relate to the handling of friendship and work groups. For example, in Colin's class, Karen is a member of a clique of girls who form the strongest friendship group in the class; Benny is both an isolate and isolated. In a formal situation their identities would be superficially lost in their similar roles, for most of the time they would both be in audience roles with equal access to teacher-talk.

In the informal situation their identities are constantly visible — Karen works with her group of friends, Benny works alone. One of Colin's constant problems is how to extract himself from the demands made on him by Karen's group in order to get to Benny. In practice this means that his contacts with Karen's group tend to be frequent but brief and his relationship with them is one of almost constant teasing and joking. His contacts with Benny tend to be few but prolonged and conducted at a much slower pace.

We are not here trying to argue against individualized or group learning. What interests us is the kind of social system that emerges in classes that constantly operate as informal situations. One important characteristic of such classes, we feel, is that as the friendship relationships come to the surface of the lesson, so the teacher inevitably becomes drawn into them himself.

From the child's point of view, informal situations create different areas of vulnerability (which is perhaps another way of expressing the fact that they allow the creation of different kinds of identities). We noticed this particularly in an individualized Biology lesson, when quite 'innocent' questions about handling animals led one boy into a conversation with the teacher which got on to how to sex animals. Because the talk was not subject to the constraints of the group it seemed as though the teacher could steer it into areas the boy was not expecting, somewhat to his embarrassment. What often happens in such situations is that the friendship group will act to protect the isolation of the individual who finds himself in a vulnerable position. In this case the boy who found himself in the embarrassing situation (for him) of talking to the teacher about sex was protected to some extent by his friend, who came into the conversation to answer the teacher's question, so taking the pressure off him. (In another instance the teacher said to a girl who had been out of the room for some time, 'Where on earth have you been, it's ten minutes since you went out', at which her friend leaped in with, 'Oh, it hasn't been that long, Miss').

In the informal situation it is difficult for the teacher to isolate a child and ask searching questions, unless that child has already been isolated by the group, which might explain some of Benny's apparent evasiveness. He is, as it were, vulnerable twice over.

CONCLUSION

Classroom observational research has an obvious attraction for researchers interested in evaluating attempts at changing the nature of the educational process at the classroom level. With techniques like video-taping now becoming readily available and technically simpler to use, many of the problems that beset earlier research can now be overcome. For example, coding and reliability which presented enormous problems to many previous projects can now be easily handled at a level of complexity unobtainable without the use of video-tape.

However, while such techniques have made it possible to solve one set of problems, they have also created a whole set of new problems unrealized by earlier workers in the field. For example, just because these techniques preserve an enormous amount of information about the process of interaction, they make it tempting to researchers to restrict their focus to short-run events, with their associated levels of meanings and simplified notions of learning milieux.

We believe that the task of sociological research in this area should be to stress the long-term meanings of classroom events for their participants. Here we have attempted to show that classroom events involve the communication of longer-term meanings which relate to the personal and social identities of both pupils and teachers.

This kind of perspective is one which relates directly to problems of educational reform — particularly in the field of curriculum development. It seems to us that one of the things that is needed is ways of describing classroom events that are accessible to teachers, that include as major elements in their analysis the interrelations of the teacher, the child, the resource and the task, and that relate individual incidents to a wider context both in time and space.[16] Here we have been concerned particularly with relationships through time — with trying to interpret extracted small-scale incidents in terms of a concept of 'school' time that owes much to Philip Jackson's analysis.[17] The incidents we have quoted are, in his terms, trivia; but they are part of, and illuminate, a total set of meanings which is powerful and deep-rooted in the identities of all of us who have been educated in schools.

Acknowledgements

The research reported here was carried out at the Centre for Science Education, Chelsea College of Science and Technology, between 1968 and 1972. Part of this time we were supported by grants from the SSRC, and we also received grants from the Ford Foundation and the University of London Central Research Fund. This paper also reveals glimpses of our more recent work at CARE, University of East Anglia, and we are indebted to our colleagues Barry MacDonald and John Elliott for any unacknowledged insights they have shared with us. We are grateful for the help of Miriam Smith-Philipson, Colin Muge and Jim Binham in allowing us to observe and record in their classroom and to quote from those observations here.

Earlier versions of this paper were presented during 1972 at seminars at the Centre for Research in the Educational Sciences, University of Edinburgh, and at the Sociological Research Unit, University of London. We are grateful to participants at both for their comments and criticisms. A brief version of this paper first appeared in a research report written to the SSRC, grants nos. HR996/1 and HR1442/1 October 1972.

Notes

1. This has been a predominantly American research tradition until very recently (for references see Note 5). Even in the U.S.A. the research has been geographically restricted to a group of universities in the mid-west, and more recently the far-west. In this country until recently, we have lacked an interest in social psychology in educational research (with the exception of sociometry), and sociological research in education has been securely founded on a dominant ideological position which rarely questioned variations and discontinuities in the educational process at the cultural level.

2. See, for example, Hamingson (1973) for reports on the fate of the Humanities Curriculum Project in schools.

3. Adelman and Walker (1974).

4. Walker and Adelman (1972).

5. When we refer to established research we mean those systems recorded in Simon and Boyer (1971). The best known are those which attempt to analyse different qualities of teacher–pupil interaction (Flanders, Withall, Anderson, Medley and Mitzel) and those which attempt to analyse the logical structure of lessons (Bellack, B. O. Smith and O. R. Anderson).

6. Groups that are rather more self-contained than school classes have often been studied by sociologists and they are often found to have developed a lexicon and linguistic routine which separate 'inside' from 'outside'. (See, for example, the writings of Becker (1963), Goffman (1961), Whyte (1943), Polsky (1971, especially pp. 105–114) and Labov (1973)). Some teachers seem particularly skilled at creating personal styles through their talk (though to some extent this is something we all manage) and this may create a private domain which functions to protect both them and their classes from the abrasive demands of the institution. (In some ways the patter of Jimmy Young creates a similar cultural niche for the housewife).

7. From Walker and Adelman (1972, pp. 6–8).

8 We use the term 'identity' rather than 'role' because it has both personal and social aspects. See Goodenough (1965) for an elaboration of this usage.

9. The emergence of a 'jester' in a class has been strikingly described by Smith and Geoffrey (1968).

10. This relates to the point made in Note 6.

11. We have looked more closely at the functions of joking elsewhere: Walker, Goodson and Adelman (1974).

12. Bernstein (1971) uses the term 'frame' to refer to the degree of control teacher and pupil(s) possess over the selection, organization and pacing of the knowledge transmitted and received within pedagogical relationships.

13. See Goodenough (1965).

14. The figures in brackets are pauses in seconds.

15. The relationship here appears to be a 'joking relationship' in much the same sense as the term was used by Radcliffe-Brown (1952) in that the 'jokes' reveal aspects of ungrammatical identity relationships in this case a sexual relationship and a teacher–pupil relationship.

16. See Withall (1956).

17. Jackson (1968).

References

Adelman, C. and R. Walker, 1974, 'Stop-frame cinematography with synchronized sound: a technique for recording long-term sequences in school classrooms', *Journal of Society of Motion Picture and Television Engineers,* March 1974.

Becker, H. S., 1963, *outsiders,* Free Press, Glencoe, Illinois.

Bernstein, B. B., 1971, 'On the classification and framing of educational knowledge', in B. Bernstein, *Class, Codes and Control,* Vol. 1, Routledge, London.

Goffman, E., 1961, *Asylums,* Doubleday-Anchor, Garden City, New York.

Goodenough, W., 1965, 'Rethinking status and role', in M. Banton (ed.), *The Relevance of Models for Social Anthropology,* A.S.A. Monographs 1, Tavistock, London.

Hamingson, D., 1973, *Towards Judgement,* Schools Council, London.

Jackson, P. W., 1968, *Life in Classrooms,* Holt, Rinehart & Winston, New York.

Labov, W., 1973, 'The linguistic consequences of being a lame', *Language in Society,* **2,** 1, April 1973.

Polsky, N., 1971, *Hustlers, Beats and Others,* Penguin, Harmondsworth.

Radcliffe-Brown, A. R., 1952, *Structure and Function in Primitive Society,* Cohen and West, London.

Simon, A. and E. G. Boyer (eds.), 1971, *Mirrors for Behavior,* Research for Better Schools, Philadelphia.

Smith, L. M. and W. Geoffrey, 1968, *The Complexities of an Urban Classroom,* Holt, Rinehart & Winston, New York.

Walker, R. and C. Adelman, 1972, *Towards a Sociography of Classrooms,* Report to SSRC, Chelsea College of Science and Technology, mimeo, (available through National Lending Library).

Walker, R., I. Goodson and C. Adelman, 1974, 'Teaching, that's a joke', unpublished paper available from CARE, University of East Anglia.

Whyte, W. F., 1943, *Street Corner Society,* University of Chicago Press.

Withall, J., 1956, 'An objective measure of a teacher's classroom interactions', *Journal of Educational Psychology,* **47,** pp. 203–212.

7. Keeping in touch: Some functions of teacher-talk

By Michael Stubbs

Editorial introduction

This paper by Stubbs analyses some of the functions which teacher-talk serves. It shows with detailed reference to tape-recorded teacher–pupil dialogue, as well as observational notes, the extent to which teachers may exert *control* over classroom talk by continually explaining, correcting, evaluating, editing and summarizing.

Note some of the differences between the way in which Stubbs analyses classroom talk and the type of 'interaction analysis' described by Delamont and Hamilton in Chapter 1. Most importantly, Stubbs emphasizes the complex relationship between language, the social context in which it is used, and the underlying values and attitudes which it conveys; he explores the problematic relationship between what is said and what is meant. Any situation of talk is 'a microcosm of basic social and personal relationships', which sustains a definition of the situation and conveys sociocultural values such as power and status.

Other papers in the book bring to bear on classroom behaviour concepts developed within educational research, sociology, social anthropology, and psychology. This paper imports concepts from sociolinguistics to begin to describe aspects of classroom language. Although a vast amount of work has been done on verbal interaction in the classroom (see the introductory chapter by Delamont and Hamilton), this work has been theoretically narrow-minded and has drawn hardly at all on sociolinguistic concepts. This is paradoxical when 'sociolinguistics' is simply the study of language-use in different social contexts: such as the classroom.

The more general sections of this paper, on sociolinguistics, might be read as a background discussion of concepts partly taken for granted in the other papers in the book (by Walker and Adelman and by Torode) which specifically discuss classroom language.

Stubbs also discusses the general problem of research strategies. What is the researcher to do when confronted with what has been called the 'bloomin', buzzin' confusion' of the classroom? Where can we start looking for pattern in the awesome complexity of 'richness' of observed social behaviour? Stubbs proposes various strategies for stepping back from the complexity and for selecting data which can highlight important features of social routines.

M.S. & S.D.

As a way of describing one level of complexity in communicative behaviour in the classroom this paper applies some sociolinguistic concepts to an analysis of teacher-talk.

Teachers have to devote a great deal of time and effort simply to *keeping in touch* with their pupils — not only because of the far-from-ideal communication conditions in the average school classroom, but also because of the very nature of teaching. They have to attract and hold their pupils' attention, get them to speak or be quiet, to be more precise in what they say or write, and to try and keep some check on whether at least most of the pupils follow what is going on.

At the start of one English class which I observed, the teacher, after talking quietly to some pupils at the front of the room, turned and said to the whole class:

Right! Fags out please![1]

No pupils were smoking. So the teacher did not mean his words to be taken literally. I interpret his remark as having the primary function of attracting the pupils' attention, of warning them of messages still to come — in short, of opening the communication channels. The remark had a 'contact' function[2] of putting the teacher *in touch* with the pupils.

The problems of analysing language-use of this kind are not trivial, and yet they have not received much detailed consideration by linguists. For example, how did the pupils know that the teacher did 'not really mean' that they had to extinguish their non-existent cigarettes? What shared knowledge and expectations concerning appropriate speech behaviour did they draw on in order to successfully interpret what the teacher actually meant?[3]

In this paper, I begin by discussing various concepts which can begin to answer these questions. I then take these concepts as a basis for isolating the particularly striking 'contact' features of teacher-talk. The general concepts are therefore introduced in order to show how teaching can be considered as a particular kind of speech event and thus constantly compared with other situations in which people speak to each other.[4] The concepts and descriptive framework are illustrated by samples of teacher–pupil interaction collected by tape-recording and by taking field-notes during periods of classroom observation.

I hope, incidentally, that the title of this paper and these opening paragraphs have themselves performed a 'contact' function of preparing the reader for what I want to talk about and, hence, of putting us both on the same wavelength.

I continue now with a straightforward description of how the data were collected. I then discuss what I mean by a 'sociolinguistic' approach to language in the classroom. This leads into some more general discussion of research strategy: how can one begin to notice interesting features of how teachers talk to their pupils? The rest of the paper then discusses specific observational and tape-recorded data, proposing various categories, concepts and descriptive rules for handling classroom talk.[5]

HOW THE DATA WERE COLLECTED

The classroom observation was done over a period of about six weeks in 1971, in an Edinburgh secondary school. I sat in on English lessons with two teachers, mainly with their second-form and fifth-form classes. During the periods of observation I was simply concerned to write down as much as I could of what the teacher said, concentrating mainly on noting ways in which the teacher controlled or organized the lesson. Otherwise, in order to provide as much context as possible for the teacher-talk, my field-notes included as many other details of pupils' responses and other classroom events as I could write down in longhand.

The tape-recordings are of small group lessons at a summer school in July 1970. I decided to record small groups from a purely practical point of view of obtaining higher quality recordings than is often possible in a normal classroom with its echoing walls and some thirty to forty children. As I was interested primarily in *how* to describe the teachers' speech behaviour, I was not too worried that this behaviour might be different with small groups and large classes. I estimated that the direct observation in a 'normal' classroom situation would in any case provide an informal check that the samples of data were not too incompatible for my present purposes. Below, I quote data from both sources; the reader can judge for himself.

Prospective researchers should perhaps be aware that it is often possible to write down in a field notebook a great deal of useful data, even on use of language — but also that a tape-recorder, whilst providing more 'objective' and detailed data, is undiscriminating and may well provide too much data, unless the data are collected with a specific aim in mind. Five minutes of conversation may take over an hour to transcribe if the recording is clear, and correspondingly much longer for a poor recording.

I comment further below on some more general questions of research strategy.

SOCIOLINGUISTICS AND LANGUAGE VARIATION

'Sociolinguistics' covers a wide range of studies of how language is used in its social contexts. But all the studies have one thing in common — they deal with language *variation*. They emphasize how malleable language is and how its form and function change across different cultures and across different social situations within one culture. The aim is, of course, to find systematic patterning within the variation.

Various *social* factors determine the individual speaker's use of language. Everyone is multidialectal or multistylistic, in the sense that he adapts his style of speaking to suit the social situation in which he finds himself. Such style-shifting demands constant judgements. Yet speakers are not normally conscious of making such judgements until they find themselves in a problematic situation for which they do not know the conventions, or for which the criteria for speaking in a certain way clash. On the other hand, it is intuitively clear that a teacher, for example, does not speak in the same way to his wife, his mother-in-law, his colleagues in the staff room, his headmaster, a student teacher, or his pupils. His way of talking to his pupils will also change according to the matter in hand — teaching an academic subject, organizing the school concert, or handing out punishments. People therefore adapt their speech according to the person they are talking to and the point behind the talk. These are social, rather than purely linguistic, constraints.

As further examples of what I have in mind by talking about language variation, consider the following rather mixed bag of 'styles' or 'varieties'[6] of spoken and written English: B.B.C. English, Black English, Brooklynese, Cockney, officialese, journalese, lecturing, church sermon, talking shop, talking lah-de-dah, talking down to someone, chatting someone up, giving someone the lowdown, giving someone a dressing down, getting something off one's chest, small talk, hippie talk, men's talk, women's talk, a heart-to-heart talk, whispering sweet nothings . . . These language varieties might be distinguished along several dimensions, notably geographical, social class and functional. But their description involves questions of the same order: namely, who says what to whom? when? why? and how? In addition, more than one dimension is typically involved in any one of the varieties mentioned. For example B.B.C. English not only has geographical and social class implications, but also shows functional specialization: the B.B.C. announcer probably does not speak B.B.C. English at the breakfast table.

Some of the categories I have listed as language varieties might be thought of as speech situations, rather than styles or varieties. But speech and social situation are not really separable in this way. It is not simply the case that certain social situations demand, or make it appropriate that one whisper sweet nothings; by whispering sweet nothings, the speaker may build up specific expectations in his audience and therefore create a specific social situation! Speech is therefore not just something that happens *in* situations — a sort of epiphenomenon. It is part *of* situations. To say, therefore, as I began by saying above, that certain situations 'determine' certain kinds of language-use, is to oversimplify. It is, rather, a two-way process. I will show below how the characteristic 'contact' language of teachers creates, and is created by, a specific social situation in the classroom.

Native speakers of a language therefore command a great deal of judgemental skill at variety-shifting to suit the occasion. Linguists have recently paid a lot of attention to the competence which native speakers of a language possess to distinguish grammatical from ungrammatical sentences. But a native speaker has internalized a great deal of other knowledge about his language, including: whether language he hears is appropriate to the situation in which it is uttered, and how to use his knowledge about social relationships in interpreting what other speakers say. In this paper, I am particularly concerned with these two aspects of communicative competence in the context of the classroom.

LANGUAGE FUNCTIONS

One way of analysing speech behaviour, which has become fairly traditional over the last ten years or so, is to isolate various factors in the social situation which influence or interact with the kind of language used, and to discuss associated *functions* which language fills in different situations.[7]

Language does not play a constant role across different social situations — it is revealing to consider how *un*important language may be in certain contexts! Yet many people still assume that language has at most two general functions of referring to the external world and communicating explicit messages (a referential-cognitive function) and of expressing feelings (an emotive function). This distinction may hold as an initial classification, but it is quite inadequate as a detailed analysis. It is now something of a commonplace in sociolinguistics to say that *language can have many functions*.

For example, in a lecture or a Third Programme talk — or in this book — language may have as its primary function the task of getting a message across and of persuading the addressee of some point of view. But cocktail party chat, talk about the weather, reminiscing about old friends, a headmaster's address to the school, or even pupils' avid discussion of last night's football match, may have the primary function of establishing or maintaining social relationships and solidarity — very little new information may be communicated. Other functions of language include: organizing social effort; reliving experiences; releasing tension or 'getting something off one's chest'; crystallizing ideas or 'putting things in a nutshell'; remembering things (a mnemonic function); measuring time; simply filling embarrassing silences.

In the same way, brief utterances within longer stretches of discourse may also have different primary functions. It is important to realize that the function of an utterance may be quite distinct from its traditional grammatical description. For example, a teacher may say:

Come down to the front.

This is a clear imperative. But he may also say:

Stevie, I don't think it's a good idea for you to sit beside anybody else, do you?

Although not in the form of an 'imperative' sentence, this remark has the clear function of getting the pupil to move. Linguists have so far made little progress in disentangling grammatical forms from underlying functions.

The main purpose of the rest of the paper will be to draw out some of the social messages underlying the literal meaning of teachers' words.

THE PROBLEM OF PERCEPTION: RESEARCH STRATEGIES

Isolating language functions in this way begins to provide a method of investigating the complexity of language-use. There are two distinct problems in reasearch into social interaction: one is to see what is going on; the other is to find a way of describing it.

Much writing on 'social behaviour' or 'interpersonal interaction' expresses an almost primitive awe in the face of its complexity or 'richness'. Researchers have shown many details in the patterned routines or conventions which shape our communicative behaviour at many levels: linguistic, paralinguistic (intonation, accent etc.), kinesic (body motion), gestural, proxemic (body position), and so on, but without bringing out the functions of the different means of communication found. A commonly expressed overall conclusion is that in human communicative behaviour, 'nothing never happens' or that 'anything anyone ever says is true' (quoted by Pittenger *et al.* (1960, p. 234)). Such paradoxical statements reveal disquieting truths. A teacher inevitably communicates something to his pupils the moment he walks into the classroom — by his style of speech, his accent, his tone of voice, his gestures, his facial expression, and by whether he sits stolidly behind his deck or walks up the passage and puts his arm round a pupil's shoulder. Members of a society do interpretative work on the smallest and most fleeting fragments of behaviour.

But in another sense, such paradoxical statements are unhelpful. There is no direct way to investigate such complexity of behaviour. If a researcher wants a fruitful strategy, it does not help simply to emphasize how skilfully we all manipulate and interpret information coming and going simultaneously on many channels. Too much happens too fast in the classroom for the researcher to take account of it and describe it directly.

The linguist-researcher has been a pupil at school, if not a teacher — he has been a native member of the society whose behaviour he is trying to describe. But, as such, he pre-interprets the behaviour just as other native members do. He 'understands' what he sees, even before he has a chance to record it. On the other hand, there is no reason why the linguist-researcher should be afraid to use his intuitive knowledge of the system of communicative behaviour in order to work out its structure. Indeed, there is, in principle, no way of inducing the systematic significance of fragments of behaviour, without making use of the tacit knowledge of the system held by a native or near-native member. It would be impossible to set up an automatic procedure which would allow one to induce the rules for appropriate speech behaviour in a given speech community, without the privileged access to the meaning of the speech held only by someone with intuitive knowledge of the system.[8]

The 'seen but unnoticed' expectancies (Garfinkel, 1967, p. 36) which govern the smooth ongoing of verbal interaction are even more difficult to make visible in their relevant details than other taken-for-granted aspects of everyday life in society. Language is even closer to us than other social routines, implicated as it is in the development of our cognitive and self-regulative processes, as well as being part and parcel of our everyday social interaction. The researcher therefore needs some estrangement device[9] to enable him to step back and observe what is going on in situations of face-to-face verbal communication. It is all too easy to record data on speech behaviour — all one needs is a tape-recorder. But such data *are* too rich to be useful, unless one has also a way of focusing on the features of communication which are relevant. An undiscriminating gaze down the microscope will generally tell the researcher nothing. What events reveal depends on the nature of our questions.

One way of breaching the researcher's expectancies is to have him concentrate on the causes, forms and effects of *mis*communication. Rather than attempt to capture directly how people communicate, the researcher can concentrate on the *problematic* aspects of communication situations — points, for example, at which the communication *typically* breaks down or encounters difficulties. By looking at what happens when people fail to get the message across, at why this happens and at what speakers do in order to reinstate the normal smooth flow of interaction, one can gain insight into the routine structures of behaviour. Some researchers would go as far as to deliberately bewilder people by disrupting the routine structure of interaction, in order to study the manoeuvres they adopt to restore the balance.[10] But one need not go as far as this. Linguists are familiar with the idea that *characteristic malfunctions* of a system indicate how the system normally functions. This is one reason why linguists have devoted much effort to looking at children's language acquisition, at speech defects, slips of the tongue and various forms of speech pathology, such as aphasia.[11]

Even in everyday conversation, moments of miscommunication arise more frequently than is often realized. But there is a general rule in our society that demands that interaction proceed at a smooth flow: silences are often considered embarrassing and disagreements must normally be mitigated. So speakers immediately counteract departures from the smooth ongoing of normal face-to-face interaction by making (if necessary, violent) attempts to restore the 'ritual equilibrium' (Goffman, 1955). Normally, vigorous attempts are not necessary, since a constantly self-regulating mechanism generally operates during situations of talk — a delicately set thermostat which keeps the communication system simmering at the desired temperature. 'Gaffes' and *'faux pas'*, are only allowed to run their disastrous or farcical course on the stage. Participants in a conversation or discussion typically combine to minimize misunderstandings as soon as they appear on the horizon, by constantly *monitoring* their own language, reading between the lines of other speakers' speech and by keeping an eye on the system itself. But think of common expressions in English to do with communication going wrong and with people failing to pick up communicative cues: 'a nod's as good as a wink to a blind horse', 'he doesn't know when he's not wanted', 'he didn't get the message' and 'he can't take a hint'. All these idioms point to the need to do constant interpretative work on the attitudes underlying the overt message — the need to continually 'read between the lines'.

But these systems-management mechanisms are brought into action so fast that they are not easily visible except in problematic situations which force the speakers to take more explicit and vigorous correcting manoeuvres than usual. Examples of problematic situations which reveal more clearly the kind of strategy which speakers have for *keeping in touch* with each other include: talking to a blind person, or talking to someone on the telephone (no visual feedback); communicating with a deaf person; situations of cross-cultural communication; most situations involving someone met for the first time; teaching.

I am suggesting therefore that it is a fruitful research strategy to look at ways in which speakers compensate for difficulties inherent in the communication system. For people in social situations have not only ways of maintaining equilibrium, they also have systematic ways of dealing with problematic situations when they arise.

What kind of instructions are available to speakers who find themselves in problematic situations? What kind of competence can be imputed to them? What are the limits on this kind of ability? How do teachers compensate for the particularly bad communication conditions which obtain in the typical classroom? What kinds of sociolinguistic skills are peculiar to teaching? At what points will the teacher's strategies typically fail?

MONITORING CLASSROOM TALK

One social situation in which at least one of the participants takes particularly active steps to *monitor* the communication system, is the teaching situation. Such monitoring may actually comprise 'teaching' or at least a major part of it. Teachers constantly check up to see if they are on the same wavelength as their pupils, if at least most of their pupils are following what they are saying, in addition to actively monitoring, editing and correcting the actual language which pupils use. Teachers therefore constantly exert different kinds of control over the ongoing state of talk in the classroom.

I will refer to this communication about whether messages have been received and understood, and about whether speaker and hearer are in contact, as 'metacommunication' — it is communication about communication.[12] Paradigm examples of utterances with a pure metacommunicative function of checking and oiling the communication channels themselves, are found in situations in which speakers cannot see each other and therefore have no normal visual feedback. Typical (hypothetical) examples are:

'Hello! Can you hear me? Oh, you're still there. I thought you'd hung up'.

'Come in Z-Victor-One! Do you read me?'

'Roger! Out!'

These examples refer to the physical communication channels, in this instance, telephone and radio. But in addition, many metacommunicative metaphors, or common expressions in use in everyday English, refer to checks that the meaning of a message has been correctly conveyed: 'I couldn't get through to him', 'I managed to get the idea across', 'Do you follow me?,'We don't seem to be on the same wavelength', 'I'm sure he didn't mean what he said' or 'He never says what he means'. It is often useful to look at common idioms connected with speech and communication. In this case they illustrate that the speech functions which I have been discussing are not abstruse concepts coined by linguists, but functions which language is commonly felt to have by its speakers.

A particular kind of metacommunication is metalanguage: language about language, language which refers to itself. Again this is not something which has been dreamed up by theoretical linguists. Consider some more commonly heard expressions: 'How dare you talk to me like that!', 'She said it with such feeling', 'He likes nothing better than to hear the sound of his own voice', 'He always knows what to leave unsaid', 'Who are you to talk?', 'Who do you think you're talking to?', 'Don't use that tone of voice with me!'. All these common expressions draw attention to the constant gap between 'what is said' and 'what is meant', and therefore to the need to do constant interpretative work on speech.

KEEPING IN TOUCH WITH PUPILS

Teachers constantly use language with primarily metacommunicative functions. Consider the following more detailed examples of the kind of metacommunication which characterizes teacher-talk. The examples in italics are taken from notes made during observation of English lessons in an Edinburgh secondary school. They are the actual words spoken by teachers. For illustration, I have chosen examples which, even out of context, have a clear metacommunicative function, but the context must be taken into account in interpreting the function of utterances in this way. The different kinds of metacommunication which I illustrate here can, without much adjustment, be further formalized into a category system which would therefore comprise one possible coding scheme for classifying tape-recorded samples of teacher–pupil interaction.

(1) *Attracting or showing attention.*

A teacher constantly makes remarks primarily to attract or hold the attention of the pupils, and therefore merely to prepare them for the message still to come.

> *Right! Fags out please!* (The context of this example was given earlier).
>
> *Now, don't start now, just listen.*
>
> *Yeah, well, come on now, you guys!*
>
> *Eh, wait a minute, let's get the facts.*
>
> (The teacher claps his hands several times). *Right, right, right, right, right!*
>
> *. . . you pair of budgies at the back!*

Or he may say something to show his own continued attention to the pupils when they are speaking.

Yeah. Mmhm. Uhuh.

(2) *Controlling the amount of speech*

Teachers frequently exert control simply over whether pupils speak or not. This may take the form of an order to a pupil to say something, or a request (usually an order) not to speak.

Do you want to say something at this point?

Brenda? . . . (long pause). Morag?

Anything else you can say about it?

I could do with a bit of silence.

I don't like this chattering away.

Look, I'd prefer it if you belted up.

Who's that shouting and screaming?

Eh, some of you are not joining in the studious silence we're trying to develop.

(3) *Checking or confirming understanding.*

Teachers may check whether they have understood a pupil, or confirm that they have understood.

A very serious what? I didn't catch you.

I see.

And they may try and check whether their pupils are following.

Do you understand, Stevie?

(4) *Summarizing*

Teachers often summarize something that has been said or read, or summarize the situation reached in a discussion or lesson; or they may ask a pupil to give a summary of something that has been said or read.

The rest all seem to disagree with you.

Well, what I'm trying to say is . . .

(5) *Defining*

A teacher may offer a definition or reformulation of something that has been said or read.

Incarnate — that means 'in the flesh'.

Well, these are words suggesting disapproval.

Sonsie is just 'well stacked'.

Whore — (the word occurred in a poem) — *now you don't want to get too technical about that word — it's just a girl.*

Or the teacher may ask a pupil to give a definition, or to clarify something.

Well, Brenda, does that mean anything to you?

What's 'glaikit'?

David, what's the meaning of 'hurdies'?

Can anybody put that in a different way?

('Sonsie', 'glaikit' and 'hurdies' are Scots words, meaning respectively 'attractive, buxom', 'stupid' and 'buttocks or hips').

(6) *Editing*

He may comment on something a pupil has said or written, implying a criticism or value judgement of some kind.

I take it you're exaggerating.

That's a good point.

That's getting nearer it.

No, no, we don't want any silly remarks.

(7) *Correcting.*

Or he may actually correct or alter something a pupil has said or written, either explicitly or by repeating the 'correct' version.

TEACHER: *David, what's the meaning of 'paramount'?*

PUPIL: *Important.*

TEACHER: *Yes, more than that, all-important.*

(The teacher is correcting a pupil's essay with him). *The expression 'less well endowed' might be the expression you're wanting — men don't usually pursue women because they're 'well-built'.*

(8) *Specifying topic*

Finally, the teacher may focus on a topic of discussion or place some limits on the relevance of what may be said.

I'm not sure what subject to take.

You see, we're really getting onto the subject now.

Now, we were talking about structures and all that.

Now, before I ask you to write something about it, we'll talk about it.

Well, that's another big subject.

Note first that the criteria for the kinds of teacher-talk discussed are consistently functional. I am concerned here with the kinds of things that teachers *do,* and not directly with the 'style' of language in which they do it. A teacher may ask his pupils to 'develop a studious silence' or to 'belt up'. On my analysis, both these requests fulfil the same function of controlling the amount of talk in the classroom. Clearly, at least some of the remarks I quote also perform other functions simultaneously. For example, a remark that some pupils are not joining in the studious silence we are trying to develop might perform the function of 'being sarcastic'. I am directly concerned in this paper with only one level of language functions.

Second, the way in which I have described the speech functions means that some functions are automatically subcategories of others. For example, if a teacher defines something that has been said, then he is also performing the function of checking that his pupils understand something, as well as attracting their attention. Similarly, if the teacher requests a pupil to define something, he is again checking whether he and the pupils are on the same wavelength, as well as requesting the pupil to speak and also attracting attention. It is for this reason that I have been careful all along to speak of utterances having a 'primary' or 'main' function. For it is a characteristic of speech that utterances typically fulfil several distinct functions simultaneously, although it is often possible to rank them in order of importance.

My claim is first then that the examples I have given of teacher-talk all have a primarily metacommunicative function of monitoring the working of the communication channels, clarifying and reformulating the language used.

My second claim is that such metacommunication is highly characteristic of teacher-talk, not only because it comprises a high percentage of what teachers do spend their time saying to their pupils, but also in the sense that its use is radically asymmetrical. Speakers hold quite specific expectations that it is the teacher who uses it. It is almost never used by the pupils; and, when it is, it is a sign that an atypical teaching situation has arisen.

As a more extended example of the kind of analysis I have proposed of teachers' use of language, consider the following extract from the beginning of a tape-recorded discussion between a young native English speaking teacher and two French boys aged twelve. The communication is problematic in some of the ways I discussed above. The teacher has been asked to discuss a specific subject, capital punishment, with the pupils. Initiating a discussion is typically more problematic than continuing it once it is under way. (Consider the difficulty sometimes caused by having to initiate social contacts and 'break the ice' with strangers and how offering cigarettes and other ruses are often used to oil the embarrassing first moments). But here, the teacher has the added problem of explaining to pupils, who do not speak very good English, exactly what is required of them. Almost all his effort is therefore devoted to coaxing along the communication process itself: proposing a topic of discussion, checking if his pupils are following, defining terms, inviting the pupils to speak, editing and correcting their language. There is almost nothing he says in this short extract which does not fall into one of the categories of metacommunication as defined above. The primarily metacommunicative functions of the teacher's language are glossed down the right-hand side of the page.

(The punctuation used for written English cannot adequately represent speech, but has been used to facilitate reading the extract. It does not affect the points I am making. Dashes [—] are used to represent short hesitation pauses).

Literal transcript of tape-recording	Metacommunicative functions
T1: *Right.*	Attracts pupils' attention
as I was saying — —	Attracts pupils' attention
the subject of the discussion.	
is capital punishment —	Defines topic of discussion
Now —	Attracts pupils' attention
you don't understand	
what this means —	Checks if pupils understand
capital punishment —	
is when — a murderer	Defines a term
do you know what a	
murderer is? —	Checks if pupils understand
A murderer.	Repeats to check understanding
P1: *Yes.*	
T1: *If a man kills another man*	
P1: *Ah yes, yes.*	
T1: *he is a murderer —*	Defines a word
then — when — a	
murderer is arrested —	
and he has a trial —	
then what happens to him	
afterwards? —	Invitation to speak
What happens after that?	Reformulates to check understanding
P1: *He has a punishment.*	
T1: *Yes.*	Value judgement on answer
He is punished.	Alters pupil's language
P1: *Punished.*	
T1: *Now —*	Attracts pupils' attention
What punishment do you	
think he should get?	Invitation to speak
P2: *Prison.*	

T1:	*Prison.*	Checks his own understanding or shows attention
P2:	(Makes strangling gesture)	
T1:	*Can you tell what — ? explain.*	Explicit invitation to speak, and clarify
P2:	*They put a rot*	
T1:	*A rope.*	Corrects pupil's English
P2:	*A rope — around his neck.*	
T1:	*Yes.*	Shows attention
P2:	*And hang him.*	
T1:	*And hang him.*	Repeats to check his own understanding or show attention
	So, ah, we've got two different ideas here.	Summarizes situation reached

In this fairly extreme, and for that reason all the more revealing, example, one can see very clearly some of the strategies which a native speaker of English employs to try and *keep in touch* with a foreign speaker and which a teacher employs to *keep in touch* with pupils. Very few studies have explored what speakers actually *do* in order to communicate across this kind of language barrier.

Now contrast the example of teacher–pupil discussion above with the following extract between another young native English speaking teacher and two older French pupils aged seventeen. The main point to be noted about the following extract is that the *pupils* use language which has clear metacommunicative functions — in other words they use language which is normally restricted to the teacher. The teacher still uses language to try and direct the discussion, although he lets some mistakes go without comment. But the pupils are also spontaneously using language which refers back to things they have previously said, defines terms they have used, sums up their own position, questions the teacher's summary of what they have said and questions his right to ask certain questions. This means that the teaching situation is more like a genuine discussion with the participants on an equal footing. On the other hand, the teacher's position is threatened to some extent and this is reflected in the way he has lost his casualness. He hesitates, repeats words and phrases, and makes a lot of false starts.

A discussion on corporal punishment has been under way for about ten minutes.

T2: *You don't think corporal punishment is eh — in a school — you think corporal punishment is all right at home — but eh — but not in a school.*

P3: No. I don't say that. I said until a certain level the cane I am against.

T2: 'Until a certain level', I don't understand you.

P3: Ah yes, I explained ten minutes ago.

T2: Well, — I still don't – 'until a certain level', I don't — I don't quite understand what you mean.

P3: The cane I am against, slaps I am for.

T2: Oh — yeah — I see.

P4: I can't agree — if eh, a smack can do nothing

T2: A slap.

P4: A slap can do nothing if eh — I don't know — a text to learn by heart do nothing.

T2: You think that a text is just the same thing — thing to give eh — something like em — lines — to write out or to learn — it's just the same thing?

P4: It's not the same thing — I don't say that — it has no more effect.

T2: It has no more effect.

(The discussion continued with P4 telling a story about a friend of a friend who had committed suicide after being corporally punished in school. The teacher brought the discussion to a close as follows).

T2: Would you like to eh say — sum up what you think about — corporal punishment in general?

P3: In general?

T2: Like to sum up yeah — what you think now after this discussion — in a few words to say — what you think.

P3: I am always of the same opinion. I am against.

T2: You're against corporal punishment.

P3: Yes.

T2: And eh —

P3: There are we have too many bad consequences in the future for —

P4: But I keep the same opinion as the eh —

T2: You have the same opinion.

P4: Yes, because what you said — what you said — what you told us, it's nothing. I have destroyed — for me, I think that — it seems for me that with the last example that I give you, all your opinions are com — all your em —

T2:   *Arguments.*

P4:   *Arguments are completely destroyed.*

T2:   *For you.*

P4:   *Yes, I think.*

T2:   *Well, I think we'll leave it at that.*

The discussion ended at this point. Having provided the pupil with the word he needs to complete his attack, the teacher simply breaks off discussion with a conventional phrase. The loss of casualness throughout the teacher's speech indicates a break in the routines. As Hymes (1962) says:

> In general, instances of the breaking off of communication or uneasiness in it, are good evidence of a rule or expectation about speaking . . .

If people feel uneasy when one thing happens, then they had expectations that something else could have, or should have, happened in its place. So the extract illustrates another way in which the study of *mis*communication is fruitful. A useful way of working out what rules hold in a situation, if there is no direct way to observe them, is to study what happens when they are broken. Speakers have systematic ways of adapting to the problematic, but these ways are restricted. Some measures of speakers' rigidity or flexibility in adapting to breaks in the routines can probably be developed. One could study for example whether different teachers make different use of the metacommunicative functions listed above.

A DESCRIPTIVE RULE OF SPEECH BEHAVIOUR

What I have called the systems-management aspect of situations of talk, has two sides to it: first, the effort which goes into simply making the interaction continue smoothly: second, the expression of values which underlies this.

I have already pointed out the radically asymmetrical situation of talk which typically holds in a school classroom. One can go further and say that many forms of language which a teacher uses frequently with his pupils would simply not be tolerated in other situations in which different expectations hold about the rights which the various speakers have. For example, a typical teacher-question is 'What do you mean?'. Pupils are frequently asked to define more precisely what they are talking about. But Garfinkel (1967, p. 42 ff.) describes experiments in which people were asked to clarify the meaning of commonsense remarks made in the course of different everyday conversations and small talk about the weather, the speaker's health, activities they were engaged in, and so forth. When students asked unsuspecting friends and spouses to clarify 'what they meant' by remarks which would ordinarily have passed unnoticed, initial bewilderment sometimes passed into violent reactions of the 'what do you mean, "what do I mean?"?' type. Having described several incidents of this kind, Garfinkel does not make explicit however that only specific social situations where specific role relations hold between speakers will permit explicit monitoring of the other's speech in this way.

The quite specific expectations which speakers hold about what constitutes appropriate monitoring behaviour for other participants can be formulated as a descriptive rule as follows.[13, 14] Suppose there are two speakers, A and B. Now,

> if A makes repeated and unmitigated statements about B's speech, or asks repeated and unmitigated questions about B's understanding of A, B will accept these statements or questions as legitimate and appropriate only if B believes that A has the right to make such statements or ask such questions; and this right is inherent in only a limited number of role relationships of which the paradigm example is teacher–pupil, where A fills the role of teacher.

The various qualifications in the rule as I have formulated it, cover various cases. A pupil *may* sometimes be permitted to ask mitigated metaquestions of a teacher, such as 'I don't quite see what you mean' (hypothetical example). Similarly, I specify 'repeated' since a pupil may get away with an occasional example, but only a teacher can do it frequently. This is a case of particular difficulty in describing speech behaviour, namely that there are often no absolutes which can be isolated in conversational analysis. A feature of speech may express no particular social information about the speaker if present in low proportion, but will give significant information in high percentages. For example, little information about the social relationships of speaker and hearer is available from the fact that metacommunication occurs. I gave examples above of everyday metacommunicative statements, and said that states of talk are always propped up and coaxed along in this way to some extent. But a very high percentage of utterances with a metacommunicative function, all used by one speaker, would probably indicate a teaching situation.

Note also the kind of concepts which I have used in the formulation of the rule of speech behaviour. The rule includes explicitly sociological concepts such as 'rights' and 'role relationships'. Some problems of linguistic description can only be solved in sociolinguistic terms — notions of variety-shifting require concepts of 'appropriateness' and 'language function' to deal with them. So it seems also that some aspects of sociolinguistic description can only be formulated in sociological terms.

One of the general implications of the view of verbal interaction put forward in this paper, is that any situation of talk is a microcosm of basic social and personal relationships. The kind of language used by speakers reflects who is talking to whom, and what the point of the talk is. By the very way in which a teacher talks to his pupils, he inevitably communicates to them his definition of the situation and the form of teacher–pupil relationship which he considers appropriate. The teacher's values, concerning, for example, who has the right to control talk in the classroom, as well as basic sociocultural values and status relationships, are put into effect linguistically.[15] I have indicated one way in which one can study the social order of the classroom through the language used.

CONCLUSION AND SUMMARY

This paper suggests both how certain concepts can begin to provide a descriptive language for discussing what teachers do when they talk to their pupils, and also how teaching situations provide a useful focus for developing sociolinguistic theory and method.

I have discussed how language-use displays a speaker's judgemental skill at variety-shifting to suit the social context, and how hearers use their complementary expectations as to what constitutes appropriate language-use in order to do constant interpretative work on language they hear. I have suggested concentrating on aspects of miscommunication, both as an estrangement device to enable the researcher to get free of some of his own expectations about language-use, and also as a focus for studying the skill which speakers have for dealing with problematic aspects of speech events. Variety-shifting implies a constant monitoring of behaviour which is characteristic of all human social behaviour;[16] I have shown how this monitoring is particularly striking and central to 'teaching' as a speech event. This view of teaching gives one precise interpretation to often quoted statements to the effect that 'we are all teachers'[17] in the sense that speakers are often concerned to persuade and influence their audiences. In other words, the approach shows one way in which teaching can be studied in relation to a wider framework of social interaction theory. A weakness of many studies of verbal interaction in the classroom has been their context-bound character — the kind of description given of teacher-talk has often been inapplicable to other varieties of language-use.[18]

Much of the paper has emphasized the complexity of communicative behaviour in the classroom and the wide-ranging interpretations which pupils inevitably place on minimal perceptual cues. Data on teacher–pupil interaction in the classroom are notoriously difficult to handle. I have tried to show that, in order to deal with this complexity, more carefully thought out techniques and concepts are needed. The main concepts which I have used are: language-variation, language function, variety-shifting, expectations, speaker roles and descriptive rules. These concepts were used as a basis for developing the concepts of 'monitoring' and 'metacommunication'. Some of these concepts are explicitly sociological as well as linguistic. But I have also shown that these concepts are embedded in everyday idioms and expressions concerning language-use and therefore reflect the way in which speakers talk about their own speech behaviour.

Linguistics (socio- or other) has no fully worked-out set of techniques to offer the educationalist interested in speech behaviour; there are accepted ways neither of doing fieldwork nor of analysing and presenting recorded or observational data on face-to-face interaction. The direction for research is therefore to maintain a clear theoretical framework, but to try and make some of the concepts (concerning 'monitoring' behaviour, for example) more precise, in order to isolate the kind of cues which speakers pick up and interpret. What research on speech behaviour needs is a hard look at 'soft' theory. In this paper, I have shown how various concepts *can* be illustrated from field data and have briefly indicated how a more formalized description may be based on systematic coding of recorded data[19] together with the formulation of associated descriptive rules of appropriate speech behaviour.[20]

Acknowledgements

For help and discussion during fieldwork I am most grateful to the teachers and pupils I observed and tape-recorded. The research reported here was funded by a Social Science Research Council postgraduate award and carried out at the Centre for Research in the Educational Sciences, University of Edinburgh. For comments on previous drafts of this paper I am grateful to Mike Byram, Henry Widdowson and members of the Centre.

An earlier version of this paper appeared as 'Keeping in touch — some functions of teacher-talk', *Occasional Paper 10*, Centre for Research in the Educational Sciences, University of Edinburgh, November 1972.

Notes

1. All examples of teacher-talk given in this paper in italics are the actual words spoken by teachers and noted down at the time during periods of classroom observation. Spelling and punctuation have been conventualized.

2. Hymes's term. Cf. Note 7.

3. American readers might put a different interpretation again on 'fags'! This only strengthens my point about the problematic nature of interpreting such language-use. Readers will be able to think up many other meanings the utterance might have in other contexts.

4. For example, I have more recently been doing work on the conversational analysis of tape-recorded discussion in committees and trade union negotiations. See Stubbs 1973.

5. The papers by Delamont and Hamilton (chapter 1) and by Delamont (chapter 5) discuss the type of category systems which have been developed by educational researchers for classroom talk and some of their limitations. There is remarkably little other work which attempts to develop descriptions of classroom talk. Barnes's (1969) study is now well known. A more recent study by Sinclair *et al.* (1972) is almost the only attempt to apply a linguistic analysis to the structure of teacher–pupil talk. The paper by Mishler in Cazden *et al.* (1972) is interesting for its demonstration of how a teacher's strategies are displayed in the very fine detail of his language. Mishler's style of analysis is similar in many ways to the paper by Torode in this volume. Labov (1970b) provides a general argument for the need for direct observation and sociolinguistic analysis of language-use in the classroom. And Hymes (1962) and Labov (1970a) discuss the more general questions of why traditional theoretical

linguistics has failed to come to grips with descriptions of language-use in its social contexts.

6. Distinctions which some linguists make between 'styles', 'varieties', 'codes', 'registers' and 'diatypes' are not relevant to my argument here.

7. The best known approach to describing speech behaviour along these lines was proposed by Jakobson (1960) and slightly modified by Hymes (1962 and subsequent publications). My discussion of the different functions of utterances in this paper is based loosely on the Jakobson–Hymes approach. My use of the term 'metalinguistic' later in the paper does not correspond with Hymes's. I also use Hymes's term 'communicative competence'.

Some of the Hymes's ideas have recently been applied specifically to the study of communication in the classroom: see Cazden et al., 1972. But the papers in the book, with a couple of exceptions, provide background material or general ethnographic description, rather than analyses of spoken classroom language. For a review of this book, see Stubbs (1974b).

8. A point made independently by Chomsky, in his criticism of American structural linguistics, and by the ethnomethodologists in their criticism of classical sociology.

9. Cf. Garfinkel (1967, p. 38), where he proposes techniques 'as aids to a sluggish imagination' which 'produce reflections through which the strangeness of an obstinately familiar world can be detected'.

10. E.g. Garfinkel (1967, p. 38): 'procedurally it is my preference to start with familiar scenes and see what can be done to make trouble'.

11. A classic example in another field is Freud's study *The Psychopathology of Everyday Life,* based entirely on the notion of how revealing mistakes in speech can be.

12. For a different analysis of metacommunication, see some of Goffman's work on face-to-face interaction, where he deals with the procedural rules which initiate and terminate talk, guide messages, change topics, etc.; e.g. 'Encounters are organized by means of communications about communications' (Goffman, 1963, p. 99).

13. Labov (1970a) proposes rules of this kind for other aspects of verbal interaction.

14. This rule concerning appropriate monitoring behaviour could be considered as a particular example of Goffman's general concept of 'civil inattention'. See Goffman, 1963.

15. The notion that people hold specific expectations as to what constitutes appropriate social behaviour, links closely to the idea that teachers' expectations affect their pupils' behaviour. But research on this has failed to show the kind of cues that pupils pick up. Having written a whole book showing that teachers' expectations *do* have an effect on pupils' performance, Rosenthal and Jacobson (1968, p. 162) have to admit: 'We do not know how a teacher's expectations for a pupil's intellectual growth is communicated to the pupil'. For another study of the effect of expectations on students see Hudson (1968). And see Nash (in this volume) for other references to this literature; and Torode (in this volume) for more detailed discussion of the minimal linguistic cues from which pupils may interpret their teachers' values and expectations.

16. A recent and very full account of the concept of 'monitoring', which places it at the centre of a theory of social behaviour, is Harré and Secord (1972).

17. This particular quote is from Morrison and McIntyre (1969).

18. For example, the coding categories in Flanders's systematic observation schedule are not applicable to speech situations other than traditional classroom teaching, or at least situations in which clear authority patterns hold between speakers. Flanders' coding schedule is given in Delamont and Hamilton's paper in the present volume.

19. A more detailed category scheme and associated model of metacommunicative functions of speech is set out in Stubbs (1974a).

20. The reader will have noticed that I still have not said how I *do* know that the

remark 'Fags out, please!' has a metacommunicative contact function! Roughly, I would propose that we interpret the remark in this way because of the position in conversational sequence which it occupies: (1) at the opening of the speech event 'school lesson', (2) immediately after 'Right', which more obviously functions to attract attention, and (3), referring back to my fieldnotes, before the utterances, 'People who want to do some language stuff come down to the front', and 'Come on then, will you get on then!'. In other words, we 'know what it means' because of where it occurs in a string of other utterances which serve the general function of getting the class organized and getting the lesson under way. In the present paper, I have not directly addressed the problem of how meaning is thus attributed to individual remarks. But, taking for granted that we can agree on such meanings, I have addressed the problem: how can we characterize one level of functions which the talk characteristically serves? For ways in which my specific analysis of this sequence can be justified, see how, at the beginning of the recorded lesson quoted above, utterances with a contact function characteristically cluster. Lesson beginnings can thus be studied for this characteristic use of language. For the only detailed study of sequential structure in teacher–pupil talk, see Sinclair *et al.* (1972).

References

Barnes, D., 1969, 'Language in the secondary classroom', in D. Barnes *et al.*, *Language, the Learner and the School*, Penguin, Harmondsworth.

Cazden, C., V. John and D. Hymes (eds.), 1972, *Functions of Language in the Classroom*, Teachers College Press, New York.

Garfinkel, H., 1967, *Studies in Ethnomethodology*, Prentice-Hall, Englewood Cliffs, N.J.

Goffman, E., 1955, 'On face-work; an analysis of ritual elements in social interaction', in J. Laver and S. Hutcheson (eds.), *Communication in Face-to-Face Interaction*, Penguin, Harmondsworth, 1972.

Goffman, E., 1963, *Behavior in Public Places. Notes on the Social Organization of Gatherings*, Free Press, New York.

Harré, R. and P. Secord, 1972, *The Explanation of Social Behaviour*, Blackwell, Oxford.

Hudson, L., 1968, *Frames of Mind, Methuen*, London; Penguin, Harmondsworth, 1970.

Hymes, D., 1962, 'The ethnography of speaking', in J. Fishman (ed.), *Readings in the Sociology of Language*, Mouton, The Hague, 1968.

Jakobson, R., 1960, 'Closing statement: linguistics and poetics', in T. Sebeok (ed.), *Style in Language*, M.I.T. Press, Cambridge, Mass.

Labov, W., 1970a, 'The study of language in its social context', *Studium Generale*, **23**(1), 30–87. Extract in P. Giglioli (ed.), *Language and Social Context*, Penguin, Harmondsworth, 1972.

Labov, W., 1970b, *The Study of Nonstandard English*, National Council of Teachers of English, Illinois.

Mishler, E. G., 1972, 'Implications of teacher-strategies for language and cognition: observations in first-grade classroom', in Cazden *et al.* (ed.), 1972.

Morrison, A. and D. McIntyre, 1969, *Teachers and Teaching*, Penguin, Harmondsworth.

Pittenger, P., C. Hockett and J. Danehy, 1960, *The First Five Minutes. A Sample of Microscopic Interview Analysis*, Ithaca, New York.

Rosenthal, R. and L. Jacobson, 1968, *Pygmalion in the Classroom*, Holt, Rinehart & Winston, London.

Sinclair, J., M. Coulthard, I. Forsyth and M. Ashby, 1972, *The English Used by Teachers and Pupils*, Report to S.S.R.C., University of Birmingham, mimeo. (Revised version, 1974, Oxford University Press).

Stubbs, M., 1973, 'Some structural complexities of talk in meetings', *Working Papers in Discourse Analysis 5*, English Language Research, University of Birmingham, mimeo.

Stubbs, M., 1974a, 'Organizing classroom talk', *Occasional Paper 19*, Centre for Research in the Educational Sciences, University of Edinburgh.

Stubbs, M., 1974b, 'Review of C. Cazden, V. John and D. Hymes (eds.), *Functions of Language in the Classroom*', *Language in Society*, **3**, 1, April 1974.

8. Teachers' talk and classroom discipline

By Brian Torode

Editorial introduction

Torode discusses some of the subtle and complex ways in which classroom discipline may (or may not) be maintained by a teacher's choice of words. He compares two teachers — one who successfully deals with challenges from his pupils and one who does not; he discusses how breakdowns in discipline are visible in the detailed ways in which teachers use language to respond to pupils and to explain their own actions in the classroom. Torode points out that 'discipline' has been avoided by social scientists: it is an area where staffroom folklore holds sway. And yet it is an area which can illuminate theoretical problems in the observation and description of social behaviour.

One of Torode's central preoccupations is with the complexity of the meanings conveyed in the classroom. This is a central concern of all the other papers, but particularly explicit in the chapters by Walker and Adelman, Stubbs and Hamilton. Torode's concern is with how pupils (and the researcher) 'make sense' of teachers' talk, particularly of their commands. On this theme, Torode's paper can be read as a radical theoretical development of topics raised by Furlong and Gannaway.

Torode starts from concepts that have been used already by Furlong and Delamont: the 'definition of the situation' and the 'presentation of self'. Torode argues that Goffman's concept of the 'presentation of self', as it stands, is only partially adequate to describe classroom behaviour. He proposes in its place a 'phenomenological' account of teachers' talk. By this he means an account which pays close attention to the fine details of behaviour (especially language) and which then tries to describe these details in their own right without imposing our presuppositions on them. Rather than simply labelling a teacher as, say, an 'authoritarian' who 'acts tough', Torode argues that one topic for research is to specify *how* the teacher *performs* such as character, and *how* he sustains such a definition of the situation.

All the papers in the collection assume the need for direct observation of classroom behaviour. But Torode takes this assumption a stage further by putting forward a theoretically radical argument that *observation* of a teacher's *own* way of 'presenting' himself to a class is essential if any rigour is to be achieved in our descriptions. He argues that the observations of outsiders are of less interest than the observations made by teachers and pupils themselves as part of their own talk within the classroom.

Torode's paper is the most theoretically oriented in the collection. It can be read as an implicit commentary on problematic aspects of observational research which the other papers avoid. Although Torode takes a different line from Walker and Adelman and from Stubbs, these other two papers on classroom language can be read as easier introductions to the problems of language, meaning and interpretation which Torode raises.

M.S.

Discipline in the school classroom is usually considered to be above all a practical rather than a theoretical problem. It is a field which sociologists have largely avoided, and one where teachers' folklore consequently retains a powerful hold. Yet one viewpoint current in social psychology seems at first sight tailor-made for the study of the teachers' work. This is the 'dramaturgical perspective' advocated by Erving Goffman. I shall argue that, in the form in which he presents it, this perspective can illuminate the performance of the teacher in only a limited way, but that it can be transformed so as to describe that performance from the teacher's own point of view.

Goffman's central notion is that, when an individual appears before others he 'effectively' projects a certain definition of the situation and 'effectively' fosters the understanding that a certain state of affairs exists. Goffman employs the term 'effectively' to allow that the individual concerned may not intend to convey any particular impression, but that nevertheless the others present may act *as if* he had done so. But generally, each individual in the setting will have various reasons for seeking to control the impression the others have of him. Goffman's interest lies in the techniques employed to sustain such impressions, both by the performer himself and by those who make up his *audience*. Generally, Goffman argues, the audience will cooperate; it is in their interests to do so since each in his turn as performer will expect cooperation in what ever role he himself assumes. Goffman writes,

> Ordinarily, the definitions of the situation projected by the several different participants are sufficiently attuned to one another, so that open contradiction will not occur . . . The maintenance of this surface of agreement, this veneer of consensus, is facilitated by each participant concealing his own wants behind statements which assert values to which everyone present feels obliged to give lip service. (Goffman, 1971, p. 20–21)

Thus the dramaturgical standpoint assumes a dual social reality. Its superficial appearance is of a polite consensus within which man appears as 'a *character,* a figure, typically a fine one, whose spirit, strength, and other sterling qualities the performance was designed to evoke'. But beneath the surface is an unacknowledged private world in which man appears as merely 'a *performer,* a harried fabricator of impressions, involved in the all too human task of staging a performance' (Goffman, 1971, p. 244).

It would seem that the case of the teacher's 'performance' before a class of pupils would provide a paradigm case for the application of this theatrical analogy. As such, Goffman's theory should prove particularly helpful to student teachers anxious to master the techniques of impression management as rapidly as possible. In order to apply the approach, we should need to ask, how can the theory be used to describe a particular teacher's actions in dealing with a class? Consider the following account, quoted by Goffman, in which an individual describes his performance of the role of a teacher:

> 'I start out tough. The first day I get a new class in, I let them know who's boss . . . You've got to start out tough, then you can ease up as you go along'. (Goffman, 1971, p. 23)

This teacher certainly describes himself as controlling impressions. And he appears to make some effort to identify precisely the 'character' he performs. It is the 'boss'. One attribute of this character is that he is 'tough'. But we are told no more. Presumably the teacher considered this adequate as an account of his role-performance to the interviewer. But, then he must have assumed that the interviewer was *already* familiar with the character 'boss' and that all he had to do was to *identify* the role, so that the interviewer could then refer to his own repertoire of knowledge about role-performance and fill in the details himself.

It seems then that, at least on this occasion, although there is no reason to doubt that the individual in question actually did conceive of his teaching as a dramatic performance enacting a 'type of person', his account did not contribute much towards a description of what the principles behind this performance might be. Specifically, it contributed nothing towards a knowledge of how to *perform* such a character. We are left in the dark about *how* to 'act tough'.

But there are more general grounds for supposing that no such interview could give more than accidental insights into the principles behind the action. For the interview is itself a social interaction within which, according to the dramaturgical standpoint, characters are being performed. In terms of the standpoint, then, there would appear to be two possibilities. *Either* the character being performed in the interview is the same as that whose performance was the topic of enquiry, *or* the character performed in the interview is different. In the latter case, an infinite regress seems to be involved, for to discover the dramaturgical principles involved in performing the second character would entail a further interview setting up a third, and so on. But, in the former case, what would be required is not a separate interview but *observation of the original character performance itself,* so as to record the performer's accounts of his definition of the situation presented within that situation. Then what we should be observing would be not simply his reflections on his definition of the situation after the event, but his constitution of that definition within the ongoing situation itself.

This procedure entails a modification of that advocated by the 'dramaturgical standpoint' theorists. Rather than *ourselves* seeking to describe the character(s) performed by an individual teacher, we can set out to monitor *his* accounts of the characters performed, by himself and by the others present, as a constituent feature of that performance. I shall now discuss some ways of going about this task, in the case of two teachers of a particular class of fourteen-year-old boys in a Scottish comprehensive school.

This was a lower-middle stream class of 41 boys, mainly of skilled working-class background, in a large urban school. I engaged in participant observation with this class over a period of six months from January 1970. Unless I had a special reason for absence I attended all of their lessons during this period and usually spent breaks and lunchtimes in the company of the boys. I also visited all their homes once or twice during the period. I maintained cordial but not familiar relations with the teaching staff and interviewed each teacher towards the end of my stay. However, all the data reported in the present paper were collected in the classrooms itself. I simply recorded conversations which I overheard, and which I found interesting, in longhand in a notebook. This procedure involved me in selecting a few speech acts out of a much larger corpus of utterances overheard. The basis for my selection remains to be described: roughly speaking, it involved a special concern with problems of order in the classroom and with personal relationships generally. The analysis here presented cannot therefore claim to describe more than a few features of conversations in the classroom.

MR. CRAMOND, THE ENGLISH TEACHER

Consider first the English teacher, whom I shall call Mr. Cramond. (All names of people, places and institutions are fictitious). His was the first lesson observed on my arrival in the school. His classroom was open and the boys entered before he arrived. When he appeared, I noted,

> At first, almost complete silence. As the lesson goes on, some talking, some gazing around, some whispering, hand tapping, and coughing.

The lesson dealt with etymology, e.g. 'tele-vision' means 'vision at a distance'. The teacher generally talked, then recapitulated, asking questions whose answers were the facts he had just given. I noted that there was 'lively competition' to answer and that he knew a lot of boys' christian names. Towards the end of the lesson he gave them 'seven minutes to talk quietly' and came to talk to me.

He told me that 'this class was very good — (he) never needed to reprimand anyone'. I noted, Mr. Cramond has a very relaxed air, though with a firmness of face and a hard voice which *commands* all the time'. He told me that he made a point of learning boys' christian names, because the use of surnames 'sets a barrier between you and them — I had that all through my school, surnames only'. Also, he told me, he always gave the boys five minutes to talk at the end of the lesson.

On my first encounter with Mr. Cramond, then, I made various observations which help to convey the atmosphere of his lessons. But they do so only by *identifying* features with which I was already familiar. This applies even to the points most directly bearing on character performance. To describe Mr. Cramond as relaxed, firm of face, with a hard commanding voice, summons up the image of a teacher with these characteristics — perhaps some sort of amalgam of other teachers whom one has encountered

— but it reveals nothing of what is involved in performing such a character. It is simply *labelling* the performance, employing my own past experience.

In my second lesson with Mr. Cramond, I began to make observations of a different kind. This was the second period of a Monday afternoon, which as I later discovered Mr. Cramond set aside for compositions. On this occasion, he began by naming two alternative composition topics, 'Hogmanay' or 'The Best Day of the Holidays'. He discussed some points of writing style, e.g. that paragraph beginnings should be indented but that otherwise lines should start close to the margin. Then he announced,

> *When we do compositions, we don't have any talking at all I hope that is clear* . . . (1)

This utterance repays a little attention. We could begin by asking, what does the utterance do? (Cf. Austin (1962)). A tentative answer might be, that it 'tells the boys not to talk'. But a problem arises. Obviously, this is roughly what it means. But presumably we want to be more precise about it, as precise as possible. *What would a more precise answer look like?* It might be one of the following: it 'warns' them to be quiet, it 'asks' them, it 'advises' them, it 'begs' them, it 'insists' that they do not talk, and so on. How could we choose between these?

With the information so far available, we would have no basis for choice. For the selection of one of these as more appropriate than another would have little to do with the wording of the utterance. The same wording could do any one of these things. Instead, it seems to depend on two kinds of factors. First, tone of voice, gestures, facial expressions, and so on: what Goffman calls the 'giving off' of the impression. Second, the teacher's actions, regarding the matter of talking in composition lessons, on other occasions. By taking into account either of these kinds of factors, we could judge whether his actions were more 'consistent' with one formulation of the pronouncement or another.

But either one of these procedures would simply involve *identifying* the individual's performance from among the observer's pre-existing repertoire of ideas about what utterances do. And again, as in the case of each such method so far discussed, there would then be no possibility of discovering how to perform such an action, given this interpretation of it. Unless one already knew, one could not in this manner learn what the performance of any such task entailed.

It appears, then, that to ask what his remark 'does' cannot help us to understand *in his terms* what the teacher meant. Suppose we resolve not to simply assimilate his remark to a definition of the situation which we already had available prior to encountering his remark. Suppose we assume that he means what he says and ask what it is that he means. One way to do so is suggested by the comment of Harold Garfinkel and Harvey Sacks (1970) that, in everyday conversation, stories told must be considered 'worth the telling' and questions asked must be considered 'worth the asking'. In short, conversational remarks are not to be understood as stating the obvious: they must be heard as drawing attention to unusual, or as we say 'remarkable', features of the situation at hand.

This can be done by the listener himself providing a version of the usual situation, in contrast to which he takes the speaker to be displaying the situation at hand as unusual. The 'usual' situation could take the form of a 'norm'. Thus in the present instance, a suitable norm might be, 'generally in English lessons, some talking is permitted'. The present utterance would then be viewed as adding to this rule the rider, 'but in composition lessons, no talking at all is permitted'.

However, this is not the only possible reading of the remark by this method. An indefinite number of other readings can be proposed, if we inspect the 'norm' here supplied and recognize that in several aspects it is imprecise. Thus:

(a) *The CIRCUMSTANCES specified by the norm*
Is 'in English lessons' *precisely* the usual rule? It could be that Mr. Cramond is invoking a more sweeping background assumption, namely that 'in lessons', 'in school', or even 'in situations generally', some talking is permitted. There seems to be an indefinite range of possible formulations.

(b) *The SUBJECT specified by the norm*
I formulated the rule and its rider as applying to a generalized 'one'. The teacher's own wording refers to 'we'. It seems as if his real meaning might be better expressed by 'you'! More precisely, this could be stated as 'boys' or, to save ambiguity in case other boys entered the room, 'J2 boys'. Doubtless there are many other possibilities.

(c) *The CONDITIONS specified by the norm*
The word 'generally' is only one possible formulation. More precisely, we could have 'on average' or some similar expression such as 'taking the rough with the smooth' or whatever, or 'as a matter of course unless otherwise stated' or something similar to this. Again, there may be many more alternatives.

(d) *The QUANTITY specified by the norm*
'Some' is only one possible way of putting the amount of talking permitted. Others would be for example 'a little', 'a reasonable amount', or 'only such as is absolutely necessary'. Many other formulations of quantity can be imagined.

(e) *The ACTIVITY specified by the norm*
I followed Mr. Cramond in formulating this as 'talking'. However in using this word he might have had in mind *either* 'shouting', 'raised voices', or some other variant of *disturbing* talk, *or* on the other hand he might have been concerned at the principle of the thing, and intended to refer to 'communicating of any kind'.

(f) *The IMPOSITION specified by the norm*
I formulated the norm as stating what was 'permitted'. However, this is only one possible version. Others, for example, would be 'welcomed',

'encouraged', 'reluctantly tolerated', 'ignored unless I see who is responsible', or whatever.

(g) *The AGENT specified by the norm*
I have assumed a silent 'by me' attached to the end of the norm. But there are many other possibilities: 'by the headmaster', 'by school rules', 'by a consensus of opinion within the school', and so forth.

Overall, then there is a great wealth of possible interpretations available, as to the unstated 'usual' backcloth against which Mr. Cramond drew attention to the situation at hand as unusual. In a similar fashion, the rider proposed to the 'usual' norm, by Mr. Cramond's utterance, can be formulated in an indefinite number of ways. We have, then, a vast range of possible constructions, the outcome of interpretative work by a listener to the remark. How is it possible to choose between them?

The account just given of my own interpretation shows that in practice one way is simply to 'jump to conclusions', that is, to produce one version of what the 'usual' norm and the rider might be, without noticing the indefinite family of alternative possible readings. A more systematic procedure would presumably rely on *either* asking the speaker for clarification as to precisely what he meant, *or* by observing his further utterances over a period of time. But each of the further remarks collected would itself be subject to the same indefiniteness of interpretation. This would only postpone the problem. At some point a decision would have to be made. How could this be done? One procedure would be as follows. We could simplify the choice dramatically by only admitting of two alternative readings as plausible alternatives. We could do this by attempting to separate out extreme alternatives from the choice presented by each parameter. In the present case (see Figure 3) these might be:

A. In lessons generally only such talking as is absolutely necessary will be tolerated by school rules.

B. As a matter of course unless otherwise stated I encourage anyone to talk to the extent that he does not disturb others, in my lessons.

In the teacher's remark itself, no evidence is given as to which of these alternatives should be taken up; indeed, they appear as alternatives only as a result of our understanding his remark. How are we to resolve our dilemma? Alfred Schutz (1971) has stressed the part played by *types* in the interpretation of actions of other people. Here we could resolve our dilemma by judging the teacher to take up one *type* of position or another. The one type would be the kind of teacher whom we would judge capable of producing statement A. We might label him the AUTHORITARIAN/ LEGALISTIC type of teacher. The other type would be the kind of teacher we would judge capable of producing statement B. He might be labelled the LIBERAL/PERMISSIVE type of teacher.

Figure 3 The indefinite family of alternative versions of the 'usual' norm presupposed by Mr. Cramond's first remark, 'When we do compositions, we don't have any talking at all. I hope that is clear'.

This family is generated by *first* 'jumping to conclusions' and assuming that the norm has the form, 'generally in English lessons, some talking is permitted' *then* reconsidering each feature of this rough version to see what possible alternative versions could be imagined.

(a) CIRCUMSTANCES	(b) SUBJECT	(c) CONDITIONS	(d) QUANTITY	(e) ACTIVITY	(f) IMPOSITION	(g) AGENT
In English lessons	one	generally	some	talking	is permitted	by me
In lessons	we	on average	a little	shouting	is encouraged	by school rules
In school	you	as a matter of course unless otherwise stated	a reasonable amount	bawling	is welcomed	by a consensus of opinion
In situations generally	boys	.	only such as is absolutely necessary	communicating	is tolerated	
	J2 boys		such as is not a disturbance to others	passing messages		
· ·	· ·	· ·	· · ·	· ·	· ·	· · ·

The interpretative procedure we have here employed is a version of what Garfinkel (1967) has called the 'documentary method', whereby an appearance, in this case Mr. Cramond's words, is treated 'as "the document of", as "pointing to", as "standing on behalf of", a presupposed underlying pattern' (p. 78). The underlying pattern, in our case the two types, is provided by the listener from his own pre-existing repertoire of such types. This procedure, then, exhibits the very properties of other methods of interpretation which we have been trying to overcome. Although we set out to describe the definition of the situation advocated by the teacher, we have only succeeded in reminding ourselves of what we knew all along, that there are authoritarian and liberal teachers, and that this teacher must be one or the other.

So far, we have approached the utterance under consideration with various initial assumptions. In the first case, we assumed that we ourselves had already a full repertoire of knowledge as to the activities of teachers, so that the only end in view in observing another one was to identify his action as one with which we were already familiar. In the second case, we assumed not that we the observers knew all about teachers, but that both the teachers and ourselves had certain background knowledge in common, which was presupposed in the interaction we observed. Neither of these approaches, it seems, could illuminate Mr. Cramond's act of production of his utterances, in the sense of showing how one could go about producing utterances like his. There seems to be only one more step which can be taken, namely, to refuse to import any prior judgement, analytical framework, or obvious background information, and instead to attempt to treat Mr. Cramond's utterance purely in its own terms. Edmund Husserl's programme for 'phenomenology', the science of appearances, is suggestive here. Stating that his method must presuppose nothing as already given, Husserl argues that whether or not our thoughts, emotions, or linguistic acts refer to existing objects in the real world, they have a describable existence of their own.

> Every intellectual process, and indeed every mental process whatever, *while being enacted,* can be made the object of a pure 'seeing' and understanding. (1964, p. 24)

In the spirit of this idea, let us set out to describe our teacher's speech in a presuppositionless fashion.

Consider what would be involved in the present case. Take the *we* and *I* referred to in the utterance. Obviously, it might be said, we know what these refer to: the boys and the teacher together, and the teacher alone, respectively. But, under our new attitude of mind, let us refrain from any such 'obvious' judgements, which begin and end with the assumption that there is nothing more to be said, that we already know what is obvious for Mr. Cramond. Let us assume that his remarks are *his* way of telling us what is obvious for *him*.

Let us ask, then, in what relationship are these two 'persons' posed as standing first to one another, second to the impersonal features of Mr. Cramond's picture? Seemingly, the *we* posed as subject to a rule, of the form '*if* A *then* B), (in this case, *when* one does compositions (*then*) one does not have any talking at all). The *I* then appears as standing back from the *we*, reflecting on its position: '*I* hope that (the position of the *we*) is clear'. It seems that here the *I* is posed as the interpreter of the rule. The *we* itself apparently has no room for manoeuvre within the rule. But doubt is possible in the province of the *I*, namely over the interpretation of the rule: the term 'hope' seems to express something less than certainty: it seems the *I* is available to the unspecified others present to make the interpretation clear if they wish.

The utterance, then, seems to convey the following definition of the situation:

(1) There are rules governing our position here, rules which can be explicitly stated.
(2) The rules affect all of us (the *we*) without distinction.
(3) My special position (the *I*) is not that I stand above the rules, but that I can interpret the rules to you if you are in doubt about them.

This definition is not simply conjured upon this one occasion. Rather is it portrayed as holding for all occasions. And on other occasions, Mr. Cramond reaffirms and elaborates the same definition. Thus, a little later in the same lesson, he said.

> '*Somebody talking. You know what will happen. No five minute break. Something else, . . .* (2)

The 'persons' portrayed here are *somebody* and you. Again, we can ask in what relationship do they stand to one another, and to the impersonal features portrayed? The *somebody* appears in a simply factual assertion. The *you* however, like the *I* earlier, is portrayed as reflecting on the situation, 'you know (no five minute break — something else) will happen'. In each case, the inner picture claims an inescapable inevitability, external to human choice: 'when we do such-and-such we don't do something else', 'no something, something else will happen'. In each case, the outer picture portrays a human figure contemplating this inner picture. The *I* 'hopes' what the *we* does is clear. It seems that the *I* has a certain freedom of interpretation, a certain looseness in its involvement with the world. By contrast the *you* 'knows' what will happen. The *you* seems to have no freedom: it seems to be dominated by the world. This, then, seems to be a fourth principle:

(4) *You* know the rules.

This second utterance, then, further elaborates the properties of the definition, in a way which also claims to go beyond the immediate occasion on which it was spoken.

Mr. Cramond did not always succeed in gaining immediate conformity with his wishes. Consider now his way of handling a problematic encounter. At the beginning of a lesson later in the term, he told the boys:

> *Right, everybody should be sitting in their own seats. As a general rule, we'll have no roaming around, because that's not a very good idea. And there'll be a lesson for those who forget . . .* (3)

Here again, we have the *we* governed by 'a general rule'. The rule is apparently non-negotiable and emphatic. It is also expressed in terms of *everybody*. In addition, we have a statement of impersonal *inevitability*, there'll be a lesson for those who forget, governing the case where the 'general rule' might be 'forgotten'. Interestingly, the *I* is absent from the whole utterance.

Almost as soon as the teacher had made this pronouncement, Alec Rialto got up out of his seat to talk to Colin Forrest. Mr. Cramond spoke to him as follows: 'Hey! Did you hear what I said? Get over there', (4) indicating that the boy stand out in front of the class. I noted, 'Rialto stands, shrugs his shoulders, . . . grins, and looks sheepish'. Having left him standing there for only a minute or two, Mr. Cramond said, 'Now, son, sit down and don't disobey orders in future, right? Use your ears'. (5) Sammy Mason now spoke to Alec, saying, 'He's a good lad, that's why he didn't give you the lash. Other teachers would have'.

In his remarks, (4) and (5), Mr. Cramond sustains a joke or fantasy, namely that Rialto had not heard his remark because he had not used his ears. In this way, he protects the integrity of the definition of the situation which he had earlier constructed from the threat posed to it by a boy's action which could have been constructed as contradicting that definition. For, in the terms of the joke, an *excuse* is provided for Rialto's action. (Excuses are discussed interestingly in Austin (1961)). This was portrayed, not as an infringement of the rule against 'roaming around', for which inescapable consequences had been portrayed, but against another rule (roughly, that one should use one's ears) for which no inevitable consequences had been postulated.

However, this interpretation was not the only one offered, by Mr. Cramond's remarks to Rialto. Another definition runs through these. The expression 'Don't disobey orders, right?' retrospectively suggests a redefinition of remark (3), as 'orders'. This expression, together with 'Get over there' (4), and 'Now son, sit down' (5), are themselves 'orders', in contrast to the previous remarks made by him. It seems characteristic of these orders that they are expressed with little of the elaboration which we have encountered in those previous remarks. They appear here when Mr Cramond was responding to a particular boy, rather than to the class as a whole. A similar case was the following. The teacher was reading a poem on the Pied Piper of Hamelin. He had different boys read each verse. After one verse had been read by a boy, Mr. Cramond turned to Jones, saying

> *'Shut up, Alan. You're a distracting member of the class. You know that,*
> *don't you?'* (6)

There are two distinct *yous* portrayed here: one within an inner picture, the descriptive statement 'You're a districting member of the class', the other portrayed in an outer picture, reflecting on the statement, 'knowing' it to be true. Jones is invited to affirm the whole, and with it Mr. Cramond's familiar definition. Mr. Cramond's location of his 'orders' within his definition of the situation is interesting. In the terminology of Max Weber (1964), the definition serves as a 'legitimate order' in terms of which the imperative is understood. The imperative is legitimated by assimilating the particular situation at hand to the familiar definition which is consistently and repeatedly reasserted on every possible occasion. Mr. Cramond treats an incident which could have posed a threat to his order as the occasion for reasserting and so strengthening that order.

A similar incident was the following. Mr. Cramond's room was in use for an examination which he had to supervise, so that the boys of J2 had to sit in a girls' classroom next door. Mr. Cramond told them:

> *'Right now. I think we know the order of events. You've got to get on*
> *by yourselves today, and I don't want to see anybody off their seats.* (7)

Here the familiar definition is reasserted. In the inner picture, the definite *we* is posed as knowing 'the order of events', watched over in the outer picture by the less certain *I*. On the other hand the *you* is portrayed as quite dominated by external necessity: 'you've got to . . . '. The *I* appears again later in the utterance, again in an indefinite outer picture contemplating a definite factual state of affairs.

The boys asked whether they could read books but the teacher said, 'I'll get you something to do', and brought in games of draughts, and comics. Then he left. Ten minutes later he returned. He at once pointed to Mears, saying,

> *'Right, next door. You were off your seat. You know the order of*
> *events. You were well warned.* (8)

Next door, Mears was belted.

As in utterance (6) above, the imperative here is contained curtly in the first three words. The remainder of the remark legitimates the imperative by locating it within the familiar definition, which is thereby re-affirmed. Three pictures portray three *yous*, thereby achieving some rhetorical force. They are not all the same *you* however. The first and third portray the *you* descriptively: they refer to a factual state of affairs. The second picture by contrast portrays the reflective *you*, in its familiar stance of 'knowing' Mr. Cramond's definition of the situation. Had we adopted a 'dramaturgical standpoint', and attempted a description of Mr. Cramond's role performance, we might have had to view this interaction as a breakdown in the teacher's impression management. Even after being 'well warned', we might have noted, the boy still acted contrary to the command. But in view of our focus on *the teacher's own* portrayal of the situation, we come to a different conclusion, namely that the incident provided the teacher with yet another opportunity for reasserting his definition.

Consistently, then, Mr. Cramond was able to treat the sequence of events in the daily life of the classroom as a continuous series of occasions for sustaining his definition of the situation. Only in part did this definition involve 'presenting a self'. This dramaturgical conception is incomplete in two ways. Firstly, Mr. Cramond does not merely present his own 'self'. Certainly, the *I* is prominent in his remarks, and it has certain distinct characteristics: it 'hopes', 'thinks' and 'wants': its presence is concerned, but detached. But the *I* is no more prominent than other 'persons' in his portrayal notably the *we* and the *you*, who each have equally well-defined features. And the *I* is just as likely to be absent from a particular portrayal when they are present as the reverse. Secondly, Mr. Cramond does not portray 'persons' in a vacuum. He situates his *I, we* and *you* in a context. This context, as we have seen, comprises 'rules', and inevitable laws (what will happen), which together Mr. Cramond calls 'the order of events'. He portrays this 'order' as having an existence external to the 'persons' in his world, as being, in the famous phrase of Emile Durkheim (1950), a 'social fact'.

These observations, of the teacher's portrayal of 'persons' present in the situation, and of the teacher's portrayal of a 'context' within which to situate them, have only been possible because, within the phenomenological point of view, we have refused to import our own assumptions. We have refused to assume, as the dramaturgical approach or common sense would presumably be forced to do, that the *I* is really Mr. Cramond, the *you* is really the boys, the 'order of events' is, perhaps, the official school rules. Instead, we have sought to 'see' and understand these phenomena in themselves. In this way, we have begun to open up Mr. Cramond's definition of the situation *in his own terms*. Of course, the brief analysis presented here only partially achieves this objective. But it seems to confirm that a speaker such as a teacher does indeed constitute his definition of the situation within that situation itself ('while being enacted', in Husserl's expression) and that this constitution is open to the sociologist's description. In so describing it, the sociologist is not simply viewing the matter through conceptual schemes imposed by himself *a priori*. Instead, he is coming to terms with the conceptual scheme of the Other whom he describes. We may say, alluding to George Herbert Mead's well known phrase, that he is learning to take the point of view of the Other (cf. Mead (1962)). Let us now turn to a brief comparison with another teacher.

MR. HOWIE, THE MATHS MASTER

In contrast to Mr. Cramond, Mr. Howie always seemed to be in trouble with the class. This is best illustrated by quoting a sequence of interaction taken from one of his lessons, before discussing it. The following occurred in my fourteenth week in the school.

'Teacher enters lesson, ten minutes late.

ALISTAIR MUNROE: *Boo! Boo!*
(no one else joins in)

TEACHER: *Right, would you turn to page fourteen* PLEASE*!*

CANNON: (shouts) *Where's Barrie?*

TEACHER: *Right, would you all stop talking, please?*
Cannon, sit down.
(no change in overall level of noise)
Now, just before we went away — '

VARIOUS BOYS: (interrupting) *Are we going away?*

TEACHER: (continues, ignoring interruption) *We were talking about sets.*

BOYS: *Sex! Sex!*

TEACHER: (interrupts uproar) *Scott, why is your book not covered?*
And Davis, yours as well.

DAVIS: *I just got it.*

TEACHER: *You didn't just get it today.*
The next thing I want to talk about is the interaction of sets.

CANNON: *What was that word you used?*'

Some explanatory comments may help in setting the scene. Mr. Howie was habitually late for lessons, largely because like other teachers in their first year at the school he was allocated many lessons in the Annexe, a quarter mile from the main school buildings, yet was allotted no time to walk between the buildings. When he arrived late, boys usually hissed or booed. On this occasion, however, Alistair Munroe, an unpopular boy, was not supported in his booing. The point about covering books was a frequent bone of contention between the boys and teachers. A school rule stated that all boys were responsible for providing paper covers for the books with which they were issued. The rule tended to be enforced only in the case of new books.

A characterization of what occurred in this conversation could be as follows. As the teacher enters the classroom, he is met with a form of communication (booing), but he ignores it. His first remark is a simple imperative. He is then asked a question. He directs an imperative at the class as a whole, then turns his attention to the questioner. But his response to him is simply a further imperative. The question itself is ignored. A little later, he allows a third question from the boys to pass unnoticed. A fourth interruption (Sex! Sex!) is the occasion for uproar from the class. Mr. Howie treats this as the occasion to ask some boys about their books not being covered, a topic which refers neither to his own previous remarks, nor to the interruption, nor to the uproar.

But these are simply commonsense judgements. What does the phenomenological approach tell us about Mr. Howie's way of speaking? As before, we can look at the 'persons' his words portray, before at the 'context' within which he situates them. For the first, his remarks portray a *you*, a *we*, and an *I*, as well as several named individual boys. How are their characters described in his words? The *you*, the first to appear, is persistently indefinite: 'would you . . . please?' appears twice. So also is the *I*, in the expression, 'I want to talk about' the *I* appears to have an uncertain relationship even to its own future activities. Mr. Howie's *we* is more definite, but only in a purely descriptive way. Overall, the persons portrayed are far simpler than those portrayed by Mr. Cramond. Consider for example the kind of consciousness which each teacher attributes to his 'persons': those in Mr. Cramond's presentation 'hope', 'think', and 'know', all rather thoughtful activities which permit some subtlety in his definition of the situation. Those in Mr. Howie's conversation, at least that so far reported, mainly simply 'do' things. The *I* alone is explicitly credited with a thought-process: it 'wants' a certain state of affairs. This term, also employed by Mr. Cramond among his other words (utterance (7) above), is not one which accounts intelligibly for the situation to which it refers. The boys are invited to talk about the interaction of sets simply as a want of the *I*. These wants seem to be the sole basis of any legitimate order to which Mr. Howie appeals.

This interpretation is confirmed when we consider the context within which Mr. Howie's persons are situated. For we see at once that he offers no definition which claims to go beyond the immediate situation and set up an enduring reality. His world involves no external social facts to which the boys could have independent recourse. The only recourse they can have is to the *I*, more precisely, to the *I*'s wants from time to time. Yet there is no reason offered why they should do so, and in Mr. Howie's portrayal (would you . . . please?), it is quite uncertain whether they will. The world portrayed in Mr. Howie's speech, then, is a world in which persons simply behave from moment to moment as they please, a world in which only one person has a clear view of what he wants, namely the *I*, but that person can offer no reason to the others as to why they should want it.

Our commonsense account simply presented an external characterization of Mr. Howie's unfortunate conversation with his class. It left unexplained why events occurred as they did. The phenomenological method has brought about a significant improvement. Now, we are no longer concerned to describe events in our imported terms. Rather, we attend to the teacher's own description of the situation, a description made while the situation was being enacted. There is no longer a separate problem of why events turned out this way, for we observe the manner in which those events were constituted, directly in the speech of those present.

Thus far, we have considered only the speech of the teacher. According to our analysis, his speech posed a dilemma for the boys in that it involved on the one hand imperatives and other expressions of what the *I* wanted of the boys, while on the other hand it offered no reason why the boys should conform with those expressions. This dilemma was well summed up by one boy who said that Mr. Howie 'tried to be a hard man'. One way in which the boys responded to this dilemma is exemplified in the sequence quoted. The boys treat his commands as the occasion for conjuring up fantasies as to what his definition might be — booing, 'going away', and 'sex' — all portray vague pictures. But however vague, they have one property in common, namely that they are beyond the pale of whatever definition of a Maths lesson Mr. Howie's *I* might be portrayed as wanting. Their production allows the boys, momentarily, to indulge imaginatively in very different wants. Mr. Howie says nothing to suggest why they should do likewise. Indeed his way of talking provides for the unlikelihood of their wanting what his *I* wants.

More generally, there were three main ways in which the boys responded to the dilemma posed by Mr. Howie's speech. First, they directly challenged his imperatives. Second, they indirectly challenged his imperatives, by offering their own readings of them (the fantasies we have seen so far are a simple example of this). Third, and most interestingly, they themselves acted in support of his position, by issuing imperatives of their own.

The first of these may be illustrated from an incident on my first day in the school. In the middle of the Maths lesson, Alan Jones loudly called out to me, to enquire what the time was. The teacher simply ordered him to leave the room. Jones replied, 'Get stuffed'. The teacher said, 'Leave the room', louder than before. He then unlocked a cupboard, and took out his leather belt, telling Jones to come outside with him. Jones did so. After a short time, the teacher returned, leaving Jones outside. A little later, Jones burst into the room again, saying, 'He's calling me names', indicating Gordon Russell. This was plausible, since he could have been watching through the glass window in the door. The teacher said, 'Get out Jones'. After some pushing from the teacher, Jones did so, while someone shouted, 'Alan, I'll stick up for you, pal'. A few minutes later, Jones came in again, strode across the room, and hit Russell lightly. The teacher again said, 'Get out, Jones'. Jones replied, very defiantly, 'Not if he's calling me names. Don't push me', and left the room again.

In each of his utterances, the teacher simply presents an unadorned imperative. No enduring legitimate order is posed *within which to make sense of his commands*. Jones replies in kind. He responds to the teacher's first order with an expletive and to subsequent orders with simple defiance. Since the teacher offered no definition of his position, he was unable to argue with a boy who offered no definition of his. The two simply confronted one another, with no common ground between their remarks.

Other boys could challenge Mr. Howie indirectly by re-reading his commands. For example, John Cannon was slow in entering the class one day, when Mr. Howie was directly behind him. The teacher said, Get in, Cannon, and pushed him. Cannon held his ground and engaged in struggle.

He laughed, and appeared to find it a great joke, for he said, 'What a weakling!, as the teacher had to concede defeat. Mr. Howie participated in Cannon's joke, saying to me, 'He's got some strength!'

Here it seems that, as usual, the teacher simply produced an imperative in his opening remark to Cannon. But Cannon, by his response, refused to take the teacher seriously. Instead, he treated the command as part of a game, wherein each party could play at being absolutist, whilst laughing to show that they did not really mean it. Once Cannon had himself set up this definition of the situation, the teacher retrospectively confirmed Cannon's claim.

But some boys acted to support Mr. Howie's position in the classroom. For example, Russell would shout out, 'Munroe, shut up!' to a boy he disliked. Mears nicely captured the hypocrisy of his position on one such occasion by commenting 'Russy, shut up, and dinnae shout!' Occasionally Mentone would assert himself over all the rest, saying 'Shut up, the lot of you, or you'll get a kicking. Do you think I'm kidding?' Intriguingly, in this last remark, Mentone himself portrays a definition involving a legitimate order involving precisely the features missing from Mr. Howie's speech. The inner picture here, 'you'll get a kicking', portrays an impersonal inevitability within which the *you* is subsumed. In the outer picture, the *you* and the *I* are presented as reflecting on the inner reality. The relation between the two pictures, though common enough as a form of speech, is of some analytic interest. The appearance of the Maths classroom, and indeed of the world portrayed in Mr. Howie's speech as a whole, belies Mentone's assertion as to the underlying reality. His irony, 'you think I'm kidding', makes sense of this appearance. His remark, then, sets up a distinction between an underlying real context on the one hand, and persons' reflection on it on the other, which we also found in Mr. Cramond's speech. Such a distinction is not allowed for within Mr. Howie's way of talking. Thus Mentone's way of lending support to Mr. Howie involves remedying this gap in the teacher's way of speaking.

The same can be said of Mr. Cramond's way of lending support to Mr. Howie on an occasion when he raised the issue of rowdiness in the Maths class during one of his own lessons. He told the boys.

> *'It's been brought to my notice that some boys have been having a jolly good time in the Maths class . . . If there are any more complaints, you'll be brought down here for one or two little jobs like cleaning the lavatories. If you don't settle down and realize that you need two basic subjects, Maths and English, for S.C.E., then you'll be brought right down here'.*

(The reference to 'S.C.E.' here is to a Scottish Certificate of Education examination somewhat equivalent to the English C.S.E., Certificate of Secondary Education). Despite the ingenious complexity of this remark, its overall structure is simple, and familiar. Following a descriptive point which sets the scene, Mr. Cramond launches into two statements which define plainly the social facts within which context the *you* is immersed. Like Mentone's remark ('you think I'm kidding'), but unlike Mr. Howie's, his speech makes intelligible the present appearance of things ('some boys have been having a jolly good time in the Maths class'), but affirms that this is not the underlying reality. The reality (you need two basic subjects, Maths and English, for S.C.E.) 'has not yet been realized' by the *you*. The distinction he is making here could not be made within Mr. Howie's way of speaking. Thus, both Mentone and Mr. Cramond posit a reality structure outside the setting of the Maths lesson itself, in terms of which what happened in the Maths lesson itself was to be understood. Despite these interventions, Mr. Howie's difficulties continued, and his ways of talking to the boys remained much the same.

According to my interpretation, there is a necessary connection between these two observations. Mr. Howie's problems were not, in my estimation, a consequence of his non-verbal communication patterns, his poise, dress, or tone of voice. In all of these respects he performed precisely the character of the normal teacher if, as Goffman would presumably have us believe, there is such a thing. The incessant and sometimes violent conflict which characterized his lessons was directly attributable to the teacher's failure to give an enduring definition of the situation while that situation was being enacted. The boys behaved, in the main, precisely as he portrayed them as behaving. Some occasionally tried to portray another way of behaving, in their own speech. The resultant situation was one which any dramaturgist could recognize as a breakdown in order, a failure of impression management. But from our standpoint, the breakpoint was visible before the dramaturgist could have become aware of it. It was visible, not in the shouting or the physical violence, which were merely features of the world as I, the outside observer, could portray it, but in the world portrayed by the participants in the situation themselves.

The case of Mr. Howie, then, seems to confirm the argument that has been developed throughout this discussion. This is that if we are to understand the nature of the teacher's work, his skills or lack of them, his successes or failures, then to treat his action as the theatrical performance of an identifiable character is unhelpful. For the processes of choice which supposedly constitute such a performance can never be open to inspection, either by ourselves as observers, or the others in the situation. In describing such performances we should therefore be bound to rely on external judgements which, however complete, would always be made from the viewpoint of one other than the actor himself. Such a description could never therefore reveal the dramaturgical principles which constituted the performance.

Instead, our concern should be with the talk by which the teacher constitutes his definition of the situation, a definition which may well claim to go beyond merely 'presenting a self' and may in particular involve the portrayal of numerous 'persons', including or sometimes not including his own self, situated within a 'context' posed as a social fact external to them as individuals. As we have seen, this talk can be investigated in a manner which displays the point of view advocated by the individual who produced it, in a manner which does not depend on prior conceptualizations or assumptions imported by the observer. Furthermore, this method holds out the possibility of a precise analysis of the response of others present to the definition of the situation offered by a speaker.

The role of the teacher would appear to be a paradigm case for the application of the theatrical analogy, since the teacher works in a setting where so many of the features of the stage which Goffman employs metaphorically, are literally present, built into the institutional framework (above all the performer/audience distinction). If his standpoint is, as I have argued, inadequate in this context, then its applicability to social action in any setting is seriously in question. The study of classroom interaction, and social interaction in general, I suggest, must shift its attention away from giving descriptions of actions to a closer examination of the speech which constitutes those actions as social for the actors themselves.

Acknowledgements

First and foremost I must acknowledge the friendly and unembarrassed cooperation I received from the two teachers I have named Mr. Cramond and Mr. Howie over a period of two terms during which time I observed their lessons daily. Thanks also to David Hamilton, Mike Stubbs and Peter Sheldrake for comments on earlier drafts of this paper. I have not always followed their suggestions. This research was financed for three years by an Edinburgh University, Special Postgraduate Studentship.

References

Austin, J. L., 1961, 'A plea for excuses', in his *Philosophical Papers*, Clarendon Press, Oxford.

Austin, J. L., 1962, *How to Do Things with Words*, Clarendon Press, Oxford.

Durkheim, E., 1950, *The Rules of Sociological Method*, Free Press, Glencoe.

Garfinkel, H., 1967, *Studies in Ethnomethodology*, Prentice-Hall, Englewood Cliffs.

Garfinkel, H. and H. Sacks, 1970, 'On formal structures of practical action', in S. McKinney and E. Tiryakian (eds.), *Theoretical Sociology*, Appleton-Century-Crofts, New York.

Goffman, E., 1971, *The Presentation of Self in Everyday Life*, Penguin, Harmondsworth.

Husserl, E., 1964, *The Idea of Phenomenology*, Nijhoff, The Hague.

Mead, G. H., 1962, *Mind, Self and Society*, Chicago University Press, London.

Shutz, A., 1971, 'The dimensions of the social world', in his *Collected Papers*, volume II, Nijhoff, The Hague.

Weber, M., 1964, *Theory of Social and Economic Organization*, Free Press, New York.

PART 4

An Applied Study

The final paper demonstrates one way in which the types of methodology and theory developed throughout the book can be applied to an educational problem area: in this instance, the implementation of new teaching methods. This study is, however, no less of a theoretical contribution to the explanation of classroom events than the other papers.

9. The advent of curriculum integration: Paradigm lost or paradigm regained?

By David Hamilton

Editorial introduction

Hamilton discusses the difference between educational ideals and the 'murky reality' of the classroom. The paper is a case-study of events in two Scottish secondary schools following the introduction of a new integrated science scheme. It documents the impact of particular school and classroom settings, and of particular teachers, on the ideal presented by curriculum planners.

The type of organizational problems which Hamilton describes — concerning timetabling, access to equipment, attitudes, interests and classroom practices of teachers, and coordination and communication between teaching and ancillary staff — could only be revealed by a classroom *observer,* present in the schools over a period of weeks or months, in the classroom and in the staffroom observing and talking to pupils as well as teachers. It is precisely such real-life situations which are inaccessible to a researcher armed only with questionnaires and 'tests'.

Concerning methodology, note how Hamilton combined classroom observation with other techniques. He used questionnaires and interviews, but not out of context: the researcher knew what questions to ask, through his own observation of problem areas, and his methodology was flexible enough to allow him to return to his informants for further observation or further discussion of areas which remained unclear. The nature of the problems determined the methods, rather than the methodological tail wagging the dog.

Whereas several papers in this book are concerned with describing classroom behaviour for its own sake, Hamilton brings a range of techniques to illuminate a specific problem area in education: what organizational complications arise in the classroom when a new curriculum is implemented? As a framework for his argument, Hamilton uses an abstract curriculum model, proposed by Bernstein, which distinguishes between 'integrated' and 'collection' (compartmentalized) curricula. The observational data likewise fill out this ideal-typical schema.

Note finally the analysis of the conflicting messages which pupils may receive in such a situation, from teachers, from teaching materials and from class-groupings and subject-organization. As with all the papers in this book, Hamilton takes as his topic the complexity of the communicative situation in the classroom.

M.S.

When any curriculum — however 'teacher-proof' it may be — is translated into classroom practice, it take on a reality of its own. Occasionally it may match the expectations of the curriculum planners but more often than not it develops in a variety of forms, some intended, some unimagined. Clearly, the impact of an innovation can be severely modified by the milieu in which it is used and by the uses to which it is put. In an extreme case 'innovation without change' may result.[1]

In this paper I would like to describe and interpret certain phenomena associated with the introduction of integrated curricula. Central to the argument is that introducing integrated studies implies a radical change of emphasis in the organizational context and thinking of secondary education.

The data for this paper were collected in 1970–71 during four-week periods of participant observation in two schools using the Scottish Integrated Science Scheme. During the observation periods I attended the science lessons of four first-year classes in each school. As far as the children were concerned I sat at the back with notebook and pencil and took no formal part in the lessons. When asked, I described myself as a former science teacher who was collecting information for a book on 'science'. During the lessons I kept a general record of events. Using a spiral-backed, pocket-size notebook I made long-hand notes on the left-hand side during the lessons and subsequently, used a different colour pen to add explanatory comments and subheadings on the right-hand side. In addition I collected a small amount of questionnaire data, attended a variety of staff meetings and interviewed the teachers and pupils observed.

Since there were few related studies available at that time the general tone of the investigation was exploratory. The approach was problem-centred rather than method-centred. In this case, the problem (the need to examine classroom phenomena associated with curriculum innovation) was instrumental in focusing the enquiry. The methods were developed, therefore, as the problem became clarified.

By relating the Scottish Integrated Science Scheme to a curriculum model proposed by Bernstein, the first part of the paper illustrates how a change from subject-specific to integrated modes of organization is not simply a matter of introducing a new syllabus but, rather, involves a range of complex questions only gradually being understood. It is now clear, for example, that immediate questions of curriculum content cannot be separated from more fundamental questions of selecting and grouping children, from questions of 'responsibility' and authority, or even from questions of school democracy. The added fact that the new 'integrated' forms of organization may be in opposition to the old increases the urgency and potency of these matters.

Besides these organizational and management aspects of the changeover from subject-specific to integrated studies there is a further series of barely-understood questions concerning its effect on children's thinking, knowledge and understanding. The second part of this paper focuses on this problem and describes two ways in which the organization of integrated studies may have a recognizable and potentially important impact on children's school careers.

INTEGRATED SCIENCE AND THE ORGANIZATION OF KNOWLEDGE

The Scottish Integrated Science Scheme covers the first two years of secondary education. It is designed to be followed by all pupils, streamed or unstreamed. In some shape or form the Scottish Integrated Science Scheme is currently being used in almost 90% of Scottish schools.

The Scheme is based on a Scottish Education Department report[2] and a set of 144 worksheets published concurrently in 1969. Curriculum Paper Seven — as the report is popularly known — contains not only a general discussion of the course but also a series of recommendations, a 24-page outline syllabus and 210 specific educational 'objectives' related to the 15 sections of the course. Although the worksheets cover the entire course they are not intended to serve as its text but merely as 'props' to support 'discovery methods'. Besides the features already outlined, the Integrated Science Scheme also intends that equal weight be given to Biology, Physics and Chemistry, that Science be presented in the form of an integrated study of the various disciplines, that the basis of the teaching be 'stage-managed' heurism and that multiple-choice exams be used for testing the stated objectives of the course.

Integrated and collection curricula

In a recent theoretical paper, 'On the classification and framing of educational knowlege', Bernstein (1971) discusses the social organization and transmission of educational knowledge and distinguishes two types of curricula: *collection* and *integrated*. In Bernstein's terms, collection curricula are characterized by a 'closed' compartmentalized relationship between the subjects; integrated curricula by an 'open' relationship.[3] The traditional curriculum of the British secondary school is therefore a paradigm for the collection type.

Furthermore, Bernstein argues that these two curriculum types can be linked to a range of distinct sociological phenomena that collection types, for example, are associated with strong subject loyalty on the part of teachers, a range of different subject ideologies across the curriculum, didactic instruction, a hierarchical conception of valid knowledge (principles more important than facts) and oligarchic control (vertical hierarchy of staff) within subjects. He also maintains by contrast, that integrated types are associated with weak subject loyalty, a common pedagogy, practice and examining style, emphasis on self-regulatory instruction, early initiation into basic principles (deep structures) and strong horizontal relationships among staff.

The Scottish secondary education system clearly illustrates certain of these second order collection features. For example, all Scottish secondary teachers — with the exception of craft and P.E. teachers — are graduates.

At the end of a year's obligatory subject-based postgraduate training they are certificated not to 'teach' (as in England) but to teach specified subjects.[4] Thus, there is a strong compartmentalization of subjects, strong subject loyalties induced, and a wide range of different subjects ideologies allowed. In addition, within each subject a hierarchical as well as a financial distinction is made between honours and ordinary graduates.[5] Until recently the latter were precluded from holding Principal Teacher (head of department) positions in five-year (cf. grammar) schools. Thus the vertical differences between honours and ordinary teachers are reinforced and made rigid.[6]

Despite the inherent collection characteristics of the Scottish system as a whole, much of Bernstein's paradigm for an integrated curriculum matches the intentions of the Scottish Integrated Science Scheme, viz.

Content openness	'Science should be in the form of an integrated study of the various disciplines'. (Curriculum Paper Seven, Recommendation 4).
Common pedagogy, practice and examining style	This is implied by Curriculum Paper Seven's advocacy of worksheets, behavioural objectives and multiple choice examinations. (Curriculum Paper Seven, paragraphs 33, 44 and 45).
Self-regulatory instruction	'The discovery method should be used wherever possible . . . ' (Curriculum Paper Seven, Recommendation 5).
Early initiation into deep structures (ways of knowing)	'a much reduced emphasis on the retention of the factual content of the syllabus. Instead . . . (pupils should be exposed) . . . to many other aspects of the work of the scientist . . . the experimental methods he uses, the different processes of thought by which he arrives at his conclusions and the language which he uses to communicate these conclusions to others'. (Curriculum Paper Seven, paragraph 8).
Strong horizontal relationships among staff	'Science teachers in a school should all be free together at least once a week'. (Curriculum Paper Seven, Recommendation 32).

Bernstein's analysis is elegant. It presents a theoretical basis for understanding not only the intellectual but also the social and organizational difference between subject-specific and integrated studies. In developing such an analysis Bernstein points out that integration — though perhaps thought to be a 'good thing' — may well present its own educational problems. He suggests in this context that 'if four conditions are not satisfied then the openness of learning under integration may well produce a culture in which neither staff nor pupils will have a sense of place, time or purpose' (p. 64). What are these four conditions?

First, Bernstein declares that the integrated idea may only work when there is 'high ideological consensus among the staff' (p. 64). By this he means that if integration is to become a reality rather than an ideal, there should be widespread agreement on its aims and objectives.

Second, he maintains that 'the linkage between the integrating idea and the knowledge to be coordinated must also be coherently spelled out' (p. 64). What is meant by this? With any integrated curriculum there is rarely a body of common knowledge (facts, principles, etc.) which can form a substantive basis for curriculum content (i.e. the syllabus). Rather, to retain the idea of integration the various contributing subjects must be linked at a higher, conceptual level. For example, the first three sections of the Scottish Scheme are concerned respectively with measurement, principles of taxonomy and energy, rather than with 'the metric system', 'the biosphere' and 'heat, light and sound'. They are thus at one remove from mere facts. Their subject matter is more diffuse. However, insofar as the higher level concepts must emerge from the content of the course, then teachers working within an integrated curriculum should be aware of the particular high-level concept being endorsed. Clearly, a teacher's pedagogic approach to the variety of animal life in a laboratory will differ according to whether he wishes to demonstrate that there are many (equally valid) ways of categorizing animals or whether he merely wishes to reconstruct the Linnaean system. Nevertheless, whichever the goal, the raw materials are the same.

Thirdly, Bernstein suggests that, as 'evaluation criteria are less likely to be as explicit and measurable as in the case of collection' (p. 65) there should be close face-to-face liaison, discussion and feedback between staff and students.

Finally Bernstein points out that if confusion is to be avoided, clear criteria of evaluation (i.e. what is to be assessed and the form of the assessment) should exist. With regard to these last two caveats it is no doubt significant that the development of new curricula has gone hand-in-hand with a concern for new forms of evaluation and assessment.[7] For example, among its recommendations Curriculum Paper Seven points out the following (emphases added):

> Tests should be designed to assess all aspects of teaching in science, they should *not* be limited to recall and simple comprehensive exercises. (Recommendation 7).

> Tests should be used for *other purposes besides* ranking pupils. (Recommendation 9).

> Testing should have a limited place in education. (Recommendation 10).

> An investigation should be made of what should be tested in science. (Recommendation 13).

THE REALITY OF INTEGRATION

Throughout his paper, Bernstein treats integrated and collection curricula as ideal types, that is, in pure form as analytical constructs. Here I want to turn my attention to the murky reality of curriculum development and curriculum change.

The essential tension between science and its component parts has a long history in science education. Throughout, the customary tension has been attended by other than purely pedagogic concern. In secondary education 'science' has been a low-status subject, taught by poorly qualified 'generalists' to poorly endowed or very young pupils. After the Second World War, secondary modern schools, recognizing the character of this ascription rejected 'general science' and made considerable efforts to raise their status by presenting science in subject-specific form; that is, as was taught in grammar schools.[8] By the 1960s the expression 'general science' was one of the shibboleths of science teaching. It was scarcely mentioned, rarely advocated. The fact that current variants of general science are now called 'integrated' science or 'combined' science is, therefore, not without significance.

The two Science departments I studied had an organizational structure that was essentially subject-specific; that is, each had separate organizations for Physics, Chemistry and Biology. When integrated science was introduced at the first school it was grafted onto the pre-existing subject-specific organization. At the second, a new school, the two organizational forms were developed side by side.

'Simpson' School

Simpson comprehensive school is on two sites, about one and a half miles apart, and serves a large prewar council estate. Observation took place at the Annexe (a former senior secondary school) where the first year (c. 500 boys and girls) were taught Science in thirty groups, each for five periods per week.

Early in the observation at this school I gained an impression that the pattern of teaching was constrained. Compared with the tone of Curriculum Paper Seven it seemed restricted in style and scope. Instead of being support materials the worksheets had become *the* syllabus and, as teacher demonstrations were often substituted for pupil practical work, class teaching had become the dominant activity.

Although there was only enough teaching for four full-timers, ten people taught Science at the Annexe; only one of them full-time. Most of the remaining teachers commuted from the isolated subject-specific departments at the main school, five of them for less than six periods per week. For timetable reasons eleven of the thirty groups had more than one teacher. Indeed, one group was taught each week by the three different teachers.

These factors: school on twin sites, excessive numbers of teachers and multiple teaching of classes, were basic constraints on the Science teaching. At Simpson, conditions were further exacerbated by teacher absences, by the shortage of apparatus, by the lack of laboratory accommodation appropriate to the needs of Curriculum Paper Seven and, not least, by the fact that integrated science was a new scheme.

The essential problem with such a large number of teachers was one of communication. At no time were all ten teachers in the building together; there was no opportunity for general discussion of the new scheme or for discussing pupil progress. For some of the teachers the only means of communication was a record book kept in the preparation room. In it each of them indicated the work or worksheet completed each lesson. If this was forgotten, chaos ensued.

When classes were taught by more than one teacher the communication problem was particularly acute. At Simpson, teachers sharing classes tried to maintain continuous progress through the course. (The alternative strategy was to divide the course — usually along subject lines). Thus, each teacher was required, week by week, to begin where the previous one had left off and to finish at a recognizable point. In a situation like this there was little scope for free-wheeling. As one teacher described it: 'All you can do is paddle along'.

For most special demonstrations or experiments there was only enough apparatus for it to be used by one class at a time. As several groups were taught simultaneously, complicated organizational bartering took place to avoid localized shortages. If it was a teacher's turn to use a certain piece of apparatus he had to use it when available or, as sometimes happened, forfeit the opportunity. The fact that some of the apparatus had to be ferried from the main school further added to this difficulty.

Finally, teacher absence was a reality rather than a prospect. At Simpson school it was customary for the absent teacher's class to be split among the remaining classes rather than to be taken by another teacher. Sometimes teachers did not return from their periods of absence. In the previous year four Science groups had been taught by a succession of five different temporary teachers. When a further teacher left without being replaced, five groups were distributed among the teachers that remained.

Each of these factors suggests reasons why the teachers were tacitly forced to follow the course closely. Anyone in this situation who had sought to develop his own ideas or even to fulfil the prescriptions of Curriculum Paper Seven would have received little sympathy from his or her colleagues; particularly if it involved their reluctant cooperation. A further reason for sticking to the course was that, as most of the teachers spent very little time teaching the integrated science course at the Annexe, they had little incentive to develop the 'additional materials' recommended by Curriculum Paper Seven. Finally, the various staffing problems at Simpson School had produced an instability that effectively precluded any long-term planning or development of the Science teaching.[9]

De facto responsibility for integrated science at Simpson Annexe was retained by the only Science teacher in residence there full-time. The fact, however, that he had no formal authority, nor yet a responsibility allowance, undermined the efforts he made. Most of this free time was spent easing the organizational work-load of the teachers who commuted from the main school.

Much of the day-to-day coordination, however, was not in the full-time teacher's hands but the responsibility of the laboratory assistant. Far from being an ancillary, she held a key position. Besides being the only person who knew where everything was, she also performed the essential task of ensuring the maintenance of entries in the work diary.

'Maxwell' School

Maxwell contrasts strongly with Simpson. It is a custom-built suburban comprehensive school that draws its intake from a mixture of public and private housing. The Science department is housed in a separate one-storey block and comprises sixteen laboratories built around a central store, lecture theatre, workshop and darkroom. First year integrated science was organized around 16 mixed-ability groups. At the time of the observation there were no pupils in years 4–6, and only about 60% of the possible total in years 1–3. For this complement of children there were three heads of department, two assistant teachers and three laboratory staff, none of whom had previously worked together. No one had special responsibility for 'Science'; the heads of department rotated the task termly.[10]

Conscious of their position and responsibilities, the teaching staff at Maxwell recognized many of the problems involved in setting up a new department and running a new science scheme. To meet the difficulties they soon established a sophisticated organizational structure to facilitate the implementation of what, for most of them, was an untried scheme. At weekly staff meetings after school, strategies were developed for keeping pupil records, for monitoring the use of apparatus, for preparing multiple-choice examinations, for making the most economical use of technical staff and for generally programming the sections of Curriculum Paper Seven.

At the staff meetings considerable discussion centred on the presentation of the course and the best possible use of the worksheets. Even the content and form of written work was discussed. Needless to say, as a result of this activity, the members of the Science department spent a considerable time preparing materials, worksheets and examinations outside school hours.

It is obvious in such a situation that the staff meetings were essential to the smooth running of the organization. At them, much of the long-term planning of work and the negotiation of responsibility was carried out.

In many, if not all respects, this system functioned successfully. Undoubtedly it resolved many of the day-to-day problems of the integrated course. However, it also created its own set of problems when the organizational structure began to exert its own hegemony over the work of the individual teacher.[11] As one teacher put it: 'We're so well organized at times I don't know what I'm doing'.

One problem that arose concerned the devolution of responsibility. Considerable time was spent at the staff meetings discussing who should be responsible for preparing the succeeding sections of the course, or who, for example, should be responsible for liaison with the laboratory staff. Very often these discussions revolved around subject loyalties and responsibilities. Was a 'Biology' section really a Biology section or was it a 'Chemistry' section? Was a malfunctioning fish tank the responsibility of the head of Biology, the head of Science or the persons whose room it was in? Who reported it to the lab assistants? Which assistant?[12] In situations like these there was an organizational tension between the informal 'parity of esteem' among the staff, and the formal hierarchical structure of the department. A further example of this tension was that, although the preparation of additional materials was shared out equally, only the heads of department had keys to the Science block (which was kept locked outside lesson time).

A second problem that arose at staff meetings concerned timing. In the interests of organizational clarity (and maintaining a 'common pedagogy'), dates were fixed well in advance for the completion of the various sections and for the setting of the multiple-choice section tests. Unfortunately, however, as various factors usually intervened a considerable time was spent at successive meetings rescheduling deadlines fixed previously.

A third problem concerned furthering the aims of the course. However explicitly they are expressed in curriculum papers or teachers' guides, aims or objectives need reinterpretation in practice. Considerable discussion took place at Maxwell School around what should be done. In the interests of presenting a unified course, this generally meant seeking agreed common ground rather than allowing for divergence of content and method.

From the data presented it is apparent that certain features of the model proposed by Bernstein were exemplified at Simpson and Maxwell. In their own ways — as quite distinct schools — Simpson and Maxwell represent two distinct types. Simpson is an example of a school where a new integrated curriculum was *assimilated* and then *redefined* in terms of an *old* collection curriculum (cf. 'innovation without change'). Thus, integrated science at Simpson retained certain important features of a collection curriculum: didactic (factual) instruction predominated; teachers maintained their subject identities; and, as horizontal relationships among staff remained weak, effective control rested with the only full-time teacher (cf. 'oligarchic control').

As foreshadowed earlier, the general 'collection' effect — characteristic of secondary education in Scotland — swamped attempts to introduce the integrated ideas.

By contrast, Maxwell is an example of a school where a *new* integrated curriculum was introduced, albeit rather precariously. However, relative to Simpson where the process of assimilation was almost complete, the future career of the integrated curriculum at Maxwell was less determined. As a new school—with all its associated benefits—Maxwell has ample opportunity to successfully establish the new curriculum. Yet, the fact that there were two or three years before it achieved a 'stable state' (full quota of staff and students) and the fact that it intended developing collection curricula in years three to six, meant that it could easily fall back on traditional subject-specific patterns of organization in years one or two. As a partially formulated and yet dynamic situation, Maxwell clearly presented a more changeable aspect than Simpson.

COLLECTION AND INTEGRATED CURRICULA: PROBLEMS OF MANAGEMENT

As already stated, Bernstein's curriculum model only applies to clear-cut situations.[13] At this point I want to go beyond his analysis and consider the situation where integrated and collection curricula coexist side by side. Such a mixture of curriculum types is a widespread phenomenon. It exists not only in the schools I have studied but also in those secondary schools which have introduced integrated curricula in their junior years while retaining collection curricula for their examination dominated senior years.[14]

Although it is logically possible for the 'organizational' problems to be reduced in a situation of mixed curricula, it is more often the case that they are heightened. This may be for the reason that certain features of the curriculum types outlined by Bernstein are in direct opposition to each other. At the theoretical level, for example, the integrated idea is sustained by stressing the unity of science, the collection idea is sustained by stressing its diversity.

Where integrated and collection curricula operate side by side, a considerable amount of time is spent on negotiation and management. This is particularly so if large numbers of teachers are involved. When rooms, time and equipment are shared (is this a Chemistry beaker or a Science beaker?) and when, as in a large school, cross-cutting patterns of responsibility exist (heads of Science *and* heads of Physics, Chemistry and Biology), the allocation of resources must be negotiated and administered among the parties involved. Each, however, may have divergent views on priority. (For example, the 'integrationists' might emphasize the early years, the 'subject-specialists' the later years).

If a collection (hierarchical) model of staff meetings is employed (e.g. only heads of department) ill-will may be created among other members of staff who expect the more 'open', democratic form of organization characteristic of integration.

In a situation of mixed curricula there may also be a need to acknowledge the individuality of members of staff who teach within the integrated set-up. Thus, if teachers have been used to the autonomy of a subject-specific curriculum they may feel cheated of their independence when forced to relate to a 'common pedagogy, practice and examining style'.

As much of the teaching under integration involves coordination and cooperation, the actions of individual teachers can become the public concern of their colleagues. Under conditions of reduced autonomy, each teacher may be forced to give an 'account' of his actions, that is, to explain, even defend his methods to others. Some teachers may feel threatened by such a situation, particularly if they are precluded from withdrawing to the ready alternative of a collection curriculum.

Under these conditions of coexisting curricula it is sometimes possible for individuals, particularly those in authority, to play the features of one curriculum type against another. It might be possible, to take a scurrilous example, for a head of Geography who is also in charge of Humanities, to increase the supply of Geography books at the expense of the Humanities allowance.

In a similar way, ancillary staff (librarians, audiovisual technicians, and secretaries) can also become powerful figures. Sometimes, as the only people who span both curricula and know exactly what is happening, they too can wield one curriculum against another.

So far, I have described how the organization of an integrated curriculum in two schools affected the teacher and his task. In outlining certain positive and negative constraints and certain contradictions, I have documented various responses to the introduction of an integrated curriculum. By describing innovation in these terms and relating it to real-life situations it is possible to see the operation of a socio-organizational influence that, at times, swamps the niceties of curriculum development. The adoption of an instructional system such as the Scottish Integrated Science Scheme may involve far from trivial modifications in the workings of a school. As has been shown above, its constituent elements can be emphasized or deemphasized, expanded or truncated. Although the instructional system remains a shared ideal, abstract model, slogan or shorthand, it takes on a different form in every real-life situation.

Every school has a distinctive network of institutional and social variables that interact in complicated ways and influence much of what takes place there. The impact of this social-psychological and material environment or learning milieu can mask the good intentions of teachers and curriculum planners and be important in shaping the learning situations they provide.[15]

By reference to the authority of the teacher, and to a feature of the pupil's value system, I would like to use the remainder of this paper to illustrate two areas where the children at Maxwell felt the impact of the constraints and contradictions of curriculum change.

PUPIL RESPONSES TO INNOVATION

During the period of observation at Simpson, small groups of children were interviewed inside or outside the classroom. By using an exploratory approach to the interviews it was possible to identify those areas of the curriculum on which the children could express and substantiate an opinion. These preliminary interviews were used to construct a small one-page questionnaire which was given to all classes being observed (see the appendix at the end of this chapter). Follow-up interviews with a small group of children at Simpson showed that they had made choices on the questionnaire for widely different reasons.

To overcome this difficulty at Maxwell each child who completed a questionnaire (total=77) was asked individually a few days later what reasons they had for their choices. Each interview took about three minutes and was conducted in the laboratory during class time. By this method of *backtranslation*[16] (establishing attitudes qualitatively (first pilot interview), measuring them across a population (fixed response questionnaire) and returning to the individual child for further information (second interview), it was possible to collect a considerable range of qualitative and quantitative data.

Authority and the teacher

One of the questionnaire items asked the children whether they preferred to 'wait for the teacher to explain the work' or to 'start straight away' (using the worksheet). 87% of them chose the former. Further questioning revealed that this was because the children went in intellectual *awe* rather than in punitive *fear* of the teacher. When questioned on this by backtranslation all but two of the children referred directly to the teacher (e.g. 'he tells you everything to do', 'he knows a lot more than we do') or to the consequences of starting without him (e.g. 'you'd be lost', 'you might muck it up if you didn't know what you were doing'). Only one child felt there was the possibility of falling foul of the teacher. He preferred to wait because he felt he 'might do it wrong and *get into trouble'*.

It seems there were several practical reasons why the children related strongly to the teachers in the situations I observed. By intention or otherwise the teachers appeared to be closely monitoring the progress of both the lessons and the pupils. This showed itself in four ways. First, the teachers developed the practice of opening the lessons by issuing instructions modifying or altering those already on the worksheets. ('Use a 100 ml instead of a 250 ml beaker'; 'Cross out instruction 4'). Second, and partly for the previous reason, all the teachers introduced the contents of the worksheets in their own words, in one case not giving out the sheets until after this introduction. 'I don't use them as you're supposed to. I give them out after the experiments'). Third, all the teachers spent time 'summing up' each worksheet and giving extra sheets, notes and diagrams. Finally, the teachers assessed pupil progress using multiple-choice (one correct answer) tests.

While the teachers felt, justifiably, that this action was essential to efficient, well-run lessons and necessary in the circumstances, the children interpreted it quite differently. They saw the teachers not only telling them exactly what to do but also following them up to see if they had done it.

Although it was not the teachers' deliberate intention, by making such remarks as: 'All of you write the same thing . . . '; 'You should still have got it to be 100° . . . '; 'Can anyone guess what the answer *should be* for number five?'; and, 'The results haven't worked out too well. You should have, in fact, found that . . . '; the children were introduced to the view that there is a right and a wrong way of doing everything. The fact that this questionnaire item provoked so many teacher-related responses suggests the *de facto* teacher-centredness of this particular pattern of organization.

This general response by the children reflects a contradiction already existing in Curriculum Paper Seven. At one point it advocates a didactic, 'closed' approach: 'The introduction to the work on the worksheets, the discussion afterwards, all of the demonstration work and the actual teaching which will establish the concepts under investigation, are still completely in the teacher's hands . . . the teacher still has complete control over the end products of the various activities'. Elsewhere, however, it 'recommends' a more self-regulated, 'open' mode of learning: 'wherever possible, class and laboratory work should be so structured that the pupil is allowed to exercise selection of approach and method' while organizing information 'in *his own way* and in his own time.'[17] From my results it seems that certain patterns of teaching appropriate to the former may well preclude the latter. In presenting coherent, well-organized lessons, the teacher may create an intellectual climate that stifles and disallows the divergent behaviour hoped for by Curriculum Paper Seven.[18]

Transfer from primary to secondary school: A question of values

An important hiatus in the academic socialization of children in Britain is the transfer from primary to secondary school. Certain differences in organization between the two levels are readily apparent. For example, in Scotland most primary schools are unstreamed, most secondary schools streamed. Generally speaking, these more obvious organizational distinctions conceal an equally important range of sociological and pedagogical differences. It has been argued, for example, that the primary and secondary schools have different 'languages', that the primary school is more person-oriented, that it is less competitive etc.; in short, that it embodies a different value system.

In a study of primary–secondary transfer, Nash (1973) showed that such values, or assumptions are held by pupils and teachers. He suggested that primary and secondary teachers operate with false (or out-of-date) notions about life in each others' schools. As a result he found that teachers prepared their pupils in the last two years of the primary school for a much stronger (or rigid) system than, in fact, they were about to enter. Nash offered this as explanation for some children perceiving secondary teachers as 'soft' and consequently regarding freedom as licence. Here I want to use data collected at Maxwell school to illustrate the opposite effect; that is, misperception of the secondary school by children who *retained* a primary school ethos.

One questionnaire item asked the children whether they preferred to 'keep the same speed as the rest of the class' or to 'work as fast as possible'. 78% preferred the former. Some felt it was socially preferable: (e.g. 'the whole class is working together'; 'you're not working on your own'). Others felt that it was intellectually or organizationally better: (e.g. 'if you do anything wrong everybody can learn and get everybody's opinion'; 'the teacher can speak to us all'). A small but significant group of children felt that it was morally or ethically wrong to want to go as fast as possible; they seemed confused about the expectations of the school and gave such reasons as: 'if you go ahead you feel you're going too fast — making them (the other children) rush'; 'it's as though you were showing off'; 'if people get more speed they boast about it'; 'some folks might think you're awfie brainy if you go too fast'.

Of the thirteen children who provided reasons for preferring to work as fast as possible, only three felt they were held back by the rest of the class. ('If you have to wait you get bored'; 'you're always hanging around'; 'you've to wait for them if they're not very good'). The remainder felt merely that it would help them to cover the work (e.g. 'you get more done'; 'if you finish you can get on to something else').

In moving from a primary to a secondary school the children at Maxwell had moved from an *integrated* setting to a *collection* situation; that is, to a school where, as far as they were concerned, all subjects were taught by different teachers. By contrast, the teachers at Maxwell changed from a *subject-specific* to an *integrated* curriculum. They too were involved in changing from one curriculum type to another, but in the *opposite* direction.

The children had moved from an 'open' system to a relatively 'closed' setting; the teachers (again relatively) had moved from 'closure' to 'openness'. In each case the participants were involved in relinquishing one set of (albeit unclear) values and adopting another. Insofar as these values and assumptions are one of education's unspoken languages this curriculum shift becomes more complicated. Clearly, as these responses reveal, the pupils as well as the teachers were unsure of the resultant value-system.

For the children in particular, the school may have been signalling contrary messages. By organizing classes on mixed-ability lines (as in the primary school) the school implies it is anxious to keep children socially integrated. But, simultaneously, by organizing the Science instruction on overtly linear lines, awarding grades etc., it signals a contrasting message; that it is concerned for their intellectual differentiation.

The ability of children to grasp this distinction and to 'manage' the inherent contradiction between these two messages would seem to be an important prerequisite for a 'successful' intellectual career in the secondary school. There is no doubt that many children can make such a distinction by this stage in their education. However, it appears that some children are still confused. They apply the 'social' message to their 'intellectual' life.

SUMMARY AND CONCLUSIONS

In concluding this paper I would like to present briefly the kernel of my argument.

First, I have tried to present a valid picture of the Scottish Integrated Science Scheme. Second, I have discussed two organizational forms taken by the scheme by comparing them with a model proposed by Bernstein. Finally I have considered the classroom impact of certain features of the Scottish Scheme.

The coexistence of integrated and collection curricula in secondary education points to a fundamental dilemma, if not a crisis, for the comprehensive school. Until recently, the role of the secondary school was, overall, clearly defined. Both secondary modern and grammar schools were governed by purely academic values. In this and other ways they exemplified the collection type of curriculum.

Today, comprehensive schools are expected to retain this academic/intellectual function while at the same time paying tribute to new patterns of organization, new boundaries of knowledge and new conceptions of education. In other words they are expected to run collection and integrated curricula side by side. Thus, teachers are expected to be 'interdisciplinary' *and* subject-specialists, to be concerned with teaching sixth-formers *and* slow learners, and to be responsible for both the academic *and* social welfare of their pupils.

As shown in this paper, the tension that these expectancies promote are readily apparent among both teachers *and* pupils. In that they represent a fundamental dilemma, the challenge they present to educational practice is both pressing and profound.

APPENDIX

The administration of this questionnaire was conducted by the investigator. Each item was read out and the children were invited to write in their answers or circumscribe their choice. Items 11 to 20 were introduced by a suitable lead-in (e.g. *'Would you prefer* working with a partner OR on your own'). At Simpson school this questionnaire was tried out with two different formats and two different colours of paper randomly presented to each class. Since observation and subsequent analysis revealed no evidence of 'response sets' or children copying from one another, only this version was used at Maxwell School.

1. Name	2. Form	3. Science teacher
4. Name of partner	5. Names of other people you have worked with this year	
6. Why do you sit where you do?		
7. What would you like to be when you leave school?		
8. Subjects you like at school	9. Subjects you *don't* like at school	
10. Next year, would you like: less Science more Science		

11. Working with a partner	OR	on your own

12. Less experiments	OR	more experiments

13. Keep the same speed as the rest of the class	OR	work as fast as possible

14. Use worksheets	OR	use textbooks

15. Less written work	OR	more written work

16. Sheets get harder	OR	sheets get easier

17. One sheet at a time	OR	several sheets at a time

18. Writing on separate sheets of paper	OR	writing on the sheets

19. Wait for the teacher to explain the work	OR	start straight away

20. Do something different next year	OR	carry on the same

Acknowledgements

Without the acceptance, forbearance and trust of a group of necessarily anonymous teachers and pupils, this research would have foundered during my first days in the field. My hope is that this report does justice to their work and also to the assistance I have received from my colleagues and fellow contributors.

Notes

1. A version of the early part of this paper can be found in W. A. Reid and D. F. Walker (eds.), *Case Studies in Curriculum Change: Great Britain and the United States*, Routledge, London (forthcoming). It is based on 'The integration of knowledge: practice and problems', *Journal of Curriculum Studies*, 5, 146–155 (1973). The concept 'innovation without change' is drawn from MacDonald and Rudduck (1971).

2. *Science for General Education* (Curriculum Paper Seven), Scottish Education Department, 1969. The worksheets are published by Heinemann Educational Books Ltd.

3. Here, Bernstein's ideas are a development of his earlier paper (Bernstein, 1971).

4. For the relevant Scottish teaching regulations see: Scottish Education Department (1971a).

5. As a result of the teacher shortage this regulation is breached by placing 'non-qualified' science teachers *in charge* of the various departments but, of course, without the status or salary of Principal Teachers. A recent S.E.D. (1971b) discussion document 'suggested' that this honours–ordinary distinction be abolished and that all promoted posts be open to qualified teachers. Since the period of observation took place this has been ratified. Nevertheless, qualification by subject still remains.

6. Such distinctions begin while the students are still in training. In at least one college of education, honours and ordinary graduates — even though they may end up in the same school with equivalent timetables — are trained separately.

7. See for example: Educational Testing Service (1969) and Bloom *et al.* (1971).

8. The expression 'general science' seems to derive from the idea of 'science for all' the title of a Science Masters' Association pamphlet prepared at the request of a government commission (chaired by J. J. Thomson) set up in 1916 to 'inquire into the position of natural science in the education system of Great Britain'. When the commission reported in 1918 it advocated a general course of science for *all* pupils up to the age of 16. Subsequently however, 'science for all' was transformed into 'general science' and developed as a scheme for elementary rather than grammar schools. (See Turner (1927) and H.M.S.O. (1939)).

9. Even the teacher 'in charge' of Science had plans to move elsewhere. In an unpublished paper, 'The foster teacher' (1970), I have considered more fully the impact of teacher turnover on the organization and expression of teaching.

10. Although integrated science was introduced when the school was opened, 50% of the labs were subject specific. Thus, the accommodation, the teachers, and to some extent the laboratory assistants, came to the school with pre-existing subject identities.

11. The extent to which the organization was developed to tackle the problems and the extent to which it helped to create or perpetuate them is itself problematic. What might have happened in a different set of circumstances is difficult to envisage.

12. It is important to note parenthetically that these were not cases of 'passing the buck' but quite the reverse. In each case the staff were anxious to define, establish and fulfil their responsibilities. As most of them had no experience teaching integrated science they were quite willing to substitute their own interests with those of the department.

13. To the extent that this is an area not considered by Bernstein, its absence might be considered a deficiency in his analysis. Generally, Bernstein's structural analysis, based as it is on two logically distinct ideal types cannot, by definition, be applied directly at classroom level. It always refers to a 'Utopia'. (See Weber, 1964)).

14. Some of the first secondary schools to implement integrated curricula can be found in areas which have a two-tier or middle-school comprehensive system. The autonomy of the 'lower' schools has allowed them considerable scope to experiment with this form of organization.

15. The terms 'instructional system' and 'learning milieu' are taken from Parlett and Hamilton (1972).

16. Backtranslation is a technique used in linguistics for assessing the comparability of words and expressions in different languages. See Deutscher (1968).

17. Curriculum Paper Seven, paragraphs 38, 32 and 33 (emphasis in original).

18. Douglas Barnes (1969, p. 75) has commented on the same problem: 'Teachers should learn how their behaviour in the classroom may embody teaching objectives

of which they are unaware'. A large part of Goldhammer (1969) is devoted to an analysis of this 'incidental learning'. Holt (1969) and Mager (1968) also discuss the same phenomenon in classroom terms.

References

Barnes, D., *et al.*, 1969, *Language, the Learner and the School,* Penguin, Harmondsworth.

Bernstein, B., 1969, 'Open schools, open society', *New Society,* 14 September 1969.

Bernstein, B., 1971, 'On the classification and framing of educational knowledge', in M. F. D. Young (ed.), *Knowledge and Control,* Collier-Macmillan, London.

Bloom, B. S., *et al.*, 1971, *Handbook on Formative and Summative Evaluation of Student Learning,* McGraw-Hill, London.

Deutscher, I., 1968, 'Asking questions cross-culturally', in H. Becker *et al., Institutions and the Person,* Aldine, New York.

Educational Testing Service, 1969, *Towards a Theory of Achievement Measurement,* Princeton.

Goldhammer, R., 1969, *Clinical Supervision: Special Methods for the Supervision of Teachers,* Holt, Rinehart & Winston, New York.

Hamilton, D., 1970, 'The foster teacher', unpublished.

H.M.S.O., 1939, *The Spens Report.*

Holt, J., 1969, *How Children Fail,* Penguin, Harmondsworth.

MacDonald, B. and J. Rudduck, 1971, 'Curriculum research and development: barriers to success', *British Journal of Educational Psychology,* 41.

Mager, P. F., 1968, *Developing Attitudes Toward Learning,* Fearon, California.

Nash, R., 1973, *Classrooms Observed,* Routledge & Kegan Paul, London.

Parlett, M. and D. Hamilton, 1972, 'Evaluation as illumination: a new approach to the study of innovatory programs', Occasional Paper 9, Centre for Research in the Educational Sciences, University of Edinburgh.

Scottish Education Department, 1969, *Science for General Education,* (Curriculum Paper Seven), H.M.S.O.

Scottish Education Department, 1971a, *Memorandum on Entry Requirements and Courses,* H.M.S.O.

Scottish Education Department, 1871b, *The Structure of Promoted Posts in Secondary Schools in Scotland,* H.M.S.O.

Turner, D. M., 1972, *A History of Science Teaching in England,* Chapman & Hall, London.

Weber, M., 1964, 'The ideal type', in K. Thompson and J. Tunstall (eds.) *Sociological Perspectives,* Penguin, Harmondsworth, 1971.

Notes on Contributors

Clem Adelman

Born 1942. 1964: took Science degree, University of London. Taught in secondary schools and as Liberal Studies Lecturer in a polytechnic 1969–73: Centre for Science Education, Chelsea College of Science and Technology, initially in educational technology, then with Rob Walker on classroom research project. 1973–: Senior Research Associate, Ford Teaching Project, Centre for Applied Research in Education, University of East Anglia. Current interests: sociolinguistics, cultural anthropology. Active musician and classroom photographer. Published articles in *Cambridge Journal of Education, Classroom Interaction Newsletter* and, with Rob Walker, in *Times Educational Supplement* and *Journal of Society of Motion Picture and Television Engineers.*

Sara Delamont

Born 1947. 1965–68: read Social Anthropology, Girton College, Cambridge. 1968–71: postgraduate research, Centre for Research in the Educational Sciences, University of Edinburgh (Ph. D. awarded 1973). 1971–73: Research Associate, Bionics Research Laboratory, School of Artificial Intelligence, University of Edinburgh, 1973–: Lecturer in Sociology, School of Education, University of Leicester. Current research interests: classrooms, the status of women, professional education. Published articles in *Race Today, New Edinburgh Review* and, with David Hamilton, in *Research in Education.*

Viv Furlong

Born 1947. First degree in Business Studies, Enfield College of Technology: developed a particular interest in the sociology of organisations. 1969–70: travelled widely in U.S.A. and West Indies. 1970–74: took part-time post as remedial teacher in secondary school to establish position for participant observation. At the same time (1970) registered as postgraduate student, City University, London, to study the sociology of education, with particular reference to pupils' perceptions of school life.

Howard Gannaway

Born 1947. 1965: worked in Paris as research assistant at building research institute. 1966–69: studied Social Anthropology, King's College, Cambridge. 1970: Centre Organizer for Task Force, Greenwich. 1971–73: taught

History, English and Drama in secondary schools, Gravesend. Now working as teacher in charge of small unit for disturbed girls.

David Hamilton

Born 1943. Studied Geology and Education, University of Edinburgh. Joined Centre for Research in the Educational Sciences as research student in 1969 following three years teaching in Leicestershire. 1973–74: Temporary Lecturer, Department of Education, University of Glasgow. Present research interests include classroom research, curriculum evaluation, history of educational research. Published articles in *Journal of Curriculum Studies* and *Research in Education*. Editor of forthcoming volumes on educational research and curriculum evaluation.

Roy Nash

Born 1943. Studied Psychology, University of Sussex; taught in a comprehensive school for a year. 1969–72: postgraduate research, Centre for Research in the Educational Sciences, University of Edinburgh. (Ph. D. awarded 1973). 1973–: Lecturer in the Sociology of Education, University of North Wales, Bangor. Published articles in *New Society, British Journal of Sociology, Sociology* and *Sociometry*. Author of *Classrooms Observed* (1973, Routledge & Kegan Paul).

Michael Stubbs

Born 1947. 1966–70: read Linguistics and Modern Languages, King's College, Cambridge. 1968–69: taught English in France. 1970–73: postgraduate research, Centre for Research in the Educational Sciences, University of Edinburgh. 1973–74: Research Associate, English Language Research, University of Birmingham. 1974–: Lecturer in Linguistics, University of Nottingham. Present research interests: sociolinguistics, conversational analysis, language in the classroom. Published articles in *Language in Society* and *Thema Curriculum*.

Brian Torode

Born 1947. Read Mathematics and Social Anthropology, King's College, Cambridge. 1968–71: postgraduate research, Centre for Research in the Educational Sciences, University of Edinburgh. 1970–71: Editor of *New Edinburgh Review*. Presently lecturing in Sociology, Trinity College, Dublin. Present interests: approaches to the study of social action and ordinary language use, and the bearing of these topics upon social theory. Published articles in *New Edinburgh Review* and *Economic and Social Review*.

Rob Walker

Born 1943. Initially trained as industrial pharmacologist, Chelsea College, then switched to Sociology; studies for first degree, London School of Economics, 1966. Taught in inner London schools until 1968, then research fellow at the Centre for Science Education, Chelsea. 1973: briefly Lecturer

Department of Education, University of Keele. Now Senior Research Associate, Ford Safari Project, Centre for Applied Research in Education, University of East Anglia. Safari is a project tracing the legacies of four major curriculum projects in Britain. Many times rejected by funding bodies, interviewing committees and publishers. More interested in classrooms than education. Published articles in *International Review of Education* and, with Clem Adelman, in *Cambridge Journal of Education, Times Educational Supplement* and *Journal of Society of Motion Picture and Television Engineers*. Co-author with Clem Adelman of *A Guide to Classroom Observation* (in press, Methuen).

Author Index

218

Subject Index